Kirklees
COUNCIL

Library and Information Centres

Red doles Lane

Huddersfield, West Yorkshire

HD2 1YF

This book should be returned on or before the latest date stamped below.
Fines are charged if the item is late.

SBr

You may renew this loan for a further period by phone, personal visit or at
www.kirklees.gov.uk/libraries, provided that the book is not required by
another reader.

NO MORE THAN THREE RENEWALS ARE PERMITTED

ZIDANE
THE BIOGRAPHY

PATRICK FORT & JEAN PHILIPPE

EBURY
PRESS

1 3 5 7 9 10 8 6 4 2

Ebury Press, an imprint of Ebury Publishing
20 Vauxhall Bridge Road
London SW1V 2SA

Ebury Press is part of the Penguin Random House group of companies
whose addresses can be found at global.penguinrandomhouse.com

Penguin
Random House
UK

First published in the UK in 2018 by Ebury Press

First published in France by Éditions de l'Archipel in 2002, 2006 and 2017
under the titles *Zidane, le roi modeste* and *Zidane, de Yazid à Zizou*
and *Les deux vies de Zidane*.

www.penguin.co.uk

A CIP catalogue record for this book is available from the British Library

ISBN 9781785038488

Typeset in 11/18 pt ITC Galliard Std
by Integra Software Services Pvt. Ltd, Pondicherry

Printed and bound in Great Britain by Clays Ltd, St Ives PLC

In memory of Jean Varraud, without whose help and encouragement this book would never have been written.

CONTENTS

PREFACE

Five thousand people: more than could sometimes be found at the Stade Coubertin in La Bocca when AS Cannes were playing in the Première Division. Only slightly less than the population of Marseille's La Castellane district.

Five thousand people: that was the estimated number of spectators who attended Real Madrid's first-team training session on 5 January 2016. On the eve of the Epiphany, a public holiday in Spain, it was the only training session of the year open to the public. More importantly, it was the first to be overseen by Zinedine Zidane.

The day after his appointment as a replacement for Rafael Benítez, the former Real Madrid number 5 visibly embraced a vocation he had been extremely sceptical about ten years earlier, when he brought his career as a player to an end. But he did eventually become a manager, someone who no longer wears a numbered shirt but has numerous responsibilities on his back instead.

He may have already been managing for two and a half years, but not in such an exposed fashion. He was now in charge of the first team at the most successful club in the world – and in UEFA's terms the best, ahead of Barcelona and Bayern Munich – as well as the richest.

Football is no longer a sport; it is a huge market, an economic sector in its own right, a spectacle with coveted audience shares, and a subject of passionate debate. Not everyone plays football, but everyone talks about it, particularly in Spain.

In Barcelona, for example, two days after Barça's defeat at the hands of Real following an unbeaten run of 39 matches, talk of football even encroached into the corridors and lounges of the luxurious Majestic Hotel at the top of Las Ramblas. On the roof terrace, the hotel's French general manager, Pascal Billard, pointed out the Camp Nou Stadium, home of FC Barcelona. He explained that it is almost impossible to avoid football here; in early April 2016, the name of Madrid's new manager was on everyone's lips, including those of its rival, Barcelona. The name of the coach who had just won his first Clásico was famous. Even better, he was respected.

In the land of passion, Zidane was attractive ... and he could sell. In Real Madrid's stores, Zidane's shirt was still a force to be reckoned with, bearing his name and the number 5 he wore as a player.

Ten years after hanging up his boots, the novice manager had rekindled the memory of the champion he had been, a genius passer of the ball and goalscorer, elegant and virtuous, successful and legendary. The eagerness for images on this January day revealed what the public were subconsciously waiting for: to see the player again. A subtle flick of the ball from him caught on camera during a training session was enough to trigger hundreds of thousands of views online. A piece of unexpected ball control at the edge of the pitch during an official match resulted in applause from the crowd and slow-motion replays for television viewers.

But the player would not return. If his style reappeared on the pitch, it would only be by proxy in the movement of his team.

He might play no longer, but he continues to be a playmaker when he coaches. He is not unaware of the laws of the sport, of the market. He manages, confronted by the risks of the new profession he has chosen for himself. Victory is a reprieve; defeat the beginning of a challenge.

Madrid, the Valdebebas training centre. Enough tiresome drills. The time to play has come.

'Come on, let's have some fun!' He coaches with plenty of spirit. When he started out as a player he was still a child, and he's a man who never lost the energy of that youthful innocence.

When he started out as a manager he was unquestionably an adult, a father to four boys, a father who has often reflected and acted by thinking of his own father, aware of the efforts and demands that sport at the highest level requires. But also the immense joy the game can bring – just like life.

1

THE CHILDHOOD GAME

It was cold. It was winter 1953 in Saint-Denis. Ammi Smaïl Zidane had just left his native Kabylie, where he had been an agricultural labourer. He had come to work on a building site in the Paris *banlieue*, far from his village of Aguemoune in a mountainous region of Algeria where the economy was based mainly on agriculture, olive harvesting in particular. Smaïl's daily life was gruelling. Homeless, he sometimes slept in makeshift shelters on the building site, exposed to the cold. This life lasted for three years, swallowing up his youth. But he pushed on.

Ten years later, Smaïl started a family with Malika – also originally from Kabylie – with whom he emigrated first to Paris, then Marseille. She gave him five children. First, three sons, Madjid in 1963, Farid in 1965, Noureddine in 1967, and a daughter, Lila, in 1969.

The youngest of the brood arrived on 23 June 1972. They named him Zinedine. At the time, the family was living in an apartment in La Castellane, a housing estate in the north of Marseille. The baby slept in the same room as Madjid, better known as Djamel.

When he was old enough to decide, Zinedine preferred to be called Yazid, which was his middle name, and so that was what

1

they called him. He was doted on by the family, as the youngest often are. He would sometimes fall asleep clutching his football. A lively child, he was passionate about the game. As in working-class neighbourhoods all over the world, life for many children in La Castellane revolved around the round ball. Football was both their primary occupation and preoccupation.

Yazid grew up in a relatively new housing development, one with a reputation for hardship. In such a delicate social setting he was at risk from any number of dangerous influences. With his mother constantly keeping an eye on him and surrounded by his brothers, Yazid spent hours playing in Place de la Tartane, particularly after school.

When it was taken over by kids, this long rectangular concrete slab resembled a kind of stretched football field, bordered by buildings, including Yazid's, Building G, near one of the goals. It was there that he perfected his tricky footwork, often in the company of Noureddine; he was particularly gifted when it came to football. When not with his ball, he had plenty of time to tease his sister, with whom he got on very well, as well as the odd moment to think about school. There he was boisterous, spirited. He needed to use up his energy, to play and to interact. On the pitch, he struggled to resist the urge to go on the attack. With his peers, he struggled to resist the urge to defend a teammate, if the need arose.

Sent off! Sent home. That particular day, Yazid had to come home early because he had tried to avenge a teammate at school. It was the sign of an impulsiveness that contrasted with the placidity of his father, a peaceful and altruistic man who did everything to give his children a good education and instil principles in them.

Smaïl worked at a shopping centre; he had a variety of responsibilities. Whenever he was not working, he took over from Malika looking after the children, including, of course, the youngest, who was showing glimpses of real footballing talent.

The game became a sport. After Place de la Tartane came regulation pitches. The sport became a competition; the mismatched outfits were replaced by official jerseys, those of the Association Sportive de Foresta in La Castellane. These were followed by those of the Union Sportive in Saint-Henri, then of the Sports Olympiques in Septèmes-les-Vallons, a town near Marseille's northern suburbs with a predominantly working-class population. Poverty was not uncommon. Football was an exciting and inexpensive escape.

At each of these clubs, just as on Place de la Tartane, Yazid's technique in motion and ball control were remarked upon and admired, as well as his enthusiasm and will to win.

Cannes, 1984. A few days before the start of the school year, term had already begun for the young players. The tenth Under-13 tournament organised by the Association Sportive de Cannes was held at the Stade Maurice Chevalier. Six teams, including one from the local club, took part in the Claude Roux Challenge, named after a former president of the Cannes supporters club. Those in their first year with the Under-13s came from Provence, the Var, the Alps, the Côte d'Azur and the Rhône-Durance region.

The players from Provence arrived on Saturday, the day before the tournament. One of them, Gilles Boix, felt a twinge during a training session. His parents came to see him the following day. As Gilles was warming up before the match against the team from the Côte d'Azur, his father could see that he was struggling. He was grimacing and clearly in pain. Increasingly so. But he wanted to play. His father refused; he wanted to take him to see a doctor first. Monsieur Varraud, a football scout, offered to drive them to the nearby Clinique des Mimosas, where he knew someone. The offer

3

was accepted. Gilles had no choice but to give in to his father's insistence and agreed to leave. He was replaced by the player in shirt number 13 and the match could begin.

Jean left the stadium. He drove father and son to the clinic in his old Citroën LN. The diagnosis was serious: a broken wrist. By the time they returned to the Stade Chevalier, the match had finished. The scout had missed the opportunity to watch the budding young players. But he had won himself a friend, Fernand Boix, who was grateful for his kind and unsolicited help.

Two years and three months later, at the Regional Centre for Physical Education and Sport in Aix-en-Provence, 30 Under-15s came together during the Christmas holidays for a training camp aimed at selecting 18 boys to take part in an interleague trial the following spring.

The first two days were taken up with trials. The third, a match between two teams of trainees. Jean Varraud had planned to attend to watch a promising forward from Cagnes-sur-Mer, Fabrice Monachino, but he was not selected. Jean decided to make use of his LN again anyway. Monsieur Boix, a manager from Septèmes, went with him. They were happy to see each other again and watched the match side-by-side.

Varraud enquired about the player in Monachino's position. Fernand knew him well because he was from his home club. Robert Centenero, the young players' coach, had pointed him out to the club president, Roger de Plano. They had offered this promising kid, who played at Saint-Henri, somewhere new where the gifts he had developed on Place de la Tartane would have the opportunity to blossom. Under the watchful and tender gaze of his family, he was always the last to leave the concrete rectangle but had yet to become as comfortable on dirt and grass pitches.

'He's the one who replaced my son in Cannes. Zidane. Don't you remember? The number 13?'

Yes, that was it. Jean Varraud remembered vaguely. Something about his physique, perhaps? Whatever the case, he did not regret having come. Although he played in positions he was not used to – on the left wing during the first third, then as a sweeper during the third – this kid in the white shirt, who played only two-thirds of the match, appealed to him instantly. His touch and vision of the game were extraordinary. Everything he did had a subtlety, a class. Varraud wanted to know more about him.

Zidane. Even in Marseille the name was not yet widely known. Except in the 16th *arrondissement*, on the Castellane estate, in Saint-Henri and Septèmes, clubs where Zinedine had played his first official matches. With well-marked-out pitches, referees and regulation kit. He had grown since the tournament in Cannes. And made progress. He was 14 and already had great technical finesse. But there seemed to be no interest in him from scouts. During the few training camps or matches for which he had been picked, his performances had not been the most eye-catching.

At the Roux Challenge, after coming on during the game against a team from the Côte d'Azur as an attacking midfielder, he played as a box-to-box midfielder in all the other matches, which came to an end with a goal against Rhône-Durance and then, to win the trophy, a crushing victory in the final against AS Cannes: 7–1!

At the end of the tournament, Zidane was not one of the players who were first on the Provençal coach's team sheet. In the coach's mind, ten of the eleven positions in his first-choice line-up were filled, but he was still hesitating about the eleventh, that of the box-to-box midfielder, the number 8. Another player from Septèmes, Gilles Manno, was in competition with Zidane, and was even slightly preferred. After the tournament, Zidane was judged 'a little disappointing given his qualities. He played a bit half-heartedly. Must definitely do better because he has the means, technique and vision of the game.'

Despite this, Robert Signoret, coach of the Saint-Henri Under-9s, had noticed his 'means'. Interviewed by the magazine *Le SeptéMois* in July 1998, Robert Centenero, the man who brought Yazid to SO Septèmes, would also remember 'a more forceful personality than that of most of his teammates'.

This assessment confirmed the character the young kid who was crazy about balls on Place de la Tartane had already developed. It betrayed a little-noted part of his adolescent character: this apparently timid boy was a warrior.

Before the Christmas training camp at the Regional Centre for Physical Education and Sport, Zidane had already been called up to Aix on 17 October and 7 November 1986, and to Puricard on 31 October, but had only played in one match of four in this inter-district trial. Absent on 14 November in Carpentras against Rhône-Durance, 28 November in Oraison against the Alps, and on 12 December in Aix against Côte d'Azur, he only played against the Var at the Huveaune Stadium in Marseille, but was replaced by Manno during the game.

Selected in fits and starts for the *département*, his appearances at the top level, the Ligue de Méditerranée, were non-existent. In two years, he had only been picked at the top inter-category level once, for a training camp at Les Pennes Mirabeau.

He had failed to attract any attention on the pitch. Off the pitch, he was excessively shy. An instructor at a camp in Alpes-de-Haute-Provence, in Volx, remembers this personality trait, summed up by the image of an uncommunicative child hunched up in his K-Way jacket. Despite this, slumbering within him were an exceptional mastery of the ball and an ease with the game, revealed objectively during the assessment of drills almost three years earlier, and confirmed subjectively by a series of observations during matches. During this Opération Guérin – a training camp for spotting young talent named after Henri Guérin, a former manager of the France team – Zinedine, then in the second year of Under-11s, got the highest scores in the technical drills. Maurice Roche, in charge of the camp, noticed his skills when it came to keepie uppies and his behaviour in different phases of the game.

But this boy whose flashes were as brilliant as they were intermittent did not seem to elicit any interest. Not yet anyway. His parents, whose incomes were modest, made sacrifices to enrol him in paid training sessions.

In a sport that was becoming increasingly commercial and business-oriented, scouts were quick to seize every promising opportunity, the slightest hope of a quick profit. They had not seen anything in him. Jean Varraud was surprised.

Was the kid to blame? Was it because of his physical fragility? (The genetic condition he suffers from, a type of anaemia called thalassaemia, leading to frequent fatigue, would not come to light until fifteen years later.) It would take time for his muscles to fill out. Was it his inconsistency? At that age this is a common failing, something that could even be seen as a silver lining. There is always the chance that a teenager playing regularly at a sustained pace could become burned out. What's more, the grind of competition can be distorting. It affects the fun aspect of the sport. It takes away the passion, or at least transforms it, as the pleasure in playing is quickly replaced by an obsession with victory. Zinedine showed clear signs of passion for the game and had the fundamental qualities. Broadly speaking, this was enough to make the scout offer him a training session at La Bocca, prior to a possible commitment.

Monsieur Varraud wanted to see him again as soon as possible, although his counterparts were not interested. So much the better for him, as he crossed the pitch at the Regional Training Centre and went to speak to the Septèmes directors. He expressed his desire to bring the player to Cannes for a probationary period of a week, which might lead to recruitment.

The response was favourable. It was also accompanied by some advice: 'If you want to get him, do it right now!' The message was clearly understood. No other clubs had their eyes on the teenager from La Castellane; all the directors at Cannes had to do was keep things quiet enough so as not to alert anyone else. But they still had to act quickly. The passing of time, the lack of good academic results, the uncertain prospect of becoming a professional footballer … and the neighbourhood in which he grew up meant that a difficult period was in the offing for this boy who was about to turn 15. On the one hand, he was exposed to the aggression of his adversaries, often unsettled by his ease with the ball; on the other, there were plenty of bad examples that might set his adolescence off course. Fortunately, he had his family. A family bound by affection around solid principles of life and education. A mother, a father, a sister and three brothers who took care of him, the baby of the family. But these strengths might still turn out not to be enough. Monsieur Varraud was familiar with the situation: 'It's always the tough guys who attract the others.' Zinedine was sweet but he lived in a difficult neighbourhood.

He had a carefree air, chatting calmly with his friends during the post-match peace and quiet. He did not know that his future was at stake. They had to take him straight away. Alain Lepeu, manager of the Septèmes Under-17s, suggested a meeting two weeks later, after the Christmas break. 'Come and see us on 11 January. We're playing at Saint-Raphaël.'

On the way home, in his LN, which took the injured to hospital, kids to the stadium and future stars to their destiny, Jean Varraud told himself he had discovered a boy with plenty of potential.

Great players are rare. Great scouts even more so. Monsieur Varraud was one of these.

A former player with AS Saint-Étienne, he joined the senior team at the age of 17. He settled in Cannes in 1941, just opposite the legendary Stade des Hespérides, since superseded by the Coubertin. He ran a cinema, the Vox, for several decades. But football was his passion. After a career as a player, interrupted by the Second World War, he became a coach and then a recruiter on a volunteer basis. Although he traded in the industry of dreams, this dignified and courteous, sensitive and lucid man did not have a mercantile spirit. He was not a trafficker of souls. Completely devoted to AS Cannes, he suggested players to the club with the intention of seeing them go on to become a part of the 'pennant team'. His interpersonal skills, kindness and straightforward nature often allowed him to attract players who, for geographical or purely sporting reasons, should logically have signed elsewhere.

Youth tournaments were his chosen field, conjuring up his own childhood back in Saint-Étienne, where his football was his day-to-day companion. Pure talent, as yet unconstrained by experience, blossoming in all its splendour. He still had to spot a good player, assess his margin for progression, his capacity to play at the highest level. Jean Varraud observed, felt ... Because he used to play himself, he knew football well. Because he had rubbed shoulders with them, he was familiar with the art of great players: Max Charbit or the Yugoslav Yvan Beck, a striker for the great Sète team, then at Saint-Étienne and scorer of three goals in Uruguay during the first World Cup. However, experience does not necessarily provide finesse when it comes to insight. In the stadiums to which he took his sharp eyes, he sometimes watched matches in the company of former international players. Some thought they had spotted great potential in a run-of-the-mill performance; others were unaware of or underestimated young hopefuls who eventually broke through. Despite never having been a professional, his insight was clear. Jean Fernandez, manager of the Cannes professional team, and Gilles Rampillon, the technical director, had absolute confidence in him.

Jean Varraud did not recruit adults, but children with the potential to become professionals. This particular child amazed him as few others have.

'I saw this guy. He had hands where his feet should have been!'

When he got back to the club, Monsieur Varraud told the general secretary, Gilbert Chamonal, about the player he had found in Aix. Still surprised by the lack of eagerness of his counterparts, he wanted to see the young player again quickly with a view to potentially offering him a trial.

He kept his appointment in Saint-Raphaël. Rampillon went with him. A frail man, a subtle player and a former international, he too made his senior debut at the age of 17, at FC Nantes, where he stood out thanks to his vision of the game and his technique, two essential components of talent. It was therefore an expert eye that he cast over the young Marseille player. But Zidane did not play in his usual position, that of attacking midfielder. The Septèmes coach came to apologise to the Cannes observers. Thanks to a shortage of players, he'd had no choice but to put him in as sweeper.

In this position as the last line of defence, the slightest error can prove fatal. And so it was thanks to some risky dribbling, intercepted by an opponent who converted the opportunity into a goal. Saint-Raphaël equalised. Zidane was dismayed, all the more so because he had shown nothing attractive to the two observers apart from a handful of pieces of skill. But his performance would soon be nothing more than an anecdote.

Septèmes won by two goals, 3–1, but lost one of their players: as agreed, he would see them again a week later. After his training camp. He climbed into Gilles Rampillon's Mercedes and headed for Cannes.

Two and a half years after the Claude Roux Challenge, Zinedine once again trod the turf at the Stade Maurice Chevalier on a week-long training camp. Initial assessments were made. Potential was gauged. Shortcomings were spotted. He had to work on his aerial game, jumping as often as possible towards the training equipment. He also had to work on his technique, tactics and physique. But the basics were there: he was insanely talented with his feet. The ball became a magic toy every time it found its way to this tall, skinny kid.

How had the scouts missed it? It became a daily question.

Jean Fernandez was immediately won over. As the professionals were coming to the end of a training session, Jean Varraud asked him to watch the Under-17s.

'Come and see. I've brought someone.' Fernandez was reluctant. He had just finished a tiring session, had work to do and was keen to put it off. But Varraud knew it would be love at first sight.

'Come on! You'll see.' The recruiter was insistent. Fernandez walked with him to the Mûriers 2 pitch at the Coubertin complex. The young player in question was in the middle of the bald pitch.

He received the ball in the air, controlling it with his chest. With ease. With consummate ease.

Fernandez, who was no novice, was impressed. Stunned even. He stayed pitch-side for 25 minutes, identifying the shortcomings and qualities of this frail virtuoso.

Why had the scouts missed it? Pierre Ailhaud, coach of the Cannes Under-17 team, had to answer another question. One asked by those who discovered the skill of this brand-new trainee with amazement: 'Who is that?' One by one, they all came to enquire.

A passing director also shared his admiration.

'He's good, that Under-18 kid!' He was good but he was not an Under-18 player. He was still an Under-17!

He was precocious. Everyone liked him, both as a footballer and as a person. With every touch of the ball he confirmed everything good that had been said about him. He knew how to be bold, as he showed in this game of six-a-side played across the width of the pitch. The goals were small but this did not stop him from shooting from distance, unleashing a shot from the middle of the park. The ball flew over the keeper's head and ended up in the back of the net. This tricky shot, requiring speed of vision and execution, revealed a great sense of improvisation, a real skill.

The recruiters seemed won over. The coach Charly Loubet, a former Cannes player and French international, as well as an important figure at the club, got on the phone to Septèmes. His opinion was categorical: 'We're interested in him. His basic skills really are above average.'

All that remained was to convince the boy's club, and his family. More determined than ever, Jean Varraud asked a local government employee, Daniel Delsalle, to plead Cannes' case with Loïc Fagon, a director at Septèmes he had known since childhood. There was no need. On returning to Marseille with his trainee, Gilles Rampillon had no trouble convincing them.

He was given a warm welcome at the Septèmes ground one Saturday morning. The club president, secretary general and coach met with Smaïl, Zinedine's father, to talk about the future.

Money did not come up. Monsieur Zidane asked the question everyone was waiting for: 'Monsieur Rampillon, do you think he can become a professional footballer?'

As always, whenever he is asked that question, the coach remained cautious. Instead he preferred to insist on the need to continue normal schooling alongside the boy's football training. He was all too well aware of the importance of psychological and physiological factors, the hazards of adolescent development, to be categorical. He took up the argument that Maurice Desvignes, director of studies at the Cannes club, often summarises with a single sentence: 'We don't want the trainees to regret coming through the door of our academy,' especially if it ends in failure.

On the other hand, Gilles Rampillon was almost certain: AS Cannes, playing in the Deuxième Division, were headed towards the elite. He was a firm believer, although the end of the league season was still some way off. Once the team reached a certain level, it would intensify its training efforts – staff at the Cannes academy was already expected to be increased by half – and more trust would be placed in their young players, who would consequently have the opportunity to begin their careers at the highest level. His words were clear, devoid of pretence. Attractive.

Jean Varraud had another, decisive argument: a bag. Zinedine's bag. A bag that did not contain the jumble of laundry you would expect to see at the end of a week spent by a kid away from home.

It was all perfectly clean and organised! And this was thanks to a mother who had welcomed the trainee into her home: Nicole Élineau.

Cannes may well be close to Marseille, both in terms of distance and climate, but Smaïl and his wife Malika would only let their son leave on one condition: that a host family had been found. In their eyes, nothing could replace a family atmosphere, something that was so important to the Zidanes. Nothing. Not even a football academy. Whatever the case, AS Cannes did not have it: there was no specific building at the academy for accommodating professional apprentices.

Several weeks passed before the signing of the non-solicitation agreement that would grant AS Cannes priority when it came to recruitment. Madame Zidane only gave her consent once the question of accommodation had been settled. There was an obvious solution: the friendly and committed Élineau family would host Zinedine. Jean Varraud went to see Jean-Claude, Nicole's husband.

'Do you want to take a child into your home?' He may have wanted to, but could he? The Élineaus had three children of their own. They were already hosting another trainee, Amédée Arnaud. Theirs was only a three-bedroomed house. This was not just about a week but a whole year.

Despite this, they agreed. They were already fond of Zinedine, so much so that, like those closest to him, they never called him by that name.

2

A TEAM OF
DREAMERS

'Hi, I'm Yazid.'

The tall boy was sitting in the living room. He got up and held out his hand. He had arrived at the Élineaus' house in the afternoon but Jean-Claude did not meet him until the early evening when he returned from the 'factory', the name he used to refer to the company where he worked, Aérospatiale. Factory: the word hardly fits with the image of Cannes conjured up by the tourism, La Croisette, congresses and festivals that make up the mainstay of the city's economy. In terms of numbers, Aérospatiale is its largest employer. On its western fringes, near Mandelieu-La Napoule and the sea, from which they are separated only by the RN 98 motorway, the company buildings are home to, among other things, parts for satellites. The site of this industrial zone is placed under vigilant protection. It is top secret.

Dressed in a white shirt with a badge, Jean-Claude was a workshop technician; he made carbon antennas in a hangar. Previously employed by the same firm in Bouguenais, near Nantes, he had obtained a transfer to the Cannes site 13 years earlier. Several times a month, he would work into the evening. He worked shifts: from 4am to noon, from noon to 8pm or from 8pm to 4am.

That night, the Élineaus found out that Zinedine preferred to be called by his middle name, Yazid. That was what everyone called him at La Castellane.

He was polite, well brought up, spoke little and had a nice smile. He inspired a desire to help him, to protect him whenever he seemed to withdraw a little, through embarrassment or fear of being in the way. Yazid won his hosts over during that rainy week.

Jean-Claude, his wife Nicole and their children – Dominique, Laurent and Virginie – had been living in Pégomas for three years. A town in the Cannes *banlieue* with a rural feel, not yet suffocated by the real-estate projects threatening to rid the plain of its farmers, one by one.

Pégomas, pronounced Pégoma or Pégomasse, is peaceful fruit and vegetable country, with villagers who still remember Provence and are perplexed or irritated at the developments and homes they see constantly going up. In the heart of the village a shady bridge crosses the river, the Mourachonne. It makes for a pleasant stroll. The new hamlet, where the Élineaus lived, is a little further on, near a busy road. Their two-storey maisonette was surrounded by a piece of land waiting for a fence.

Upstairs, next to Virginie's bedroom, two bunk beds were occupied by Laurent and Amédée, who was also training at AS Cannes. Dominique slept downstairs, on the sofa bed in a corner of the living room, with a curtain dividing the room.

For Nicole and Jean-Claude, taking in boarders was a way of thanking Raymond Gioanni, the president of the Côte d'Azur district of the French Football Federation. It was thanks to him, who had welcomed them in Cannes with kindness and friendship, that they were able to continue their involvement in football. In Rezé, in the Nantes *banlieue*, Jean-Claude Élineau supervised the trainees, while Nicole helped with administrative tasks. They gave a lot to ASC, just as they had previously given to the Pont-Rousseau schools association. There was more that they could have done, but things were cramped. Nevertheless, they agreed to welcome this new aspiring professional. The sporting year begins in July, and Dominique, the eldest of the children, had to leave in June to carry out his military service. This left a spot free. The corner of the living room would not remain unoccupied for long.

Monsieur Varraud did well to work this out in advance. Zidane's final months at Septèmes confirmed the scout's judgement: on 5 June 1987, the future Cannes player, still registered in the Bouches-du-Rhône, was called up to the national junior team. With the delegation led by Jean-Pierre Escalettes – who would become president of the French Football Federation years later – he travelled to Ireland. There Yazid would discover a world that would leave its mark on his life: the France team. His call-up letter showed his first name as Sincédrie! Zinedine was definitely not yet a household name …

Yazid's destiny followed a course that became increasingly favourable. In just a few weeks, his existence had been turned upside down. Still closed or even unimaginable six months earlier, the door leading to professionalism was now ajar. What had been on the horizon was coming into view. After the insight and insistence of Monsieur Varraud, attracted by a match he had little reason to attend; after the host family, at which Yazid had found a place, it was the turn of the Cannes team to reach the top flight, Division 1!

This rise was all the more deserved as it was obtained at the expense of the D1 club that finished third from bottom, in this case FC Sochaux. During the return match, played in the pleasant atmosphere of a Saturday in June, a record crowd occupied the stands at the Stade Coubertin. The 2–0 win, making up for the 1–0 defeat suffered at Montbéliard, brought about a joy that would not be short-lived. An era of a passion for football had begun in Cannes.

For Yazid, the prospect of playing not only with the professionals but also at the highest level, in the Première Division, was no longer just a dream. But the club would need to stay in D1. At the Coubertin, in the offices under the stands, the idea of spending only one season among the elite had clearly not been ruled out by anyone. But a rare cohesion, a calm environment and a competent workforce were transforming one of the best clubs in D2 into an efficient and solid club capable of establishing itself in the top flight for seasons to come. They were set on one idea: training young players who, at a lower cost, would strengthen the squad and, over time, become first-team players.

It was in this serious and committed atmosphere, combined with Cannes' traditional laid-back attitude and persistent euphoria, that, 29 days after the victory against Sochaux, the baby of the Zidane family arrived.

If all went well, he would not return to the family apartment in Marseille for several weeks, until the holidays. If all went well, it would be a long time until he would be able to return home after the holidays. Maybe it would not be possible again. Ever.

Maybe it was a farewell to his childhood … After 20 days, Yazid turned 15. His new life and career were beginning. He had waited a long time for that moment, and he would have to deal with it whilst far away from his loved ones. Far from Malika, his mother. Far from his elder siblings, his sister Lila, his brothers Noureddine,

Farid and Djamel. And far from his father, who had decided to go with him to Cannes when he left to see him off. A two-hour train journey. A long way.

Jean-Claude Élineau nearly arrived late. His Citroën had broken down. He had had to come to the station with Nicole's car, an Austin Mini that was aptly named; Smaïl struggled to fold his long legs into the back. Yazid, who was not much shorter, climbed into the front with his bag.

It took them 25 minutes to reach Pégomas. Monsieur Zidane left again that night. He only stayed a few hours. The goodbye was low-key and brief; all emotions were contained. What can you say when you are leaving a child? As well as a childhood? A pivotal year in the course of a life would take place away from home.

This was not a normal goodbye. But Smaïl could leave calmly. He had already seen that his son had been entrusted to sensible people. The substitute parents would do their duty. There was also a boy of his age, he would make a good pal, before becoming a friend for life: Laurent, known as Lucky since missing a cinema trip. While in Nantes, Nicole and Jean-Claude had wanted to take him to see a cartoon, *Lucky Luke*, before they were told by a cinema employee that they could not take such a young child in to see the film. His parents turned this misadventure into a nickname.

Lucky Luke, a reference to the speed of the hero of the same name, was also the nickname of the footballer Bruno Bellone. He played at Monaco. He had grown up in La Bocca, near Avenue Chevalier, where he would dribble and shoot for the first time on a small neighbourhood pitch surrounded by trees. The start of his career, six years earlier, had been dazzling. He was still one of France's best strikers. There were rumours of his transfer to ASC.

In Cannes, in the summer of 1987, in the absence of any news other than the usual influx of tourists, there was plenty of talk of football. It had not been spoken about so much since 1949, when the club left D1 for the first time, or since 1932, when the team had won the Coupe de France. At the time it was the only national competition, a few months before the first professional league began. This victory remained the only trophy won by the players in red and white. With Bellone, climbing to Division 1 would be even more intoxicating.

In Pégomas, Yazid was at a safe distance from the local excitement. He spoke little and enjoyed his first moments of relaxation quietly. The day after his arrival was a national holiday. He went to the village dance with Lucky and two friends. He gave the impression of being bored, barely moving his legs when he danced. Nonchalant? Reserved? Thoughtful? What went on inside Yazid's head was a mystery. There was a tendency to see it as nothing more than shyness. But it could also have been seen as maturity, an innate understanding of adulthood, into which he was getting ready to dash headlong without being weighed down by the torments of adolescence. Holding on to the most precious thing of all: the soul of a child.

As for dancing, he did it in silence rather than to music. On the football pitch. And it was he who chose the rhythm, as the inspiration took him. A waltz, for example, when he spun around the ball and back on himself. During a training session with his fellow Under-17s, Lucky was not content to admire the virtuosity of his friend, whose Marseille turns had got the better of more than one opponent. He too tried and succeeded with this daring move, as Yazid watched on. It was a source of pride that would be discussed at home, fuelling the conversation.

Unfortunately, the enjoyment of a piece of skill or the game is not what makes up the majority of training. When you are destined for a professional career, you have to run, jump, stretch and build muscle. The sport is not just a game. And the competition is not just a sport. There is a lot at stake. When you set foot, literally and figuratively, in a major club, you also set foot in a world of struggle. It is not just about having fun with others, as on Place de la Tartane in La Castellane, or on makeshift pitches all over the world, where those who are young at heart can enjoy themselves. Sometimes you have to learn to fight, with madmen in command and cowards who obey.

Luckily for Cannes, Gilles Rampillon was neither of those. He had been a great player and an exemplary champion, punished only once by a referee. Lucid and determined, Jean Varraud, another hard-line opponent of the warrior sport, was keen to skip the intermediate and dangerous steps. He wanted Yazid, although only 15 years old, to join the club's second senior team as quickly as possible, without going through the Under-17s. He had complete confidence in Gilles Rampillon, who was in charge of the professional reserve team. Playing for that team was the final step before the elite. Playing for that team at 15 meant that it would probably not be an end in itself, provided it was backed up by relentless work.

Of course, Yazid and his teammates also had to get used to working without a ball. Without playing. Without pleasure. Without football at all. In the mornings, they would meet in the car park of the Stade Coubertin before heading off towards the trails of Parc de la Valmasque. Long running sessions in the forest were on the agenda. Such is the lot of competitive sportsmen. But not everyone has the opportunity to play under the gaze of such a noble and attentive coach. The former Nantes playmaker was still keen to stress the importance of group performances, but without countering individual initiatives. Yazid's physique was a source of hesitation: should he be played as an attacking midfielder, as he had at his previous club? Rampillon had excelled in this position, with a style based on one-touch passing to his teammates, with his back to the opponents' goal. He believed that someone of Zidane's build could take more play than a number 10. He imagined him wearing the number 8 shirt – usually given to the box-to-box midfielder, positioned less often near the goal, covering more distance across the pitch. More space.

Rampillon hesitated. There was one thing he was sure of. This young player, this adolescent who was discovering a new world, rubbing shoulders with the seniors and playing at a new and higher level of competition, should in no way have his playfulness drilled out of him. He liked playing with the ball. This love had to be channelled.

Jean Fernandez, keeping a discreet eye on his progress, recommended a useful, if not enjoyable, drill. He noticed that Yazid, excellent when it came to his natural sense of the game when facing the opposition's goal, was relatively slow to spin around on himself when he picked up the ball in the opposite direction, with his back towards to the goal.

'Kick the ball against a wall. As soon as it comes back to you, bang! Spin quickly until you're facing the direction of play.'

He committed the advice to memory.

Every evening, Yazid was picked up by Jean-Claude Élineau or Charly Loubet, who made the journey back to his home in Grasse. Pégomas was halfway there. But going home did not mean the end of football. A day of drills did nothing to blunt the passion. Quite the contrary. The demonstration in the street was enlightening. The fun – a word dear to all the great players, strikers in particular – is always to be found in manipulating the ball, controlling it and dribbling with it. Dribbling, getting past the opponent blocking your way with the ball at your feet, is one of the fundamental building blocks of football. In absolute terms, however, a great team can dispense with it if each pass is well measured and received. It turned out that Yazid also liked passing the ball, finding the opening and sending it on without it being intercepted.

But outside the front door of the house in Pégomas, there was no one to pass the ball to. There was only Laurent and Amédée. It was just a kick-about before dinner. No one missed it. Despite all that they had done during the day, the two trainees came together with enthusiasm and good humour. In Allée des Violettes, Yazid felt a bit like he was back on Chemin de Bernex in Marseilles. There were no matches here though, no passes, just a competition; the winner was the one who could perform the most nutmegs. This piece of technical skill held no secrets for Yaz. More often than not, he won the friendly challenge.

Yaz. From one diminutive to the next, he became ever closer to his host family. Yet he still spoke few words. He preferred to listen to music on his cassette player. But his looks and smiles spoke volumes. As did his absences, when his thoughts seemed to fly elsewhere. A long way. A two-hour train journey away.

Brutally uprooted, he missed his nearest and dearest, who did not come to the Riviera as often as they would have liked. In size he was the largest of the Zidanes, but he would always be the youngest, the baby of the family. He missed them more and more. And they missed him too. Despite the odd Saturday or Sunday of freedom, when he was not required to play in an official match, he rarely returned to Place de la Tartane, where his teammates often thought about him. Time with his friends had become episodic: brief, snatched moments. When he came back to Marseille, he had to be content with days here and there, a few hours carved out of a busy schedule.

He was finally a footballer, almost full-time. So he would not cry. At least not in front of everyone. Jean-Claude, Nicole, Dominique, Lucky, Virginie and Amédée did not notice anything. Not even a tear. Given that his words were rare, it was difficult to tell the difference between happiness and pain.

Yazid spoke little and opened up even less; except to Laurent, rarely. Sometimes he would chat with a neighbour, originally from Argentina, who was very interested in football and lived at the other end of the hamlet to the Élineaus' home. Zinedine was not very talkative but not at all asocial. He liked people but preferred to listen to them. He would only talk over and over with his two friends, once he had had his fill of his football … or after the neighbour had confiscated their ball, annoyed at seeing it mistakenly land in her garden.

It was finally time for dinner. There were plenty of people around the table, in a kitchen in which everyone came together after a day at the factory, school or on the pitch. Nicole drew lots to assign chores to each of the children. Luck would determine only the turns, not the share. The responsibility was the same for everyone. There was no lack of work, especially since the mistress of the house aspired to a little relaxation after hours spent at the community centre where she worked.

Two parents, one girl and three boys. Like in Marseille, almost. For Yazid, it was not the same family, but the same kind of family. Large and close, with little room in the house but plenty in the heart.

The families of Chemin de Bernex and Allée des Violettes had got to know one another and respected each other. Laurent was particularly fond of Monsieur Zidane, whom he regarded as a philosopher, a sage. He liked to talk with him, to immerse himself in his vision of life, influenced by both his respect for others and self-sacrifice, knowing that nothing can be achieved without effort, nor without rest.

At Pégomas, Yazid was kept away from the temptations of Cannes city centre. He went to bed early and slept a lot, as much as he could to counter the tiredness. Dreaming of victories, in a red and white striped shirt, at La Bocca or elsewhere, with the number 10 or 8 on his back, it mattered little.

Near the house, on the right, outside the front door, was somewhere he could give his parents good news: he rang Marseille from the phone box next to the boules pitch. This precious link reassured both parties. Everything was fine.

Over the passing months, spectators in the French Première Division learned all about this unknown club, avoiding the superficial clichés attached to the city known for its International Film Festival. The Cannes team was like a solid block, not an assortment of former champions awaiting retirement or fading artists. Only Bruno Bellone, who had been transferred from AS Monaco, was a big star.

Recruitment was not based on any image or reputation; management was rigorous and training was planned over the long term. Complementarity, the paramount objective of every technician, was a watchword. In the Division 3 league, in the reserve team, or two steps down in the Division d'Honneur league, one particular duo demonstrated this complementarity. Taking advantage of Yazid's precise passing was a forward to whom he indirectly owed his place in Cannes: Fabrice Monachino, whom he had replaced at the training camp in Aix. Together they tasted the ultimate joy in 1988: the France Under-17 team!

For Yazid, the future was becoming clearer. If he was already one of the best Under-17s in the country, what was stopping him becoming a professional? Or even an international? Making his mark at the youngest level would be an ideal springboard. In Spain, in Malaga, during the final phase of the European Championship in their age group, the two Cannes players could not take their places in the starting 11 for granted. But they did play. Yazid played for the whole match against Turkey, during which Fabrice was substituted, just as he was in the next match against Spain. This time, Yazid did not play. A Bordeaux player, Christophe Dugarry, was picked ahead of him.

In the room they shared, the two players from Cannes talked about their life playing for the *Tricolore*. Serious and keen to apply themselves, they intended to remain faithful to the principles instilled in them at La Bocca. They only deviated from this under friendly pressure from their teammates looking for a distraction. In two-seater electric cars intended only for use in the grounds of the hotel where they were staying, they took to the road, without permission or driving licences! Led by the troublemaker Francis Llacer, a Paris Saint-Germain player, the merry three-vehicle band surprised Spanish drivers, stunned by this convoy worthy of the *Wacky Races*! Yazid and Fabrice were in high spirits, enjoying this short-lived entertainment that gave them a brief escape from their strictly regulated world.

Footballers do not lead the unrestrained existence so typical of adolescence. High jinks are forbidden, at the risk of seeing the long-hoped-for possibility of a career vanish into thin air. You have to comply with a healthy lifestyle, be careful not to blunt the sensibilities that competition sharpens ... and take care of your body. Fabrice had a painful cough. Yazid had the solution, always at hand, in his bag: 'Here, take that, you'll be fine tomorrow!'

He gave him a round box, containing an ointment for soothing respiratory complaints. Fabrice applied it. The following day the pain had gone. He understood that his partner in crime already had the soul of a professional.

The two AS Cannes players began the third phase of the tournament but did not finish it. The match against Hungary was also their last. France were knocked out. But Cannes' Under-17s returned to the Coubertin with a wealth of experience and an air about them.

The pair often became a trio at La Bocca. One would pass, the other would cross ... and then his friend Noureddine would score. Yazid knew the scorer well. He had been recruited at the same time, also by Jean Varraud. He was originally from Saint-André, a Marseille neighbourhood just two kilometres from Septèmes, and played at the Saint-Antoine club, in whose shirt he proved to be a fantastic goalscorer. Two weeks after they both joined Cannes, Yazid came to see Noureddine to pay him a touching compliment: 'You were my idol! I would come and watch you with my brother. The goals you scored...!'

While still in Marseille, Yazid had had plenty of admiration for two great players named Noureddine. One was called Zidane; his brother. The other was called Mouka; he was now playing alongside him!

Over the months, the Cannes players got to know and admire the man with the initials ZZ. But few directors took much of an interest in him. His skills were enough to seduce the purists and hint at something better. He was inconsistent but promising. Most importantly, he was different. He had style, of the kind that can attract spectators all on its own. As well as aggression from opponents.

During a match in Marseille, in the Sainte-Marthe district, a player temporarily banned from competition was sitting on the opposing team's bench. Yazid was sent off. On his way back to the dressing room, he saw the suspended player get up quickly and petulantly, before he came over and punched him. Behind the fence, his parents and two of his brothers, obviously distressed but helpless, watched on at a scene that was unfortunately all too commonplace. The path to professionalism can also be strewn with these kinds of obstacles. Dominating your opponent is not always enough. You also have to know how to control yourself, not to respond to provocations and to endure violence.

Fortunately, there was Allée des Violettes and the serenity of the hamlet. Yazid was at home there, where the only fight involved a tennis ball. Two against two when Dominique was visiting. Now his military service had ended, he had started a catering course in Nice and only came back to Pégomas to sleep once or twice a week. He had to share the living-room bed with Zinedine.

One night, coming back from the Beach Regency, a hotel on Nice's Promenade des Anglais, Dominique found Yazid asleep, across the bed, his long legs stretched across the diagonal. Getting into bed without waking him up would be too difficult. Thankfully, there was the sofa. The following day, Yazid, confused, apologised to Dominique.

A rope was stretched across the alley, between the Élineaus' house and the neighbours'. A box was marked out with chalk on the tarmac. The two apprentice footballers faced off against the two brothers. Moments of happiness and serenity, in the calm hinterland of the Riviera, when the light of dusk disappeared behind the Tanneron Mountains. Carefree moments in Pégomas. Moments that would be the last.

Some weeks later, Dominique would come home to an empty room. Yaz would no longer be there, nor would Amédée, who had spent three years on the banks of the Mourachonne. They would no longer wait for Jean-Claude to pick them up in the late afternoon, putting an end to their table-football or billiard games with Sandra, the club secretary.

The year of transition came to an end. It was time for a second separation, to say goodbye to his second family. A cherry tree, planted one morning by Yazid, would stay in the Élineaus' garden and would grow as he had done. One day, no doubt, it would dwarf his six feet one. That would be the measure of time passing, the shadow of the memory of an endearing and quiet boy.

It was time to put away the Walkman, whose tunes had filled quiet moments, to say goodbye to Pégomas and, this time, to say farewell to family life for good, at least as a child.

Zinedine Zidane, aged 16, was moving house. He went to live in Cannes, at the Logis des Jeunes de Provence, in room 207. He was on his own, but had plenty of people around him, including an old family friend: Noureddine Mouka.

Michel Almandoz, Frédéric Dufau, Franck Gomez, Jojot Moussa-Madi, Gilles Hampartzoumian, David Bettoni, Éric Giacopino, Zinedine Zidane, Denis Armbruster, Noureddine Mouka and Fabrice Monachino. Eleven teammates – some close, others not – who would make up a team that, thanks to absences and their involvement in other categories at the club, would never exist.

They shared the dream of a professional career, belonging to AS Cannes, and daily life at the Logis des Jeunes de Provence.

The Boulevard de la Croisette and the Rue d'Antibes were not far away. The prestigious centre of Cannes was nearby, on the other side of the railway line. It could be reached by an underpass, just a few seconds from the Foyer Mimont, the 50 rooms and 18 studios of which, with a small auditorium and a cafeteria, made up the Logis des Jeunes. It was a good step along the road to adulthood and independence.

The buildings were modern, functional and unadorned, decorated with the posters, classifieds and leaflets that are invaluable when setting out on an independent life, sometimes without close family nearby. The residents were usually accommodated according to social criteria. Some individuals required special attention from the staff. But the atmosphere was relaxed and easy-going. Those involved in sports contributed a lot. These included the aspiring trainees from AS Cannes, about 20 in total, who were accommodated here while waiting for the training centre to be built. They formed a rowdy group, whose collective mood was rarely in tune with that of the neighbours, but, paradoxically, it helped maintain a happy atmosphere. Days were strictly organised. They would train twice, from 9am to 11am and from 4pm to 6pm; they had lunch at the Collège des Mûriers near the Coubertin, and dinner at Mimont, to which those aged under 18 were required to return no later than 10.30pm. Their presence at this time was attested to by a notebook they had to sign each day. Rent and meals were paid for by the club.

Life could certainly be more difficult, especially for athletes in sports other than football. Olivier, known as Billy, a volleyball player at Cannes Aéro Sports, the joker of the residence, organised disco nights … when he had time: training sessions at his club, dependent on Aérospatiale, were held from 8pm to 10.30pm as his teammates, amateurs and students, had jobs or activities that occupied their time during the day.

In comparison, the football routine was worry-free. Apprentices were paid in increments, at 25 per cent then 35, 45 and 55 per cent of the statutory minimum hourly wage. But they were placed in conditions conducive to training and had few material concerns. They could enjoy the nightlife and delights of the beach.

Some of them, those who were old enough to drive, had a licence and a car. This was true of Lionel Firly, who, whenever he went back to visit his family, would give several of the players from Marseille a lift: Giacopino, Gomez, Hampartzoumian, Madi, Mouka and Zidane ... a subgroup within the group, not all of whom knew each other. Although originally from the same *arrondissement* but a little older, Lionel had never heard of Zidane. Now it was different.

Quietly, whether in the car or at the residence, Yazid had made his mark, not thanks to a kind of leader's authority but because of a natural kindness and talent that commanded respect. His kindness was appreciated on a daily basis by a newcomer: David Bettoni. David came from Saint-Priest and owed his arrival to the goalkeeper at his previous club, ASPTT Lyon. During a match against Cavigal in Nice, the keeper had attracted the attention of Alain Moizan, the general manager at ASC. But the goalkeeper declined the recruitment offer from Moizan, who then asked Bettoni to come to Cannes for a trial. Jean Fernandez, passing the trainee pitch, spotted him and asked his colleagues to sign him.

When he arrived in Cannes, David struggled to adjust to the daily repetition of training sessions because he was not used to the pace. The club chiropodist advised him to bathe his feet.

The ideal place in which to do this was a bidet. His room did not have one but Yazid's did and he immediately offered to let him use it.

Over ten evenings, the two boys got to know each other. They would chat for at least ten minutes, during which David would soak his feet while Yazid was on his bed. A friendship was born. It extended beyond the walls of the room, to a pizzeria near Mimont called Chez Xavier, where the Cannes players were regulars. But rarely any further, to nightclubs or elsewhere.

'Come on, Yaz!'

'No, I'm going home.'

It was a regular discussion. Night owls often have trouble with form. They knew the response, which was often also David's. Once, only once, did those who had been at the residence longer succeed in making them give in. Yazid, who never drank alcohol, consumed more than he should have. But he held his own and made it back valiantly to his room ... unlike Fabrice Monachino, his unfortunate companion at the initiation at the Malibu, who had to miss training the following day.

Despite appearances, Yaz was a willing joker. But not to excess. An observer ready to listen to others whenever they succumbed to a narcissism that increases when stardom is on the horizon, he liked to do impressions, mimicking his teammates or well-known figures. His face, so often impassive, came to life vividly when he was taken by the urge to reproduce the grimacing style of the actor Louis de Funès.

Véronique, an adviser at the Logis, underlined how much the footballers contributed to keeping a happy atmosphere at the residence: 'They were very well behaved. We didn't hear anyone talking about them. They didn't cause any problems. If only all our residents had been like them! They weren't deadbeats or the types to sneak out at night. There was an emptiness when they left!'

And leave they did. A few months later. All of them, off to La Bocca. 'It's going to be tougher,' said one of them, Ludovic Pollet, well aware of the remoteness of the planned buildings, next to the Coubertin, a long way from the city and its diversions. 'They saw lots of people here!' remembers Véronique. A world that it was hard to believe could be entirely masculine, group spirit or not.

'There were also female residents,' Véronique explains. 'Dancers,' the footballers had told her, not insensitive to the charms of the trainees at the Rosella Hightower School.

Far from Pégomas, Yazid was still under the watchful eye of the Élineaus, with the consent of his parents, of course. 'Children need a family nucleus to guide them from time to time.' Jean-Claude has not forgotten Nicole's words. Sensing the emergence of a peer group with a negative influence, at the club rather than at the residence, he decided to prepare for any eventuality and resolved to make his authority felt with a telling-off. For the first and last time.

He had never previously needed to lay down such a clear boundary. He thought his intervention would help keep his protégé away from bad influences, or at least from influences that had not been lucky enough to have parents like his own. Lucky enough to have received 'an extraordinary education . . . as you owe it to yourself to give,' clarifies Guy Lacombe, future successor to Rampillon, expressing in one sentence the rarity of something that should, by rights, be taken for granted: an education, morals and affection.

For Yazid, the Élineau family was still reassuringly close. At Mimont, his colleagues were friendly and focused on the same professional goal. Thanks to them he could begin his adult life with points of reference. Affinities. Complicity, even. With one or two of his friends at least. But nothing like back at La Castellane, of course. The context was different: Malek, Richard, Yvon and Jean-François were his friends; Denis, David, Fabrice and Gilles were his colleagues. They had a shared goal: turning professional. Several of them had a good chance of getting there. But none had Zidane's style.

One day, in the early afternoon, while he was working in his office, Jean Fernandez heard a knock at the door. It was Yazid, who had come to get a ball. His friends had gone into town, to the cinema or for a walk; either on their own, in groups or with girlfriends. He wanted to work on his speed. He took a ball and went to the stadium entrance near the ticket booths, to the little artificial pitch where there was a section of wall used for drills. He remembered Fernandez's words. He kicked the ball against the wall. It came back to his feet. At the moment of contact he turned around, as quickly as possible. Once, twice, a hundred times.

None of the trainees had Zidane's style. None had his desire. None had his diligence. How could he not succeed? Smaïl and Malika would have liked to have been sure. They came to the office of Gilbert Chamonal, the secretary general, for an important moment. Gilbert left them briefly and went to speak to Fernandez: 'Zidane is about to sign his training contract. His parents are here. Come and meet them.'

The coach arrived. For the first and last time, he saw the sweet and timid-looking woman. For the first time, he saw the man, proud of his son, just as his wife was, and eager to ask the same question he had asked Gilles Rampillon two years earlier. Smaïl took Jean by the arm, led him to one side and spoke in a low voice.

'Monsieur Fernandez, do you think Yazid can make it?'

It was no longer time for logical prudence. The answer was clear: 'Don't worry, Monsieur Zidane. He's a boy with a fantastic mindset and plenty of talent. He'll become a great player. He will make it.'

3

16 YEARS, 10 MONTHS AND 27 DAYS

The prospect of playing in D1 had never been so close. Especially when Yazid was doing astonishing things on the pitch. During a match with the Under-18 team, a clearance from the opposing team's goalkeeper landed in the centre circle. Yazid stuck out a leg and waited for the ball, which came down stuck to his foot. His control was flawless. Perfect. Spectacular!

The kid from La Castellane already had exceptional skills that allowed him to transform a badly measured pass no one else could do anything with into something amazing.

He had lost none of his qualities. He had also been given the chance to acquire new ones, starting by correcting his faults. He had an inimitable and exhilarating way of making the ball stick to him like a magnet, of controlling it and sending it on to a teammate 30 or 40 metres away. But Gilles Rampillon thought his ball-striking could be improved, that he could be quicker, did not have enough pace and that his movements followed on too slowly from one another. It was obviously not a question of his natural skill level. The Division d'Honneur, and even more so the Troisième

Division, was a blessing for such a motivated and gifted boy. He knew how to put in the work required so he could be compared to experienced adults.

Despite looking like a lanky beanpole, Yazid's manager considered him a sportsman with great athletic potential. But that did not mean all his efforts had to be focused on his physique to the detriment of technical development. Gilles Rampillon was not one of those who advised against dribbling. He realised it was Yazid's greatest skill; he strove to improve it, to steer it towards an awareness of depth so an opponent could be taken out during the lead-in to a pass.

Such a brilliant young man could have been damaged by authoritarian coaches, at academies where physical performance was a determining factor, easier to judge than development on the pitch. Distance travelled can be measured. Positioning can be observed, by definition, by the human eye, without the help of figures. But technology has infiltrated the sports field. Quantifications, computer and statistical analysis have entered a domain previously reserved for pure subjectivity. The art of football nevertheless remains resistant to scientific explanation.

At Cannes, creative players were not forced to take people on; their intensity was not drilled out of them by exhausting running sessions. Work was not tailor-made for the individual, but it was at least varied. Endurance for some, speed for others, etc.

Gradually, a pleasantly surprised Gilles Rampillon noticed that Yazid had a large margin for progress, the limits of which were hard to assess. He was of the opinion that neither his height – now six feet one, just an inch off his eventual height – nor his relaxed approach were exploited enough. He was impressed more than anything by his ability to listen and his intellectual qualities. This receptive and attentive boy, who was also modest and ambitious, was not yet familiar with the world of professional football. But he was aware of the path that separated him from it. So he listened.

'Yazid, there's a principle here. You have to see quickly. You have to know who you're going to pass the ball to even before you've received it.' Zinedine listened to the theory and put it into practice.

'Yazid, you've got to get free from your marker,' his coach insisted and repeated. The quality of the play depends on the number of calls for the ball, on the variety of solutions offered to the person with the ball, and therefore on the number and availability of players in motion. Zinedine went back again to practise, training in moving without the ball, which was not something he was fond of, nor the basis of his game.

This message was not understood by all the apprentices. Zinedine understood and learned. He listened. He was brilliant. And he was lucky, as he would also be understood by Gilles Rampillon's successor: Guy Lacombe. He was also a former Nantes and Cannes player, also forced to bring an end to his career because of injury, also someone who had transformed himself into a technician; he would define and apply an effective training policy, profoundly transforming the structure of the club. In January 1989, when Rampillon was still director of the centre, Lacombe took charge of a young group of players in 'post-training'. Yazid would have to rise to their level and redouble his efforts, forced to progress because he was the youngest. He was lucky.

What's more, apart from the very talented but older Philippe Carrat, there was little competition for his position. Even luckier.

Guy Lacombe did not tell him that he would become a professional. He didn't say that to anyone. He said the same thing to everyone, but addressed them all in a different way. Several methodologies allowed him to better understand his charges and refine his teaching methods. Among the instruments he used was a sporting personality questionnaire, the model of which was designed by a professor from Clermont-Ferrand for use with any type of athlete. The questionnaire consisted of 240 questions, the responses to which came in the form of yes or no boxes to be ticked.

Three points became clear from Yazid's responses: his motivation was very high, his self-esteem quite low, and he did not put himself ahead of others. This final point did not surprise those around him, but confirmed a very unusual characteristic among players of his technical level. Usually, great technicians use their skill to make themselves stand out. The attraction towards the opposing goal is frequent, even systematic – because scoring a goal is also the best way of getting individual recognition.

A football fan always wants to get at least two pieces of information about a match he or she has missed: the score and, if relevant, the names of the scorers.

The goal, as its name indicates, is the purpose of football. Scoring is more rewarding, more appreciated than the preparatory work, and certainly more rewarding than defence, in which performance is less spectacular.

Yazid, excellent in the attacking phases, was not obsessed with scoring. His teammates had no complaints. On the other hand, he had to overcome his deficiencies in the recovery phases. He would succeed because he knew how to show self-sacrifice for the benefit of the group. He was rare in that respect. Guy Lacombe saw additional proof of this with the results of another test, aimed at determining the way in which knowledge is acquired. The least common, extremely rare case – even rarer among Latins than Anglo-Saxons – is that of auditory predominance, when an individual learns by listening. A person's 'inner voice' is the best aid to memory, better than sight or touch, the case for the majority of athletes.

Zinedine Zidane was particularly auditory when it came to learning. His trainer took this into account, and when he spoke to him chose a vocabulary rich in evocative words. Words that the player, unconsciously, retained and interpreted better than others. They really 'spoke' to him. They made sense.

These techniques are still poorly exploited in an academic setting. They would perhaps have been useful for Yazid, who was less happy and motivated at school – he achieved a vocational qualification in footballing professions – than in his sport. Like all the players in his year, he studied at the CFA. In a footballing context, this abbreviation referred to the old French amateur league. In Cannes, what first came to mind was the Centre de Formation d'Apprentis (Apprentice Training Centre), located, like the Mimont residence, on the northern edge of the railway, on Boulevard d'Alsace. It trained future chefs, pastry chefs and hairdressers.

Surname: Zidane
First name: Yazid
Address: Logis des Jeunes de Provence, 06400 Cannes
Phone number: 99 59 62

At the bottom of the blue cardboard cover of Zidane's apprentice notebook, opposite where it was printed with the words '*Prénoms*' (first names), Yazid had written only one. Yet, the cover showed the six digits of his telephone number, with or without the 93 in brackets, the dialling code that had come into force that year. In red or blue ink, the figures were scribbled in their dozens, in all directions. Diagonally, horizontally, vertically ... Was this a call for help, or at least for communication? Or simply evidence of boredom in class?

At the CFA, the apprentice pastry chefs had a laboratory, while the hairdressers had a practice salon. The footballers did not have a pitch. That was not where they learned their profession. For most of them, knowing how to write, read, count and acquire a cultural background was not a priority.

Faced with the students' inertia, the teacher in charge of the biology class decided not to teach. On Monday, between 2 and 3pm, there was no talk of anatomy applied to sport, but just of sport, or rather the matches that had taken place that weekend. The 'friendly gang' from Marseille, as the teacher portrayed them, were more expansive when describing goals and free kicks than talking about muscles or bones. They now sometimes reminisce about misdemeanours dating back to that time, not so long ago, when school was definitely not their thing. Eggs thrown at cars are mentioned, but no one owns up to other, more subtle pranks.

Yazid, who sat at the back of the class, was no more talkative than normal. But sometimes he was more disruptive. Whatever the case, there was little praise from his teachers. The comments in his quarterly reports became less and less flattering. His first year was honourable. It started quite well, of course, with an 'attitude needs work', but irreproachable diligence. In the first semester, an 'A' in Citizenship, with an unequivocal 'very good', 'good participation' and 'satisfactory overall', counterbalanced by 'attitude too often obstructive', 'poor attendance' and 'little serious work'.

In the second semester: 'should have participated more', 'little work' and an 'AB' or 'talkative'! Was the boredom so great as to drive an individual so besotted with silence to become talkative?

Despite a 'lack of work', his passage into the second year was granted. But studying soon became secondary. More and more often, the administration at the CFA received pre-printed cards in the post intended to justify absences on the dates in question: 'was not present on 3 November', 'was not present on 13 and 14 April', etc. The space allocated for a response was filled in by the club general secretary. His writing was as regular and clear as the reasons mentioned. 'Took part in a training camp at Clairefontaine, near Paris, with the France Under-18 team', 'absence due to physio'.

During the second year, eight absences partly explained his mediocre results. The comments were self-explanatory. 'Keep working hard', 'must try harder', 'little serious work', 'does not work', 'average' in the first semester, with this instruction from the headmaster: 'Act like an adult!' 'Complete lack of seriousness, childish attitude', wrote one teacher, the namesake of a former manager at Paris Saint-Germain, well known for his strictness. 'Too many absences for serious work', 'just average', 'no effort in his work, childish behaviour!' concluded a second semester, complemented by a sarcastic reminder from the deputy headmistress: 'Classes at the CFA are mandatory!'

Mandatory classes … But Yazid, who had left the Collège Henri-Barnier in Marseille after Year 8, had good reason for giving up on the world of school. Football, which had always been his preference, monopolised his time and thoughts.

In his file at the CFA, his destiny was written in black and white: 'Plays professional football and athletic sports.' This was pushed to the highest level. After joining the professional squad, after the Under-17s, here he was back with the France team. Further proof that Yazid, irreproachable on the sporting front and finally spotted by the selectors, was on the right track. He needed it.

In Cannes, as elsewhere, the directors would need to make cuts at the end of the course. Necessarily cruel choices would be made; the professional career of some apprentices would stop at the academy. After two promising years, such an end would have been a big disappointment for Yazid. He would have lost both his dreams and his job. Jean Varraud was well aware of this, and measured his selection among the best Under-18s in the country by this yardstick.

The discoverer of talent, of diamonds in the rough, was not attracted by bank accounts. He was the opposite of a mercenary individual. He was also a proud man, who did not go cap in hand. And especially not at that moment, while the club was successfully entering a structuring phase. On the other hand, he knew how important Yazid's sporting and financial success was. For him, for his family to whom he would have so much liked to bring some comfort, a future free from financial worries. Smaïl would have a happy and comfortable retirement. He would not be solely dependent on income from his jobs as a labourer and security guard, which provided the essentials and, most importantly, a dignified situation without handouts or compromises.

At AS Cannes, this mentality, as old as humanity but facing the onslaught of an upstart's world, emblematic of the decade, was shared by several influential figures. Honesty, candour and loyalty were also words with which Jean Varraud and Jean Fernandez were both familiar. The two Jeans got along well. Sometimes they would set off together by car in search of talent. They went to Saint-Étienne on a moving journey, a nostalgic detour through the neighbourhood where Monsieur Varraud spent his childhood. They saw the family home, where his parents who had worked as poultry sellers lived; an honest couple who preferred generosity to the temptations of a profitable black market during the war years. On the outside walls and ceilings, under the shelter next to the house, plenty of marks still evoked a footballing past, left by the tireless shots kicked by the young *Stéphanois* – the local term for residents of Saint-Etienne – still there 50 years later!

Jean Fernandez's childhood was more modest. Uprooted from his native Algeria, his father settled on the western shores of the metropolitan Mediterranean. He was a fisherman. Like Smaïl, he passed on his values of hard work and respect to his son.

Fernandez lived passionately; his early days in the profession were punctuated, after promotion to the Première Division, by a purely honorific but very encouraging reward: coach of the year, awarded by a specialist newspaper. He was also the youngest professional manager – two of his former players, Alain Moizan and Albert Émon, who became general manager and assistant coach respectively, were older than him. He was one of those responsible for building the club. No one could imagine him leaving, abandoning, even for a higher salary, what he had so patiently built. 'Jeannot', as everyone called him – fans, friends and family and the club's directors – was a 'hard worker'. A perfectionist and a tireless worker, shy and not particularly talkative, a child of the sun and toil, the young coach understood and appreciated his youngest player. He was aware of his qualities, his work. He also knew that, thanks to the match bonus, an appearance in the Première Division, however brief, would triple his salary. He was aware of the expectation. On a technical level, he could see that Yazid's qualities were superior to those of every other professional at the club. But he did not want to throw him into competition too early, into a demanding physical situation that could be harsh and sometimes painful, the repetition of which would subject his body to a severe test.

The end of the league season was a good time. Even without Bruno Bellone, who had gone to Montpellier in the close season but whose return was rumoured, relegation to the Deuxième Division was avoided for the second consecutive year.

On the penultimate day of competition, Yazid made his debut on a D1 pitch. At the Stade de la Beaujoire in Nantes on 20 May 1989, he came on in the 78th minute. A quarter of an hour of play, a shot that came off the post, a 1–1 draw and a good personal performance that would linger in the memory. His start had been successful, and the players' bonus was doubled by the president, delighted with the result. It represented six times the amount of an aspiring player's salary.

The some 6,000 inhabitants of La Castellane were quickly informed. For the first time, some of them heard the name of their child, brother, friend or neighbour spoken on the radio. It was a strange feeling.

One night, in the car park at the Coubertin, Gilles Rampillon felt a hand on his shoulder and heard a soft voice: 'Thank you, Monsieur Rampillon.'

The manager turned around. Smaïl Zidane was standing in front of him. Smiling. Thanks to his son's skill, he was beginning to answer the question Smaïl did not stop asking. His son, there was now no doubt, could become a professional footballer.

Zinedine Zidane was aged 16 years, 10 months and 27 days. His progression had been steady, sustained. He had not broken through abruptly; he was not in danger of collapsing. His precocity did not go unnoticed. People were keen to see him again. He was ready.

'I aspire to becoming a trainee and to one day turning professional.' For players in training, this maxim went without saying.

Two years after his arrival, Yazid was no longer aspiring; he was a trainee. This meant a tripling of his monthly salary and a higher probability of playing regularly with the professionals. Since the match in Nantes, followed by another 11 days later in Caen, the D1 was no longer a fantasy or an ideal, but a reality. A reality with a springlike feel in a stadium full of support.

The season that had just come to an end was that of his first great memories. For Yazid, it ended in the friendly rural environment of the Municipal Sport and Leisure Association (ASLM) tournament. The ASLM, probably one of the best-known acronyms in Cannes, brought together municipal service employees. On a Sunday in June, it organised matches that were open to all, whether or not they were licensed players, on the pitches of the Stade Saint-Cassien, near the Cannes-Mandelieu airport.

Yazid and his teammates, including Malek, his childhood friend, Laurent and Amédée, made a formidable team. Les Tout Fous (The Crazy Gang), as Lucky named them, progressed through the competition to the quarter-finals.

Like his teammates, Yazid left Saint-Cassien with the gift of a fondue set and an unexpected sermon. He should never have taken part in the tournament, which had exposed him to potential injury, he was told firmly by the team. His body had become his working tool; he had to protect it, not risking the slightest accident, not calling on it unjustifiably outside the normal scope of its services – of its *profession*.

Here was further proof that time with his friends was now a thing of the past.

In this case, the fear on the part of the AS Cannes directors was retrospective because the tournament was spoiled by incidents, although fortunately without physical consequences for anyone.

A fight broke out and spread into the outdoor refreshment bar. ASLM members, volunteers like Bruno Bellone's mother, were serving customers by the touchline, where people could rest and chat while standing, sitting or lying down. They suddenly dispersed in panic and began running in all directions. Someone had started waving around a handgun.

Those who wanted to protect Yazid were aware neither of the atmosphere at the time, nor his propensity to react to dirty tricks. This was not new. While he was playing for the Under-13s, the final of the tournament held in Roanne was stopped because he had head-butted an aggressive opponent … incited to violence by his coach, who went on to manage the France women's team! More recently, in Montpellier, in the Troisième Division, he was sent off for the same type of vengeful reaction. As a consequence he was banned from all competition for three weeks. It was a long time, which gave Guy Lacombe the idea of introducing 'dressing-room duty', a cleaning task that would become the responsibility of anyone suspended from then on. At the same time, with a phrase that was a little caricatured but realistic, not to mention distressing, the manager exposed Yazid to the risks of the profession, the profession of brilliant dribbler, someone who protects the ball so well their opponent has no idea how to get hold of it: 'If one day you stop getting hit, you'll know you aren't as good any more!'

At La Bocca, during the 1989–90 season that was just beginning, the blows were not visible. They were not administered on the pitch but on an imaginary chessboard, where everyone moves their own pawns. New pawns, moved by new hands. A municipal election fostered a change of mood and the atmosphere no longer felt like that of a family, unless it was a family whose members were tearing each other apart.

Football, which was being increasingly broadcast on television, a source of money and power, had long since become an instrument for businessmen and politicians. Drunk with the prospect of victory at any price and with ever-increasing budgets, those who exploited volunteers lined the pockets of backers who came out of nowhere, ready to make 'football merchandise' part of their portfolio.

These kind of psychological dramas were nothing new. From Nice to Marseille, and even in Monaco, in a less conspicuous fashion, they had long been tracing the contours of a turbulent Mediterranean, where a clan atmosphere competed with an insane attraction for the plundering of resources. Cannes had never been a violent place. Nor had the Stade Coubertin, where they could barely remember a handful of troublemakers from Nice, or the devastating visit of a group of Marseille fans who ripped up numerous wooden benches in the south stand. But the city was changing. Intrigues and administrations were no longer confined to rackets among closed groups of well-known figures or elected local officials, but to the schemes of larger networks. Cannes was no longer a provincial town of 60,000, where a somewhat outdated paternalism could still be seen to exist. It was now an international seaside resort, whose famous name carried a strong cachet, and consequently huge market value.

In this context, a football club in the Première Division was manna from heaven.

At ASC, the partial replacement of the management team and the profits to be derived from the club's elite status threatened its place in D1. At the Coubertin, as elsewhere in France and in the hectic world of football business, the long term, the durability of work carried out and the future of incumbent executives became uncertain. The choices made by Jean Fernandez, the principal architect of the team's rise to D1 and the consolidation of its position, were contested from the very first defeats on the pitch. Despite this, the atmosphere within the squad did not suffer too much. Away from home, the mood was good; betting on that day's results helped a lot. In Nantes, where the team from Cannes lost in the 16th match of the league season, the time had come for a prediction competition. The aim: the final score and names of every scorer in the match between Marseille and Paris Saint-Germain. Marseille won 2–1 thanks to goals from Chris Waddle and Enzo Francescoli.

Francescoli was Yazid's favourite player; he continued to wait, to dream of the day he might perhaps cross his path. After a succession of bad results, the team in red and white sank into the relegation zone. But the season was far from over. Fernandez was keen not to overdramatise; not to avoid criticism, but because it was logical that the club's means did not guarantee it would escape relegation every year. The vagaries of competition are irrefutable.

Faced with a latent hostility that was often unacknowledged – at least directly – Jeannot began smiling less. On a human level, he became more withdrawn; in sporting terms, he was reluctant to apply bold solutions, such as involving new young players. Such as a player who had only just turned 17, barely accustomed to the hard struggle of the negative spiral of a run of defeats, without the serenity of a comfortable league position, with the need to collect at least a point for a draw if not two for a win from every match. Only one of the 11 trainees would play that season: Manuel Nogueira, a defensive midfielder who would take part in two of the 38 league games.

The desire to prove his value, the energy, technique and ability of Yazid to keep the ball, to play for time against a pressing opposition, were nevertheless interesting arguments. But Fernandez, fearful of 'burning him out, physically and psychologically', failed to pick him. Neither at the Coubertin, where he would probably have been confident, nor elsewhere.

Five months after his D1 debut, Yazid would not make the trip to Nantes. He would not see the Beaujoire that season. In October, he would instead return to his beloved Bouches-du-Rhône. Not Marseille's Stade Vélodrome, where AS Cannes had earned a well-deserved draw despite a goal from Francescoli, but Martigues, with the France team.

The French Under-18s were playing their English counterparts. In the stands, Jean Varraud was sitting next to Guy Lacombe. Yazid played the second half. He replaced a boy he had known since the Under-17s. Someone whose fame had already extended beyond Bordeaux, where he played for the Girondins, the great French club of the decade. The player, Christophe Dugarry, was a powerful forward. Monsieur Varraud thought his game complemented that of Yazid and wondered why the two had never played together. He bluntly spoke to the manager about it, but the response was concerning: 'They don't complement each other.'

'How can people who do that for a living get away with saying those kind of things?!'

Guy Lacombe chose to laugh about it, moved by the passion and approach of his colleague: 'Monsieur Varraud, you're priceless!'

Priceless, perhaps. Unpaid, definitely. But he did not care. The scout continued to find happiness in a sport that involved him searching high and low. He would set off with Lacombe to 'far-flung corners' in search of new talent. But he did not lose sight of the club's reserve team, in which Yazid became one of the undisputed starting 11. After falling from the third to the fourth division, the reserve team's mission was to secure promotion as soon as possible.

Guy Lacombe had every reason to be happy with Yazid's performances, which were described in the same way as Jeannot: 'hard-working'. His return to D1 was not compromised, it was just postponed; by a matter of months for someone who worked so hard and was so gifted. In the words of Lacombe, he was the model of a player who 'could not be trained' but merely humbly instilled with the principles of play and behaviour.

The risk, with a sportsman like him, was instead that he would be corrupted. A risk ruled out with Rampillon and Lacombe, who succeeded him before the start of the season, in June, as head of the training academy. Yazid the artist was lucky, he continued to avoid those who loudly and obsessively accused Jean Varraud of 'championitis'. But he stood firm and reiterated: 'Shouting is pointless. This boy isn't just anyone!' And there was a precedent.

Monsieur Varraud could refer to another Jean, a great name: Jean Snella. He shared a love of great football, a noble and aesthetic art, a collective discipline with respect for others. Varraud had spent a month at Snella's home in Geneva, where he was in charge of Servette, one of the best clubs in the country. 'He never raised his voice, nor did his players; they played at 150 per cent for him, while others, now, are only playing within 30 or 40 per cent of their means.' They had gone on trips together, like those that took them to the reserve bench of a team in northern France, alongside another French manager. They got up in the middle of the match and left: 'He was screaming so much! He treated people like morons!'

There was none of that under the rule of Guy Lacombe, who could nevertheless be intransigent. Results were quick to come.

The Cannes reserve team were dominant in a fourth division in which the average level was clearly below their own. Goals and victories came thick and fast. Yazid led the play; strikers converted his passes. The gap between them and their opponents was often enormous. At the Coubertin, the game against Béziers finished with an extraordinary 7–0 scoreline, while Pont-Saint-Esprit were defeated 9–0. The setting provided the ideal opportunity to get used to playing in competition with the professionals, who strengthened the reserves when not picked among the 13 selected for each D1 game. Passing the ball to a pro was almost like being one yourself.

Zidane loved to pass the ball, to provide scoring opportunities, as Fabrice Monachino was well aware. With him he acted as a real leader, almost a guide, dispensing well-considered advice or comforting words. 'Spread out the play. I'll send you the ball over there.' 'Wait, calm down.' 'He should have made you play…' On 30 October 1989, the pair represented the football section of AS Cannes at a ceremony held at the Palais des Festivals. The city honoured its champions. They were there as junior internationals.

On the pitch, Zidane collected the first fruits of his altruism. He liked to create opportunities for others. He could have taken more advantage himself, played closer to the goal, settled into the gratifying role of scorer. But he seemed at ease and set on the role of provider, especially as he had made progress in the phases of recovering the ball. His headed game was also satisfactory. He no longer had a fatal flaw that would impede his involvement at the highest level.

The name Zidane, which was no longer unknown, was finally attracting attention – and criticism, often unfairly. In a football match, there are three main scenarios that can result in protests from the fans: when a keeper lets in what looks like a soft goal; when a scorer misses a sitter; and when a technically brilliant player gives the impression of nonchalance or an apparent lack of productivity. Yazid was sometimes reproached for the last of these. Astonishingly, during a match with the reserve team, one of the directors even said: 'He plays an old-fashioned kind of football.'

Coming from a former player who distinguished himself with a career punctuated by numerous poorly judged moves, at a time when these were less common, such a judgement would only have had limited value. But it might have had an influence. The elegant number 10 irritated fans of the sporting struggle, aroused jealousy with his flair and put the noses of those who judge too superficially out of joint; pundits like those look merely at goals scored, assists and conspicuous facts, rather than at an overall vision of the game or in-depth analysis – things they themselves are unable to produce.

This criticism was particularly difficult for a boy who was not the type to provide a minimum level of effort, or to rest on his ease in manipulating the ball. He played an eternal, relevant style of football. Not old-fashioned, but avant-garde – at least until a handful of other players would join him in achieving the same control. Was having a vision of the game or anticipation old-fashioned? Were dexterity and the ability to control the ball old-fashioned? Spoken by an anonymous fan, such criticism would have been unfair but benign. It became dangerous when the spectator was a director, and when this director thought he was a coach; especially given that his erroneous vision was combined with a foolish favouritism. Like Jean Fernandez, although on a smaller scale, Guy Lacombe was under pressure. He received advice that was often useless or even aberrant rather than relevant. The worst thing was that some influential people, when the time came to offer professional contracts, made it known they wanted other players to be preferred to Zidane.

4

IN TUNE WITH HIS TEAMMATES

Had Yazid got it wrong? Did he need to change his style or positioning on the pitch? Jean Varraud obviously didn't think so and kept repeating, 'Play like you did at Septèmes!' to encourage him. In other words, right up behind the strikers to offer them solutions and scoring opportunities.

Guy Lacombe would change nothing. Yazid was invested in his work. He had tried to make up for his shortcomings off the ball as soon as he had been told that 'you need to be in tune with your teammates'. This was evocative language. For him, the musical metaphor, of being like a conductor charged with bringing all the instruments together, was particularly powerful. Yaz's style seemed exactly like an improvised musical score, a succession of notes that corresponded to the movements of his feet.

Lacombe stuck to this principle: 'You can't train players like him.' You certainly couldn't teach them 'fistfight football', as Jean Varraud called it. This was a speciality sampled, through no fault of their own, by the reserve team playing away at Marseille. In the words of their manager, they were 'in fear of their lives' that Sunday. It is often said that it is in adversity that men are trained. But that is not how training should be. Ultimately they did manage to score and get off the pitch. Back in Cannes, a quiet place where Sunday boxing matches were rare, the story of this unusual so-called match, this brutal trap, stopped many experienced stadium brawlers in their tracks. At Endoume, in Marseille's sixth *arrondissement*, the battle had raged against US Catalans. An official match in France's D4, it turned into a sham, a caricature. André Amitrano, a goalkeeper with an irreproachable mindset, was trampled underfoot. Guy Lacombe, outraged by this aggression, which could have been much more serious, immediately shouted: 'He's a professional!' He was subsequently punched. On the touchline, Charly Loubet had to be 'saved' by some former players of his own generation. Several Cannes players were attacked by their opponents. Yazid had been abused in his home city. Just as he had been at Sainte-Marthe.

The episode was distressing. It was enough to tarnish a brilliant season. Those who had fallen victim needed to be motivated again and Lacombe got to work. The boy from La Castellane knew how to exact his own form of justice, how to avenge his teammates. They had been aware of it in Cannes since his first few weeks at the club, since a game at Nice when he had walked across the pitch to throw the final punch in a fight. But it was never something he did happily.

Although it may appear that way to the outside world, fighting is not appreciated in rougher neighbourhoods; less so on makeshift pitches, in matches that are neither competition nor sport, but friendlies. Football is played on neutral ground, surrounded by the tensions it soothes. In the street, it is about putting on a show. Even in urban settings, where violence bubbles under the surface, a match gives diplomatic immunity to brawlers, some of whom are transformed into genuine artists, who have fun. Violence is only relevant to the stakes. Yazid was having fun. The time had come to start putting the memories of his city, good and bad, out of his mind. The Marseille of La Castellane, the Marseille of Endoume.

The path towards professionalism was undoubtedly fraught with pitfalls that could cause a player to stumble. He had to gather his mind and focus on what was paramount: playing and training well. Forget red or yellow cards brandished by referees. He also needed to channel his impulsiveness, even when this was a struggle. He had to show he was as placid on the pitch as off it – where Yazid would commit only one behavioural misdemeanour, at the ticket booths of the Stade Coubertin. He was refused the tickets he had asked for, which were to be used not by him but to be given as gifts. The booth employee said he had rarely seen such an outburst ... swiftly followed by an apology.

On a day-to-day basis, Yazid was one of the quietest of the Mimont's some 150 residents. Unlike some of his teammates, he never used inappropriate tones to speak to girls passing in the hallway. Outside the residence, he was rarely seen at parties, nightclubs or restaurants. Room 207 was tidy; his shoes were organised and his bed always made. He was not one of those who would inadvertently set fire to his mattress with a camping stove while cooking pasta; not one of those whose pile of clothes had to be negotiated by the chambermaids just to get to the window.

Mimont was a welcoming place, less isolated than the club academy, which was welcoming its first residents. Consequently, there were several new employees, one of whom was anything but wet behind the ears: Jean Varraud. After half a century in the service of the club, he would finally be put on the payroll. Just reward for this man who spared no effort nor counted his time volunteering for ASC along motorways or at stadiums and grounds around France.

Since the closure of the Vox, his cinema – attendance at which had gradually decreased from 5,000 to 1,000 movie-goers per week, justifying its inevitable closure – Jean had had to rely on the resources of his wife, who ran a shop on the Croisette. In the early days of luxury ready-to-wear and in the midst of the Cannes tourist boom, long queues could often be seen at the Roseline Var boutique. Jean met several celebrities, thanks in part to his acquaintance with MGM's distributors, as well as to the reputation of the shop.

Monsieur Varraud's life found a happy balance – full of diversity, anecdotes and lessons – that revolved around the sporty kids sweating on a Sunday and customers arriving in Rolls-Royces from the Hôtel du Cap in Antibes. Yazid was particularly sensitive to this. He had also forged an instinctively close friendship with Madame Varraud, although football was only of secondary importance to her. Of the several children or young players who had passed under the watchful gaze of her husband, he was the only one with whom she had such a connection.

At the club, where close friendships were rarer still, the atmosphere began to feel less and less like a family. Weary and tired, Jean Fernandez left somewhere he could never have imagined saying goodbye to. At least not so soon. Thanks in large part to him, ASC, who had been wavering between six and eighth position in D2, finished their third season in the top flight in their best league position since their comeback: 11th out of 20, after two

12th-place finishes in the previous seasons. What was more, no team had won away at La Bocca, where attendances had never been so high.

A persistent rumour had begun to circulate before a well-deserved tribute, made over the microphone at the Stade Coubertin by Gilbert Chamonal, who delivered a fair and courageous speech before the start of Fernandez's last match at Cannes: some of the directors had apparently banned the unfurling of a '*Merci Jeannot*' banner.

The president announced 'a big foreign manager' to take over from the man who had symbolised Cannes' renaissance. Upon learning of the appointment of Boro Primorac, a former player and captain during the Première Division promotion season, commentators came up with a play on words, emphasising, with lashings of irony, that Primorac was not only foreign (Yugoslav) but also a big man in terms of stature. He was obviously not the famous manager everyone was expecting, forgetting that announcements made for effect, true lies and false joys are all part of footballing folklore.

The only promise kept was the construction and commissioning of the academy, a small one-storey building with modest facilities and great ambitions. Yazid would never stay there. He had just turned 18 but declined an offer of accommodation in the town, at an apartment he would visit with Jean-Michel, an adviser at the Logis des Jeunes. He was struck by the cost of the rent. He thought about his mother, his parents. This level of comfort, all this space for just him, was a little disconcerting. There was no doubt that it heralded the truly new life that lay ahead of him when it came to material wealth. Time would tell. Jean-Michel understood. Yazid did not let it go to his head. He remained in what he believed was his place. He decided to stay where he was comfortable, at Mimont, where he liked to play with the director's sons in the corridor. Watching on kindly and attentively, he was in his element: the truth of childhood, which he had never forgotten. But he did leave his room and moved to studio 223, overlooking the garden, on the second floor, with a telephone and a separate exit at the rear of the residence. This was already a big change.

Another came two days later with the second home game of Cannes' fourth season in the top flight; they were at home to AJ Auxerre. Zidane was to be the playmaker. He had not taken part in a D1 game since the final match of the last-but-one season, in Caen, where he had played the last 24 minutes. He had not played for the first team at all during the previous season. Nor had he played in the two first league games, at the Coubertin against Montpellier or in Lyon.

He was in the D1 starting 11 for the first time and played the whole match.

Guy Lacombe was one of those who followed his performance closely. After half an hour, in his heart of hearts, what he had seen was enough. This time he was convinced: Zinedine Zidane, aged just 18 years and 42 days, had matured into a French Première Division player.

Not everyone shared this informed opinion, however. At the same time as he joined the first team, the criticism began. Towards Yazid and his manager.

Yazid had played well. He had been one of the best players on the pitch, if not the best. But AS Cannes had lost heavily; Auxerre had won 3–0. The witch-hunt had already begun, instigated by those who thought they understood it all.

As was usually the case, the directors paid a visit to the players and their coaching staff a few minutes after the final whistle, so Boro Primorac was not surprised to see a politician step into his office. The speech made by this local official was much more surprising than his presence. In veiled terms – initially full of innuendo then more explicitly – he began to criticise the manager's most striking choice: picking such a young and inexperienced player to start as playmaker. Despite Yazid being man of the match, this influential figure laid some of the blame for the defeat on his selection and performance! With the tone of someone delivering a sermon, he listed every well-known player at Cannes before concluding: 'But instead you want to pick a team of Zidanes!'

Primorac was stunned by these laughable remarks. For him the time had come to give experience to Zidane, who was beginning to acquire a reputation beyond the Alpes-Maritimes. 'Let's see what this phenomenon can do!' commented one visiting Auxerre fan from Dijon before the game.

Phenomenal in his genius and precocity, the new Cannes playmaker would also have to be mentally strong to endure the challenges that were beginning to emerge.

Defeat did nothing to change the planned party. Alain Pédretti, the club president, a relative of the famous clown Achille Zavatta, had a circus tent set up in the car park, in which the post-match dinners were held, funded by the Club Enterprises' partners. Yazid was nearby, standing between two cars and sobbing. Pédretti saw the scene. He went to the bar and came back with a pick-me-up, a whisky and cola for his player. Zinedine Zidane, 18 years old, emotive and brilliant, a winner every day but a loser that night, would have to get used to the harshness of a world in which injustice is a tough opponent.

Absent for the next four games, he reappeared in Nantes, against Bordeaux at the Coubertin, and then in Marseille ... for an unexpected victory in front of his friends from La Castellane. Marko Mlinarić, another leader in the Cannes team but in a more attacking role, scored the only goal of the game. Smaïl Zidane arrived ten minutes before the final whistle. But, despite this success away at the defending champions and heavy favourites, ASC were languishing at the bottom of the table after the first half of the season. Just as they had been the year before.

The bad performances gave rise to mocking clichés. A columnist in one daily newspaper spoke of a 'pub team'; Mlinarić was described as a 'beach footballer' by one sports daily. For the workers at Aérospatiale, employees working long hours in sometimes difficult conditions, and the inhabitants of La Bocca's estates, who made up a large proportion of the crowd at the Coubertin, these descriptions were an annoyance. For the players they were unbearable and could not be tolerated.

Professional footballers knew that here, on the Côte d'Azur, their behaviour was subject to even harsher judgement. The quality of life afforded to them by an income no higher than elsewhere – lower, in fact, but usable with greater ostentation – left them little room to manoeuvre. They had to be irreproachable. They had to live up to the support provided by their fans.

Only a handful of brazen big-spenders, popular with a certain section of the public won over by a façade of virility, could get away without the need to justify their private life, day or night, in nightclubs or on the turf.

Just as no one dared to believe it any longer, everyone, including the well-behaved and saintly Zidane, who had nothing to reproach himself for, sparked into life, freeing themselves psychologically. AS Cannes began moving back up the table.

The 'big foreign manager' held firm and silenced the sarcasm, at a time when it was least expected, when the most pessimistic believed it was impossible – statistically at least – to avoid relegation this time. And yet ...

The team began to get the better of their opponents. The dragon costume, the club emblem worn by a mascot to drum up the crowd at home games, was once again sported with pride. Halfway through the season, results began to fall in Cannes' favour; one victory in particular was symbolic, earned away at Auxerre, 3–0.

For the iconoclasts, the dragon of the Garden of the Hesperides had long since stopped guarding its heroes in favour of overpaid wage-earners unworthy of their fees. After Auxerre – Cannes, those tired of the 'syndrome', those frustrated by waiting for the click, are keeping a low profile. Arms of honour to those so bittersweet and a guard of honour to the clairvoyants; this clever race knows that once in the arena it is both wild animal and Christian, numbering in their thousands at the final whistle ...

Thus summarised Claude Guarnieri, a *Nice-Matin* journalist in the 24 December issue. It was to be a happy Christmas.

The club was in an unusual position. In no time at all, they had gone from a relegation spot to possible qualification for the European Cup thanks to an astonishing unbeaten run. In eight games, their form was quite simply worthy of France's champions. The team pocketed 14 points from a possible 16.

Yazid played and shone. The circumstances became favourable to his development. His positioning on the pitch was somewhat less central than it had been in D4 with the reserve team; he also explained that he had no clear preference for the role of attacking midfielder or defensive midfielder. Monsieur Varraud's opinion and exhortation remained unchanged: 'Play like you did at Septèmes!'

Zidane was a topic of conversation, stirring up emotions and plenty of questions. How many players hailed as future heroes had disappeared at the first setback? This objection did not stop people noticing that this particular player had succeeded in keeping his promises. What reason could there be for a sudden downturn? For him, who believed so little in himself, the biggest obstacle, invisible and immense, had perhaps already been passed without anyone noticing; no one, not even himself.

One of the most beneficial effects of making regular appearances in the starting 11 is that pre-match pressure decreases. Off the pitch, nothing had changed. Yazid was always in the same mood. Between noon and 1pm, he would have lunch at the academy. He continued getting a lift home with the general secretary, who would drop him off near the motorway. On the way from La Bocca to the Marché Forville, near where Gilbert lived, conversations were rare. Yazid was still far from chatty.

Was he introverted? His driving instructor did not think so, seeing him as a reserved boy but not one who was disconcerted by the world around him. Neither awkward nor clumsy. He passed his test first time after a number of lessons well below the 20 hours that would become the minimum requirement a few years later.

Coordinated, thoughtful, and not someone who spoke unnecessarily, Yazid was certainly shy but, above all, very diffident, far from inclined to daring behaviour, except when in the company of friends and family ... or on the pitch. There his temperament and elegance worked wonders. The string of victories did much to mitigate the criticism. He was no longer treated as a 'dancer'.

A winner is often right. As is a scorer. On 10 February, Georges Parrain, the announcer at the Coubertin, was in full voice when it came to acknowledging the goals. In true South American style, he screamed the world '*gol*', dragging out the 'o' to what seemed like an infinity, making a much-anticipated announcement: 'That was his first goal in the Première Division! Give him a big round of applause! His name is Zinedine Zidane!'

He had finally scored. The Élineaus would smile wryly; the opposition was none other than Nantes.

Two-thirds of the way through the game, he took the goalkeeper on after controlling the ball with the outside of his right foot at top speed. With confidence, he threw up a lob; a bold move that was stunning to watch.

With ten minutes to go, Yazid was substituted. A noisy and intense guard of honour escorted him off the pitch. The applause only subsided as his slender young silhouette disappeared, swallowed up into the tunnel, out of sight of the fans.

After the game, clusters of supporters hung around chatting outside. Until the last glimmers of the setting sun shone off the Tanneron mountains, the ridges of which overlook La Bocca, they were talking about this first goal, which had also been the finest of the 26th day of the league season.

His first goal also meant his first car, a red Renault Clio, a joint gift from a car dealership and the club president. Alain Pédretti loved his brilliant player. He only had one complaint: the night when a teammate dragged him to a Palm Beach nightclub on their return from a defeat at Nancy. They bumped into ... Pédretti, who, although himself a party animal, told them in no uncertain terms that he did not want to see them anywhere like that the night after a loss.

The president organised a reception at the academy to present Yazid with the keys to his car. One new face would be a surprise to many, that of a 20-year-old girl who had been staying at Mimont since September.

As it turned out, it was not Yazid who was the dancer. It was her, a trainee at Rosella Hightower, a school located just a few minutes away in the Gallia neighbourhood. The young woman was not well known at the club. She had been spotted at the Coubertin for the first time in the west stand for the game against Nantes.

Three days earlier, during a trip out on the Croisette, his friends from the residence realised there was something going on between her and Yazid. It was an unusual day. The slate domes of the Carlton Hotel were as white as its legendary façade. Cannes was covered in snow. It was an afternoon of pure joy, laughter and snowball fights. There was Jojot Moussa-Madi, David Bettoni, Noureddine Mouka, Lionel Firly, Éric Giacopino, Magali and Fabrice Monachino, and Marie and Ludovic Pollet. It was clear that there would soon be a new couple at the residence.

Her name was Véronique. She was from Aveyron, like Guy Lacombe. Her last name was Fernandez, like Jean. She was pretty, kind and reserved, like Yazid, who was not the first to fall under her spell.

It was not to be a short-lived fling, as was often the case at the residence. They were a couple, a real couple, as sometimes happened at Mimont. Jean Varraud was reassured. He feared that the Logis would only encourage his protégé to disperse his energy elsewhere. Of course, a romantic relationship can be destabilising, but on this occasion, it represented balance. At the Lycée Carnot, where he was in his final year studying, one boy in particular understood that his friend had found happiness: Lucky, whom Yazid continued to see. Walking up Boulevard Sadi-Carnot, he went to see him, to tell him what a calming influence Véronique was.

Winter was shining yellow; the colour of the sun, of the mimosa that brightened the hills, and, in particular, of the new first-team strip. The printing of a new advertising logo for the club sponsor led to the replacement of the vertical red and white stripes. Cycling enthusiasts saw this as a quirk of fate, an allusion to the Tour de France, whose winner wears a yellow jersey.

In the D1 peloton, AS Cannes won several stages and were riding high. To heights never reached before: a European contest! The following season, the small Stade Coubertin would play host to matches in the UEFA Cup, one of the continent's three competitions.

The carnival atmosphere at La Bocca and across the city was reminiscent of promotion to D1 four years earlier. Had AS Cannes managed to take it to the next level? Qualification was celebrated in a nightclub at the Palais des Festivals. Véronique danced. Yazid kept himself at a safe distance from the noise, joking with his teammates. A charming and mysterious hint of a smile never left his lips. As someone with little time for frivolity, was he bored? Or was he enjoying moments that were finally carefree and without pressure? He was happy. In many ways, the season had been his. He had still not turned professional but had never earned as much money … some of which he was in a hurry to send to his family.

Another companion also made an appearance: fame. It was flattering but had never been one of Zinedine's priorities. He complied with it but took care never to abuse it. One night, he was at the pizzeria with two friends from Marseille. From their table on the mezzanine, one of them addressed the waiter in a somewhat threatening tone. Yazid pulled him up on it.

'Don't speak to them like that! They're nice here.'

Nice ... and keen on their football too. One of the waiters, Joseph, known as Giuseppe, paid up the hundred francs he had lost to Yazid in a bet. His beloved AC Milan had been knocked out by Olympique de Marseille.

Yaz remained humble, approachable and serious. Unlike some of his teammates, his presence could be counted on at the public and private events to which the players were invited to represent the club. It was a not-unpleasant mission that often consisted of posing for photographs, drinking champagne, sometimes listening to a speech and reaping the praise heaped on AS Cannes' impressive performances.

Every year, his birthday topped off a period of celebration and excitement: the arrival in Cannes and then the first game of the D1 season. This year there were plenty of other good things. A goal, a qualification, a car, a love story. Did this mean that the coming season would inevitably bring with it a slowdown? Or would the pace accelerate? With a bit of luck. However, realism suggested that AS Cannes' ongoing tendency towards disorganisation had yet to be overcome once and for all.

From the outside, the club appeared strong. It was one of the few in France whose three senior teams all played at the highest level: the first team was now playing in Europe, the second had stayed in D3 and the third had been promoted from the Division d'Honneur to the Quatrième Division, the league in which the second team had been playing only the year before! This overall progression was not a coincidence. The Cannes academy set the standard. In one year, the training centre had received a thousand applications.

A new season was beginning. And once again, the first half of the league season was disappointing, as in the two previous years. The word in the stands was that the players and directors had got carried away by qualification for the UEFA Cup. Whatever the case, the fans were clearly fired up and, as always, they looked for the usual scapegoats. Yazid figured prominently. Slow, heavy and fragile were some of the adjectives bandied about. Aborted dribbling, badly measured passing or a poorly struck shot were enough to awaken the critics, who are never asleep deeply enough when watching an elegant playmaker, a 'dancer', as they say.

The Coubertin faithful were no longer counting missed opportunities or lost points. It was time for criticism.

At the start of the season, however, against Frankfurt, Zidane's class had been apparent for all to see. But since this promising friendly, his partnership with the new recruit, Asanović, failed to work as well as the previous season's link-up with Simba, who had returned to PSG to strengthen their team decisively.

Too spoiled, the fans were no doubt expecting uninterrupted progress. After promotion to D1, they had consolidated their place. After this consolidation came Europe. And then, the only highlight in a gloomy start to the season, qualification in the first round of the European competition against the Portuguese team Salgueiros.

22 October 1991. The second round of the UEFA Cup. New territory for AS Cannes, who faced Dynamo Moscow. A large photo of Yazid adorned the front page of the match programme but his name failed to appear inside it. Neither in the caption, nor in the double-page spread with the list of the names of the 16 players

supposedly in the squad. The official match sheet, distributed to media representatives, corrected this mistake. He would play. Although not everyone was happy about it.

The whistles began as Cannes went 1–0 down at half-time. The players did not understand. Had the fans forgotten the previous season? Had they missed Cannes against Frankfurt?

Football is a game played by millions of human beings. Mere thousands know how to manipulate the ball in a way that looks as if the laws of gravity are being defied. Some of these, like Zinedine Yazid Zidane, have an extra gift. Aged just 19 years and 4 months, this man was one of the rare few who can turn a game into a breathtaking spectacle. Dominique and Laurent Élineau, whose interest in football was limited, only came to the stadium to see him; not because they were friends but to see an artist at work. And yet the whistling continued. Yazid, with his head down, running, exasperated, raised his arm to the whistlers.

In the dressing room, after the boos of the match had subsided, the water was not only flowing from the showers. Yazid cried as he thought about the game. He was beginning to realise it did not take much to go from champagne to bitter tears.

Cannes, despite a commendable second leg in Moscow, were eliminated from the UEFA Cup and tumbled down the table. Michel Gandolfo, a prominent member of the board, tried to put sporting events back into perspective. In the fans' magazine, he lamented that some of them had 'behaved like the very worst kind of thugs when Saint-Étienne had visited'. He gravely concluded: 'Some of the events reported day after day by newspapers, the radio or on television, are sadder, relatively speaking, than the troubles AS Cannes are causing us. After seeing the hopeless eyes of hundreds of Muscovites just a few days ago, I can assure you that they would be very happy if this was the only thing they had to worry about for the rest of their lives.' This cultured man, one of the wise men of the club, would pass away just a few months later. But for every Gandolfo, there were plenty of small minds.

Once again, climbing back up the table was imperative. The club was in a relegation spot. In January, Boro Primorac was forced to give up his position; he was replaced by his assistant, Erick Mombaerts, who had legally been the manager anyway because he, not Primorac, had the necessary diploma. This change had little bearing on results. Or on the critics.

At the Faculty of Sciences at Nice University, Lucky had lost none of his optimism, at the risk of being mocked. The prediction he had made to a fellow student was received with amusement: 'There's a guy who plays for Cannes who used to live at my house. One day he'll be the playmaker for the France team!'

Jean Varraud did not risk making that kind of prediction, or even explaining in his soft, stuttering and descriptive voice that Zidane had already proved in the senior team what he had shown glimpses of in the Under-17s: his genius. Monsieur Varraud had given up talking to non-believers. It was a waste of breath. He had even given up going to play boules in his beloved Place de L'Étang, near his home. Amateur commentators had become too categorical and, above all, spoke with a confidence proportional to their incompetence and lack of lucidity.

Whenever he happened to make a chance detour through the square, the discoverer of Zidane was quickly met with sardonic laughter and targeted by sly remarks about his protégé.

Yazid did not complain. But he needed to be surrounded by friends and family, to be supported. These moral wounds were matched by physical difficulties that may not have been unrelated. They were not mitigated by the constraints of national service carried out at the Joinville Battalion, under the direction of Roger Lemerre. This experience allowed him to get used to another form of operating at the highest level, beyond his club, but also interrupted his regular training and the alternation of competition and recovery. These comings and goings did nothing to help him prepare for the frenetic league games. And, as if that were not enough, a knee injury that required treatment by painful injection complicated the situation.

Luckily, there was Véronique. She had appeared at just the right moment, when it was not only a question of enjoying the party but of bonding. The lovebirds of the Logis had already forged a close relationship, for better or worse. The friends Yazid had had since the beginning were also still there, ready to help. Since the start of the season, there was one more who could be counted on: Alain Rouvier, the club's administrative secretary. He was a discreet, humble and attentive man. Many of the high-ranking directors paid little attention to him. Some had barely registered his name. He was not someone who needed to be flattered. He had no power but was sensible and honest.

On two occasions, Alain would console Yazid before drying his tears. He knew it was what he needed. He knew the injustice he was suffering, while others had won over the crowd, despite not having the same moral stature, far from it. They were weak, cowardly and spineless. Alain saw them posing proudly in front of the camera, shaking hands with the public but being contemptuous or selfish away from the media spotlight. He noted that, after every training session, Yazid did not throw his bib on the ground but carefully deposited it in the cart provided for the purpose. He had respect for people. Respect for equipment. Respect for the luck he had managed to seize. All that should end up paying off eventually. And paying off well.

5

ZIZOU

The club's directors may not have said it, but the future of their number 10 – who sometimes also wore the 7, 9 or 11 on the pitch – was no longer in Cannes. In a few months, he would be returning to his region. To play, despite not yet turning professional, for the current French champions!

Olympique de Marseille had come to a secret agreement with AS Cannes.

Marseille had decided to send their recently signed Croatian forward Alen Bokšić out on loan. Surprise, surprise: he was going to Cannes! At La Bocca, this arrival was met with joy, mingled with incredulity. Why would such a good player come to a modest team in a precarious league position? No one, other than those who had carried out the transaction, was aware of a clause in his contract that remained confidential. Marseille had negotiated a purchase priority on Zinedine Zidane.

In front of a small audience but to loud applause, the new centre-forward made his debut on 21 December 1991. At the end of the first half, he got himself noticed with a run towards the opposing team's goal; the Lyon keeper came out to meet him in what the referee judged to be a dangerous and illegal fashion. He was sent off. For the fans it was a happy day. Not because of the result – another draw conceded at the Coubertin – but because of the hopes raised. They would not last.

The directors at Lyon soon initiated proceedings to withdraw the loan of Alen Bokšić, proceedings that were seen to be motivated by revenge. It was less about the sending-off of the goalkeeper and more about their own failed deal. They too had had their eyes on the Croat. They pointed out that any player signed by a club could not be loaned during the first year of his contract. Their counterparts in Marseille and Cannes fired back that the deal had been done between AS Cannes and Hadjuk Split, the striker's original Yugoslavian club. However, thanks to contacts in Yugoslavia, Lyon won the case by proving that Marseille did own the player after all. Bokšić would only play a single game for AS Cannes.

Curiously, Marseille's directors no longer seemed interested in Yazid after that. The president, Bernard Tapie, hesitated. The chief executive was not – or was no longer – receptive to the arguments put forward by Henri Camous, the director of administration at Cannes. Perhaps it was a negotiating strategy. But the weeks that passed contradicted that theory. Since negotiations in the autumn, the struggles of ASC, which were not conducive to showcasing their junior international, had probably led some people to look elsewhere.

The Marseille manager, Raymond Goethals, nicknamed 'The Wizard', was more likely working from intuition than analytical sense. His judgement was negative: 'Too slow.' Negative and definitive. The assistant coach was in favour of the transfer, however. Whenever Tapie asked him, his response was always the same. It was frank, positive, enthusiastic ... and consistent.

One night, he was awoken by the phone ringing at 2am. Tapie was calling him to weigh up the pros and cons, one more time.

'So, do we do it or not?

'Do it!'

'They say he's very slow.'

'He's ten times faster than anyone else with the ball. He sees more quickly, plays more quickly and his passing is better!'

Zidane was superior to the two mainstays of the Marseille midfield, internationals whose technical background was rather crude in comparison to his own. The assistant coach confirmed it, with the information he needed at his fingertips. He knew his subject well. Better than anyone. This man was none other than Jean Fernandez. He had returned to the club where he had played for five seasons and was a strong advocate for his former youngest player. He was sure of his opinion. But his advice would be ignored ...

A few months later, Farid Zidane bumped into Fernandez and asked him if a transfer to Marseille might tempt his brother, despite the tough competition. His response was unambiguous: 'He's capable of playing. He's better than anyone on the team!' Yazid's entourage were not overly disappointed, however, too aware of the often unstable atmosphere at the club to want a return to the city at all costs.

Observers far from Cannes, even more so than others, needed evidence, goals, figures and statistics. During the league season that was drawing to a close, Zinedine Zidane was the eighth most present player for his club, with 2,568 minutes spent on the pitch, and the seventh in terms of games played: 31 out of 38. But he had only scored five times, which was not much for an attacking midfielder. His fifth goal looked like a final nod. It was scored during his last match at the Coubertin, against FC Nantes, and was another lob.

This time relegation could not be avoided. AS Cannes returned to D2. The Première Division had been nothing but a brief five-year spell, when Yazid was in the right place at the right time. Even if their stay in the Deuxième Division was prolonged, nothing would be the same as when the training policy was less structured. The quality of this policy was now a guarantee of long-term success and, in this case, of a probable return to D1.

Although fond of the player he had trained, Guy Lacombe was one of those who did not want to see Yazid stay in Cannes. The Deuxième Division and its weekly struggles, less rewarding than those at the highest level, could set him back a year or more. They could slow down his progression or even lead to a regression. He had to stay in the Première Division. The manager who had trained him was saddened that his 'good, deserving kid, who has worked hard' and become a first-team player at 18 did not seem to have sparked any interest.

'You'll have to sell him yourself!' was the response given to Guy Lacombe by Alain Pédretti, who had not been able to find a buyer. Lacombe took him at his word. For the first time in his life, he became a salesman. He started by calling the AS Monaco manager Arsène Wenger, who was of the opinion that Yazid had not confirmed the prowess he had shown in the previous season. Lacombe put this bad patch down to all the comings and goings and to his military service. Wenger nevertheless declined the offer.

Monaco did not want him. Nor did Marseille. No club wanted to engage the services of this attacking midfielder, a position that was important because of his decisive influence on team play and in an area of the pitch in which natural-born talents are rare. As had been the case at Septèmes, no clubs showed any interest. This might seem outrageous, but in a world in which supply seems to condition demand, where shopping is based on reputation rather than rigorous observation, where players are bought and sold by lot, if possible, promoted by an obliging agent, talent is not enough.

At the last minute, when preparation for the following season had already been scheduled, despite the fact that Yazid did not yet know his fate, a French club came forward. But it was not offering the 8 million francs promised by Olympique de Marseille, nor even the 6 million asked by the Cannes president.

The Girondins de Bordeaux wanted to sign two players: Jean-François Daniel and Éric Guérit. They left with a third: Zidane. A deal was done. Four Bordeaux players – Raschke, Marx, Ernst and Lestage – were exchanged in return for the three Cannes players. Zidane cost only 3.5 million francs. A great deal and a good investment for the buyers.

On a sporting front, the main objective had been achieved. Yazid would be staying in D1 and would have the chance to lead a well-drilled team with a proven logistical reputation. Although sanctioned for its management and relegated to the Deuxième Division the previous year, this great club had taken only one season to bounce back up. The Girondins, three times champions of France in the 1980s, had since put powerful structures in place but these had done relatively little to control the vagaries of results.

On a human level, his departure from Cannes could have been better negotiated. Yazid would have to leave the city of his adolescence. Having arrived at 15, he was leaving at 20 with a solid foundation. Surprised but not unhappy with his destination, he nevertheless looked a little aggrieved by the direction events had taken. As usual, he would not say much on the subject. In the car park in front of the club's headquarters and academy, he did, however, have something to say to Jean-Claude Laugénie, the president of the supporters club, who would sometimes greet him as they passed in Rue Mimont.

'They sold me like cattle.'

To be sold, you need a contract. And despite statistically being one of the first-choice starting 11, Yazid had still not turned professional. His first professional licence would be a wonderful gift, much better than all the red Renault Clios in the world.

On 4 June, Yazid passed the obligatory medical. On 1 July, the French Football Federation granted him the status he had long been waiting for. But the licence was registered in the name of the Cannes club.

Negotiations had dragged on. After the holidays, the three 'transferees' resumed training at La Bocca as if nothing had happened. It was a matter of days, they were told. Fortunately, Rolland Courbis, the manager, and Alain Afflelou, the president of the Girondins, whose boat was moored at Cannes' Port Canto, eventually concluded the transaction. Zinedine Zidane would prepare for the league season in Bordeaux after all.

He had finally turned professional but left Cannes with relative indifference. He had been looked upon kindly by those who had welcomed and supported him for five years and these unconditional admirers knew what he was capable of, as did the Girondins de Bordeaux. With them he would make progress and hit new heights. He was gifted, did not shy away from effort and had the benefit of a considerate and attentive entourage. Barring injury or an unlikely change of mood, he would succeed.

He would make his last appearance in a Cannes shirt against FC Nantes on 18 April 1992. When he left the pitch in the 82nd minute, he was replaced by Fabrice Monachino – for one last time –

and spent his final moments as a footballer in red and white. Unless he came back one day, of course.

Yazid would not forget Cannes. It was sunny like Marseille, had both pretence and sincerity like everywhere else, but was the club where he had been able to turn his passion into a profession.

He said he would come back. The two friends from Mimont went their separate ways. On a motorway, a red car and a white car took turns at overtaking. The drivers amused themselves before saying goodbye at a junction. David Bettoni was leaving on loan to Istres; Zinedine Zidane was leaving for Bordeaux, for fame and a new name.

They were both finally on their own. They had not wanted it to be that way, but Véronique and Yazid were, by necessity, isolated in a new world. With a new challenge to be met. He had to build his career, while she had given up on hers, patiently accepting the passing of days without him. The stadium, home. Home, the stadium. The first few months of life in Bordeaux were monotonous. Fortunately, there was love.

Véronique would not be a dancer. She had decided to follow and support Yazid, the young professional who had to earn his place in a squad built to reconquer the status of a great team. Together, the lovebirds of the Mimont learned to live as a couple. Often on their own. Their friends and family from Marseille would visit less often. As soon as he could, Yazid would visit the Association des Jeunes de la Nouvelle Vague, the club founded to replace AS Foresta, but La Castellane was a long way away; even further from Bordeaux than Cannes. Rodez, where Véronique's parents lived, was much closer, however.

The stadium, home. Home, the stadium. In the end it was not so bad to have to focus on the primary objective: proving a value of which informed observers were certain but which had yet to be fully recognised. Evidence would have to be provided. Actions, assists and goals, not just pretty skills.

Jean-François Daniel and Éric Guérit, the two other recruits from Cannes, had a salary twice that of Zidane's. But they were well aware that the potential of their transfer companion was not half of theirs. They were hardly less amazed by him than their new teammates, who discovered the technical prowess Zidane displayed with disconcerting ease. Sometimes, they would just stand and watch him with admiration.

In the grounds at Le Haillan, the club's headquarters, games of 'football tennis' brought Zidane's skills to the fore. 'Doubles' matches were played by teams of two and one particular pairing attracted spectators who knew their stuff: Zidane and Dugarry. Partners in the national team since the Under-17s, they got to know each other better and quickly became good teammates, with an understanding that went as far as the pretend spats that brought plenty of laughter to training sessions. Their ease with football tennis inevitably led to teasing as well as relaxation. Never hurtful, it was a way of demonstrating genuine esteem.

'Are you coming?' 'No, no. I'm going home.' This conversation became very familiar. There was plenty of mutual admiration but not to the extent that Yazid would have lunch with Dugarry and a group of other single teammates. At least not during those first few months when Véronique was at home and somewhat lonely. But this did not prevent a friendship growing when Christophe, a local man, comfortable at his club and in his city, offered to help Zinedine get better acquainted with life in Bordeaux. They would roam the surrounding area, visiting the coast or the mountains, enjoying themselves like carefree kids.

The boy from Marseille needed human warmth even more than sunshine, something less frequent in Gironde than Provence! Thoughtful, especially in a world as hectic as professional sport, he liked spending time on his own to think but this did not mean avoiding human contact entirely. A love for others, given and received, forges trust and this was essential when it came to showing how brilliant, resistant and consistent he could be in competition. He needed people around him. He needed his family, his childhood friends, the Élineaus, David Bettoni and Véronique, of course. Now there was also Christophe Dugarry.

Zinedine was determined, by nature and by nurture. He knew he had work to do. Focused in the dressing room then on the pitch, sometimes his attention would still waver over the course of the minutes, probably because his body could not cope with the intensity. He was 20 years old; his musculature could be better and his endurance improved upon. His first months in Bordeaux made him change imperceptibly. His strength came up to meet his ambition and creativity. Completely exhausted, he was often taken off during games, but it was for his own good.

Gradually, he began to make his mark. Soon he would no longer be substituted. His volume of play would increase. And he would be the playmaker, even if he would sometimes wear the number 7 jersey, which he had often worn already in Cannes. But what did the number matter, unless you were keen on numerology? You might remember his first address on Place de la Tartane, building seven, or the relevance of this passage from a book on numerology about those, like Zinedine Zidane, for whom the number seven is their 'intimate number':

Your motivations drive you to seek calm and tranquillity

to observe, meditate, reflect and satisfy your desire for knowledge, or simply to find yourself. You are attracted by understanding the mechanisms of life and the deeper meaning of things. [...] You would benefit from learning to have more confidence in your feelings, expressing yourself more freely in the emotional realm and relationships. You can sometimes be difficult to understand.

Véronique understood him. 'Duga' understood him. It was important. But his opponents did not understand what he was doing to mystify them. That was important too.

In the last match of the league season, the Girondins qualified for the UEFA Cup with an away win at Lyon. Two of the three goals were scored by Zinedine Zidane and Jean-François Daniel. A week later, ASC were promoted back to the Première Division. Just as it had six years earlier, the club beat the third-from-bottom team in D1, in this case US Valenciennes-Anzin.

But these two events went unnoticed due to a dramatic end to the season. USVA were in the news thanks to a trio of former Nantes players: Marseille's Eydelie and the Valenciennes players Robert and Burruchaga – three of Yazid's first D1 opponents in Nantes in 1989. They were involved in an enormous scandal, triggered by the match between Valenciennes and Marseille. Despite fierce denials, embezzlement by certain directors at Marseille was proved in court. From then on, there was speculation that certain brilliant results may not have been achieved by sporting talent alone. There was also a certain amount of suspicion that this was a surprisingly widespread practice, as if the sport could escape an evil, the allure of gain and cowardice, for which evidence had long been mounting up.

Some discovered with dismay that competition is not a game. And that the game has little to do with the sport dreamed of by Pierre de Coubertin, whose philosophy it was fashionable to mock.

Marseille were sanctioned, relegated to the Deuxième Division, which Yazid, who had left Cannes at the right time and been courted but not signed by Marseille, had now escaped on two occasions. Once again, fate had smiled kindly on him, preventing a falsely flattering transfer to a club with an unhealthy atmosphere little suited to a young man full of faith and illusions.

A year had passed. At the Girondins, Zinedine had earned European qualification as well as a nickname. Rolland Courbis, his manager and protector, was keen to find a way of shortening the three syllables in Zinedine. As Zidane had matured, he had reverted back to using his first name, rather than his middle name. At one of the first training sessions of the season, he thought he had heard Jean-François Daniel shout 'Ziz'. He soon added the ending himself, something he would often do to the first names of relatives or players. The nickname was quickly adopted: Zizou was born and is still being talked about, outside Bordeaux, France and even Europe.

It was thanks to Courbis, supported by Alain Afflelou, that Zidane's D1 career was able to continue. It was also thanks to him that the budding professional, easy prey for the devious, was able to play with peace of mind.

Not always successfully, Courbis would try to channel the negative energy of Zizou, who was still too quick to react violently. As on 18 September 1993, at the Stade Vélodrome, when he punched Desailly, bloodying his face. The first red card of his professional career.

In moments of distress, the young player could also count on Jean Varraud. The discoverer of the former Cannes player proved his sporting insight once again. For him, the recent season had been marked, more so than by the first team's promotion back up to D1, by another happy event. Thanks to several boys he had discovered, ASC had won the French under-15 championship.

With his customary lucidity and the experience of a sometimes carefree life, Monsieur Varraud urged Yazid to protect himself against potential setbacks.

His first piece of advice was very serious: 'Take out insurance against losing your licence.' This precaution helped calm the player's primary anxiety, that of injury. The misfortunes of Bruno Bellone, forced to give up competing before his 30th birthday, had left its mark on Cannes' players. The history of the sport is littered with other famous and lesser-known examples. 'With a million francs, you could always buy a café and run it with your parents!' joked the scout, whose second piece of advice was just as serious: 'As soon as you can afford it, set your parents up in a quiet part of town.'

His third piece of advice was unequivocal: 'Get married! You'll pay less tax if you do.'

The response was exactly what you would expect from a young man with such a proven ability for deep thought: 'If I get married, it's for life.'

On 12 December 1993, his friends from Mimont, footballers and employees alike, were in the stands at the Coubertin. AS Cannes were playing the Girondins de Bordeaux. The name Zidane was received relatively warmly, although the local fans gave a bigger welcome to a new Cannes prodigy: Patrick Vieira, who, like Zinedine, was born on 23 June and had also made his D1 debut in Nantes.

Thanks to the progress he had made in Bordeaux, the critics were less aggressive towards Zidane. But they did not disappear entirely and were still present in the newsrooms, where some still seemed not to have understood or even noticed that it was through the art of measured passing that Zizou made his mark.

His friends still provided unfailing support. After the match in Cannes, about 20 of them met for dinner in a pizzeria in Antibes. During the meal, Yazid kept pulling down the sleeve of his jumper, trying to cover his wrist. He was obviously embarrassed by his watch. A brand accessory. A designer object. An outward sign of wealth.

At the end of the meal, Véronique got up discreetly then returned to the table before anyone could notice. When the time came to pay the bill, the guests realised they had been treated. She was modest. They were generous. They loved each other and they loved their friends.

On 28 May 1994, their Cannes friends gathered at the town hall in Bordeaux. As indicated in the announcement sent by the two families in keeping with tradition, 'Véro and Zizou have decided to spend their lives together.' They gave their consent in the presence of their friends and family in the usual way.

They came from modest parts of the Bouches-du-Rhône and the Alpes-Maritimes, as well as from the more well-to-do parts of Bordeaux. Zinedine paid his guests' hotel bills personally. His eyes were fuller with joy than ever before. He was moved and delighted, always attentive and considerate to those who may have felt uncomfortable surrounded by the splendour of the reception venue, the Château du Haillan. The turrets of this 18th-century building overlook the grounds of an estate immersed in the Gironde forest in the outskirts of Bordeaux. The château was restored before the Girondins' glory days – to which this restoration undoubtedly contributed – under the leadership of the president Claude Bez and manager Aimé Jacquet.

The château was the ideal setting for a tasteful wedding, a dream location to celebrate a young lord of football. Usually discreet, but exuberant on this occasion, he danced while surrounded by an army of staff opening bottles of champagne and firing the corks dangerously close to the wood panelling! The generosity of the new couple towards all those who had marked the stages of Yazid's young life, from different backgrounds, characterised these simply happy moments, free from excessive or misplaced pride. It was a real party. Full of happiness.

What more did Zizou need to be 100 per cent happy? Hair that wasn't thinning, giving him the almost monastic style he had no choice but to get used to? In the shower, last in the dressing room with his usual modesty, he tried a lotion tested by Courbis. Bixente Lizarazu thought it was hilarious. Half cruel, half teasing, he sang a few improvised words about early-onset baldness at the top of his voice like an opera aria! Zizou forgave him and made 'Liza' one of his closest friends. As for his unusual hairstyle, the V on his forehead and the tonsure would become so symbolic of his appearance that a German newspaper would attribute it to all the players in the German team at Euro 2004. A photoshopped tribute was accompanied by the caption: 'We need 11 Zidanes!'

Zizou was now comfortable in Gironde. And he had become indispensable on the pitch. Decisive, thanks to his often stunning goals and passes, of which Christophe Dugarry was a privileged recipient, just as he had been five months earlier when he scored at the Coubertin.

Dugarry was a striker, or more precisely, a forward. He would attack but would also pull his weight in defensive work in his area of the pitch. Zidane did the same in the midfield, although he was not used to forcing himself into this defensive role, for which some technicians thought he was predestined.

The duo were well known, recognised and feared by their opponents. They did complement each other after all, despite what France's Under-18 manager had said when they were playing England in Martigues. Unlike his partner and friend, it was relatively difficult for Zinedine to find his ideal position on the pitch, one that would allow him to make the best use of his creative ability.

Monsieur Varraud had the answer. 'Play like you did at Septèmes!' The close relationship between the two men had not come to an end with Yazid's last match in red and white. It continued over the phone, giving them the opportunity to talk about lots of different subjects, including the player's performances, of course. These discussions sometime turned to banter, especially if the number 10, wearing the number 7, had had few touches; if he had seemed neither offensive, defensive nor box-to-box, cut out by a game that jumped from one end of the pitch to the other, skipping over the midfield.

Jean Varraud teased him. 'So, you didn't enjoy that then?' Yazid laughed. Calm because the results were good, both for him and for the team. He could now sleep easy. As could his mentor, with the exception of the night of 17 August.

The phone rang. Roseline and Jean were asleep. Jean got up and answered: 'Hello?' Barely awake, he heard a familiar voice, behind which he could sense the presence of a crowd of people celebrating.

'Did you see it? One goal with my head and another with my left foot!'

It was Yazid. Jubilant. Delighted! He had just woken up the man he had been thinking about a few hours earlier after scoring two goals in Bordeaux's Lescure Stadium ... but this time he wasn't playing for the Girondins. He was wearing the blue of France! Alongside another promising talent, the defender Lilian Thuram, Zinedine Zidane, aged 22, who was starting his third season with the Girondins, had just made his debut for the national team, the 'équipe de France', the most popular sports team in the country.

He had scored twice for the first time in his career. They were also the only goals scored by his side. When he was brought on two-thirds of the way through the game, the Czech team had been leading for fifteen minutes, thanks to two goals scored in three minutes. Zizou reduced the deficit, then equalised, in a five minute spell before the end of the game. Two goals in his first game! Two magnificent goals! Bold strikes: one he had had to master and the other his speciality. A step-over and a quick sidestep rapidly followed by a shot with his 'weaker' foot, the left, then a magnificent vertical jump followed by a header, cutting off the trajectory of a corner.

The tall boy who used to duck whenever the ball came towards him in the air had grown up. He had once again been able to seize the opportunity offered to him. A chance doubled by favourable circumstances. When he came on for only 27 minutes in a team trailing on the scoreboard, he risked going unnoticed, of having 'not played enough to be judged', as columnists often write.

He had everything to prove and everything to gain. Especially in the enthusiastic and familiar setting of a stadium filled largely by local fans. They had been won over by him, despite a few initial negative reactions by some who were too impatient and made their judgements based on some clumsy but inconsequential initial gestures. Smaïl and Malika, who had come to the Lescure, could breathe easy.

Such an exceptional beginning could not go unrepeated and even overshadowed any subsequent below-par performances, which would not be enough to definitively remove him from the team, although a doubt would remain.

These two goals could not be put down to luck and would linger long in the memory. There had been no opportune rebounds, no unwanted deflections or any other quirks of fate resulting in unsightly or fortunate 'ugly goals'.

His selection for the France team represented a logical success for this former Under-19 international, who, unlike some of his former teammates in that category, had succeeded in imposing himself in D1. Just as logically, his first selection would not be his last. Against Slovakia he was in the starting 11 for his third appearance in a *Tricolore* shirt. He played the first 75 minutes, which were largely sufficient for him to do himself justice, with ease, in the role of playmaker expected of him. The game was played in … Nantes.

Confident in his talent and constant in his efforts, here he was being given responsibility at the highest level, on the pitch and in life. At aged 22 and 9 months, Zinedine Zidane became a father. The child was a boy. He was given the name of a footballer containing the letter Z: Enzo, a tribute to Francescoli, the Uruguayan hero so admired in Marseille, whose photo was a window into a dream, in the bedroom that the young Yazid once shared with his brother Djamel.

Did Enzo look like his father? Would he have the feet (especially) or the hands to play with a ball whatever the cost? Would he be a restless and agitated child, a little possessive but endearing, before becoming a timid teenager who was obsessed with balls of all shapes and sizes? Would he have blond, curly hair?

The world in which he would grow up would, of course, be different. His dad was on track to ensuring that his home would never be cramped. But he promised himself he would not forget to give him love or teach him the principles that had made Yazid himself a happy and calm child. Life was waiting for little Enzo, who would find out that it is not always as comfortable as when you are being cradled by the arms of your father, a champion.

6

THE BELOVED CHILD OF THE OLD LADY

A top-flight French club, debuts for the national team and a family. The objectives that seemed like dreams became achievable over the years and were eventually ticked off one by one. Thanks to a rise in his salary, the grateful son, generous and loyal, gave his parents a gift that was long-awaited, by him as much as by them. A gift that could not be wrapped in shiny paper. A gift for all seasons: a home. For Smaïl and Malika. For the whole family.

The tall, discreet young man with black hair that was increasingly thinning remembered the child he had been. A little blond kid with curly hair, then a tall, brown-haired boy whose presence haunted the apartment and the area around the building. He was the youngest: taken to his first matches by his father, guided by his mother towards the right path, and cosseted by his brothers and sister. Loved by everyone. He wanted to say thank you.

An emotional goodbye had been said to La Castellane, left for more comfort, as well as peace and quiet, in a town in the Marseille region. But the star would, of course, still return to the old neighbourhood. To see his friends. To see what the past looked like.

During an indoor match with the Girondins in Switzerland, one particular face and voice took him back to his years on the estate. A former teammate shouted to him from the stands: it was Gilles Boix. He now lived in Haute-Savoie and played for Annemasse, near the border between France and Switzerland. Yazid motioned to him and invited him to join him on the bench. Their friendship was clear for all to see.

Just as it was with Dugarry at Le Haillan. Partners in crime both in life and on the pitch, Christophe and Zinedine suffered their first big disappointment during their third season together. Knocked out by the Polish team Katowice, they were unable to take their team beyond the second round of the UEFA Cup. In the heat of the moment, on his way out of the dressing room, Bixente Lizarazu, the left-back for both Bordeaux and the France team, called the attitude of the whole club into question, not just its first team. A reaction was required. Although the directors could comfort themselves with the club's healthy financial situation, not jeopardised by this unexpected elimination, the disappointing performance on the pitch was enough to irritate those who were desperate to see the team in navy and white back playing at the highest level.

Zizou applied himself by redoubling his work rate, raising the pace whenever he could and finishing his performances as well as he began them.

Six months later and after plenty of hard work, another European qualification punctuated the efforts made to recover in the league. The Girondins qualified for the UEFA Cup by way of the Intertoto Cup. For Zizou, Duga and Liza, a marathon season came into view, opening with this summer prelude and concluding, if all went well, with participation in Euro 96, which would bring 16 teams together in England.

After a busy summer, Zidane began looking like the great hope for French football that everyone had been waiting for. By the autumn, he finally had full confidence in himself thanks in particular to a very unusual double. Two goals scored ... against Nantes. Zizou's goals were rare but they were often beautiful to behold and sometimes truly exceptional. The one he scored in Seville would go down in the Girondins' history books. The Sanchez-Pizjuan Stadium in the Andalusian city is famous for having hosted some fantastic matches played by the Brazilian team in the 1982 World Cup, as well as the dramatic encounter between France and Germany. For the inhabitants of Bordeaux, the Benito-Villamarin Stadium would linger long in the memory for the fourth minute of play in the last 16 of the UEFA Cup.

Zizou picked up the ball in the centre circle. He spotted that the Betis keeper was off his line and took his chance. The ball flew over the goalkeeper and into the back of the net. This tricky shot, requiring speed of vision and execution, revealed a great sense of improvisation and genuine skill. He had been trying his luck in this way since the days of the Stade Chevalier. Since a six-a-side training match. This inspired attempt secured qualification for the quarter-final. The Girondins, pitiful in the league, where they regularly languished just above the relegation zone, rediscovered their lustre on foreign pitches. A surprising collective energy then cut in. They won their quarter-final and their semi-final, knocking out Slavia Prague, whom they beat 1–0 away and by the same score in Bordeaux.

So far, Zinedine had only had glimpses of European competition. By the end of this season, he would experience the last stage: a final, played against Bayern Munich. However, a very unfortunate suspension was to tarnish this apotheosis: Zizou would play only the return match in Gironde. After a yellow card for an innocuous arm movement in the previous round, he was suspended for the first leg in Munich. Dugarry found himself in the same situation for failing to stop after the referee's whistle.

The two friends, until then the decisive heroes, united even in misfortune, watched on helplessly from the Munich stand, holding Canal+ microphones, as their teammates lost. Their absence did much to help the Germans, who secured the title by a two-goal margin over both legs. Duga failed to score at the Lescure and this time Zizou did not manage to outfox the keeper Oliver Kahn, whom he had mystified with a majestic free kick when the German was playing for Karlsruhe. Bixente Lizarazu picked up a serious knee injury and had to leave his teammates after half an hour.

With the final as its highlight, this fourth season in Bordeaux, with a record number of 20 matches in Europe, had been unforgettable. Despite a constant struggle to stay in D1, it would be forever symbolised by qualification for the semi-final, achieved with panache against the prestigious AC Milan. It must have broken the heart of Giuseppe, back at his pizzeria in Cannes. Milan on one side; Yazid on the other.

It would take something special to overturn the 2–0 loss in the quarter-final first leg, a scoreline considered 'ideal' for securing qualification, particularly when combined with the experience of a big club. But that was precisely what happened. At a Lescure where the succession of wins in the previous rounds had left the Girondins buoyed with confidence, the players were in no doubt. A feeling of inexplicable certainty came over them as soon as they entered the dressing room. Zizou was focused. He went through his pre-match ritual. He had long since worked out how to behave before a game. The brilliant yet slightly fragile Cannes playmaker had worked on his physique. His body held firm and his mind followed suit. Right to the end. Zizou spoke little but knew how to galvanise his team. There was no shouting, just some well-placed encouragement. As well as some advice, in his role as shrewd and lucid leader.

His body held firm and his mind followed suit. Until the decisive move, a masterful pass sent to Christophe Dugarry, who converted it into a goal: 3–0! None of Milan's stars were able to reverse the balance of power. Not even a young recruit aged not yet 20, originally from Cannes: Patrick Vieira, whose deflated silhouette cut a sorry figure alongside the beaming Zidane, whom he had not known well at La Bocca. Logic would dictate that they would meet at other events. In Italy, perhaps.

Zizou's future was no longer necessarily in France. There were rumours that the directors at Juventus had long had him in their sights. He said nothing, unlike the Bordeaux president, who did not hold back when it came to talking about what he thought of the Turin representatives he had met with in Paris. The negotiations had gone sour and none of his players would be transferred to Turin, he promised. Zinedine, circumspect, kept his silence and continued to focus on his game. It was better not to say what he thought, knowing that nothing is ever set in stone when it comes to transfers.

From training to competition, from physical exercise to results that promoted confidence, his progress was regular, seamless. Free time was cut to a minimum. Luckily, there was always the telephone and Yazid made good use of it. He called the man who had discovered him, often from training camps or while on the team bus, during short spells when he was more or less on his own.

Monsieur Varraud would phone him too, not always at a good time. Sometimes, another voice that had become familiar and friendly would respond kindly. The voice of his roommate at training camps or when playing away from home.

'Hello! It's Christophe Dugarry. He's asleep. He'll call you back.'

Duga talked a lot. Sometimes he would have liked Zizou to do the same but his esteem and admiration for his friend as both a person and a sportsman were unwavering. The pair were closer than ever. Ready to overcome shared and individual challenges.

Unfortunately, an enforced period of inactivity would leave more time for telephone conversations. A broken gear lever, bruised skull and a hurt gluteal muscle: a dreaded injury, the result of a car accident on a motorway in Gironde in the spring of 1996, the physical consequences of which could have been much more serious. Zinedine's convalescence negatively affected his preparation for the European Championship, formerly known as the European Cup of Nations. Like the World Cup, after the first group stage it is a knockout competition, with the possibility of penalties to decide the winner. You become the champions of France by facing every club in the championship. You do not become champions of Europe or the world in the same way, but by winning a random competition. A single missed strike can rarely prevent a championship win, but it can eliminate the most deserving team from a cup. A single strike ... This is what happened against the Czech Republic in the semi-final of the 1996 European Championship in England. This time, Zizou did not score, at least not during the match itself. He scored from the penalty spot, but the French team were eliminated after a 0–0 draw. They would not play in the final. It had not been the much-anticipated revelation. Yet, the manager Aimé Jacquet did not regret picking him. Although he had not been able to take advantage of one of his strokes of genius, he had at least got used to the atmosphere of a major international competition.

However, after the event, Zizou, who had spent a long time considering whether or not to make himself unavailable, was not convinced he had been right to play in his diminished state, far below the standard he had shown for club and country. Disproportionate to the reality of his performances – he had been especially good against Bulgaria – but proportionate to expectations of his talent, he found the criticism particularly hard to take. Especially when it came from some of his teammates.

Without entering into a public debate, he would not forget these moral wounds. Just as he had not forgotten those inflicted in Cannes. Just as he would not forget the reassurance he had also received. Just as he would not forget Bordeaux and Nulle Part Ailleurs, the brasserie between Cours du Maréchal-Foch and Cours De-Gourgue that had sealed his friendship with Duga. David Dugarry, Christophe's brother, sold him his share in April.

Zizou would return to this affluent neighbourhood lined with office buildings as often as he could. During Euro 96, he had confirmed that he would be leaving the Girondins. His best season in Bordeaux was to be his last. He was leaving for the land of superstars: Italy.

The Élineaus had had one regret for almost two years now: they had not been able to attend any of Yazid's long-awaited and brilliant appearances for the France team. If they found out he was not in the starting 11, they did not even bother to watch the television broadcast despite being ardent football fans.

This time, they were in New Caledonia, in Nouméa, where Dominique was a chef. The telephone rang. They heard a familiar voice with a piece of incredible news. This time, it did not take them by surprise: 'I've signed for Juve!'

He had not forgotten. The Élineaus had hosted several apprentice footballers in Pégomas but only one had stayed in touch with them. His name would now appear on the back of a Juventus number 21 shirt. Rare at that time in a sport played by 11, the number was one of the few available. Yazid had accepted it willingly and without superstition, not demanding the number 10 that corresponded to his position and with which his image was associated. This type of attitude helped him earn respect and made it easier for him to adapt. But it was on the pitch that he had to earn esteem and make his mark in order to justify his status as a young star. A status that, in the arms of the Old Lady – Juventus are nicknamed the *Vecchia Signora* – had become more commonplace because of the many valuable players in its squad.

There was not just one star at Juve, but several. It was up to him to prove his place alongside them, or rather above them. It was up to him not to allow himself to be intimidated by this world of perfectionism, where ambition is constantly striving for first place, in Italy, Europe and the world.

'Juve are something else.' In 1985, this short soundbite became a newspaper headline, bruising the players and directors of the Bordeaux team that had just been beaten in Turin. It took on a double meaning, a form of vaguely contemptuous criticism – Juventus, an opponent that was much more dangerous than those of the previous rounds, as well as a club as solid as the Girondins, which Aimé Jacquet had led to the semi-final of the European Cup.

Juve are something else. Arriving in Turin after a few days of rest that could barely be described as a holiday, Zizou, the rising star of a Bordeaux team back playing in Europe, discovered a world that, in terms of infrastructure, was a wonderful sight to behold. Everything was impressive: the Stadio delle Alpi, built for the Italia 90 World Cup; the headquarters; the passion, omnipresent in conversations about Juve and their rivals Torino; the tactical rigour, although coach Marcello Lippi was, in this respect, a little more liberal than some of his colleagues in France; the quality of the squad; and finally, the quality of the facilities. And the fitness training. Especially the fitness training.

Juve are something else. Not necessarily 'better' in all areas, but always 'more'. More demanding. More effort. Not yet fully recovered from a thrilling but challenging season, the busiest of his young career, Zinedine could not keep up with the pace imposed by Giampiero Ventrone, known as 'The Marine'. At least not yet. His body had definitely filled out – the years spent in Bordeaux had taught him to exploit his talent – but he had had a long season in the UEFA Cup, suffered a costly injury and ended Euro 96 with a feeling of unfinished business.

As his nickname suggested, Ventrone was a demanding physical trainer who was tough on his Juventus commando unit. He not only prepared his players before a game but from the start of the season – well before the start of national competitions, later in Italy than in France. The basics needed to be worked on in order to be fit by the end of the summer.

Arriving after his new teammates, Zizou discovered Ventrone's methods in Châtillon, a charming village with a French-sounding name in the Val d'Aosta region, autonomous since 1945. But the leg work required from footballers at Juve, whose training camps used to take place at Châtillon, was 100 per cent 'Made in Turin'. In other words, extremely tough.

During the summer, the surrounding mountains were particularly welcoming. Much more so than the local stadium, with its artificial track unworthy even of Place de la Tartane. When summer storms were not crashing down around the mountain peaks, the sun did plenty to lighten the atmosphere. Laps of the track and other exertions broke the spell. Running, again and again, for three solid weeks. Perhaps the pace would slow after the camp ... but it was not to be.

Juve are something else. Weights, daily running races, endurance and middle-distance. They worked hard. Very hard. Too hard for Zinedine, who would often end the sessions exhausted, ready to give up the ghost. It was cause for concern. He wondered whether Italy, home to the world's best footballers, a country where international talent is judged, might not necessarily deserve its reputation.

Beneath the cloudy Piedmont skies, especially when temperatures dropped, morale was just as sad as the weather. In this country, where he did not speak the language, it was harder to adapt than it had been in Bordeaux. Almost more difficult than in Cannes, although there the adolescent dreamer had become a man, sure of the path he had carved out for himself.

When your heart is about to falter, it is those around you who provide comfort. Véronique, taking care of day-to-day life; Enzo, whose dad was eagerly awaiting the day when his little feet would first make contact with a ball. He would set up a goal for him in the living room of their enormous new apartment, previously occupied by Gianluca Vialli. Enzo was ready to carry on his father's tradition: Yazid, a boy who learned keepie uppies on makeshift pitches, had also been an excitable indoor player. In Marseille, one of his strikes had even broken the ceiling light in the dining room.

In these 200 square metres on Via Carlo Alberto, in the heart of the historical centre, with a certain Alen Bokšić, Juve's new striker, as their neighbour, the family was not alone. Two old friends were also there: Malek from Marseille and David Bettoni from Cannes. Both had come to help Yazid settle in.

David only stayed a few weeks. The time it took to help make a few things easier and carry out some minor work, such as setting up a television aerial. He also acted as interpreter because he spoke Italian, the language of his ancestors that he had studied at school. He too had a new club in Italy. After returning to AS Cannes following a season on loan at Alès, he was made to understand that his services were no longer required. His contract was terminated, leading to plenty of reflection and eventually a decision. He would join Avezzano, in Serie C1, the equivalent of the third division. Not so far from France. Not so far from Turin, or from Yazid.

Malek would stay for several months. He was a close friend from La Castellane, a partner in crime at never-ending neighbourhood matches. He was the mirror to a simpler past. A guarantee of stability when the media and advertising whirlwinds pointed to fame looming on the horizon. Malek, resourceful and helpful, soon learned the local language, drove Yazid to training, helped Véronique with the shopping and took care of Enzo. Above all, he provided an attentive and reliable ear, happy to take on various moods and confidences without the risk of seeing them splashed all over the front page of a magazine one day.

In his new city, the timid Zizou, not really an introvert but a true comrade, who loved nothing more than finding a shared understanding, did not take long when it came to making new friends. This also went a long way to disproving the idea that he was ascetic and closed off, obsessed only with football, like the kid he used to be. No. Zizou was also a gourmet, greedy at times. He would devour pasta and emotions, laughter exchanged without ceremony around a good meal. One new friend was called Roberto. He worked at Da Angelino on Corso Mocalieri, on the left bank of the Po. He was the son of the owner. He was a chef, like his father.

Often at lunchtime and sometimes at dinner, Da Angelino was one of the few places where the number 21 could be spotted. This homebody who struggled to get a taste for the high life, or the scrutiny of passers-by, could not escape into anonymity. Not in a country where football is king. There was no question of him wandering the streets. Nor was there any question of him accepting the help offered to players, akin to a handout. He declined the club's offers. He did not have a driver; everyday tasks, however onerous, were down to him, his wife or Malek. Not to his employer. It was less a question of self-esteem than a natural precaution, staying surrounded by the people closest to him and not disconnecting too much from the 'normal' environment from which his fame distanced him. He was one of the very few, if not the only player, to adopt this position.

The warmth of his home and the physical presence of his friends helped support him through a testing first three months. Zidane smiled little. Zidane spoke little. Zidane shied away from press conferences that had the air of a trial about them, rightly or wrongly. The language barrier would turn out to be convenient. Sometimes Zinedine would have liked to respond, but the response was obvious, and everyone knew it: at the beginning of the season, he had not fully recovered his fitness. He was not in his best shape. And football, here more than anywhere else, is a competition from the very first to the very last minute. From the first to the last match.

If the press pointed out his lack of fitness, the fans in the stands at the Stadio delle Alpi, who loved victory but also knew how to recognise the touch of genius, were not as circumspect. They had seen the extraordinary talent of the number 21. Especially since his first stunning goal, against Inter Milan, a remarkable piece of control followed by an instantaneous left-footed strike.

Zidane may have been struggling a bit, but he was already loved. And he would become even more so when Juventus won.

The first chance to win a title came in Tokyo in December. Two big clubs had their sights set on the Intercontinental Cup: Juve played River Plate, winners of the Copa Libertadores, a major competition on the South American continent, where the relationship with football is just as passionate as it is in Italy. 'River' had long since left their mark on the history of Argentine sport. The upmarket neighbourhoods of Buenos Aires identified with the club, while the working classes were more inclined to support their great rivals, Boca Juniors. But for Yazid, River Plate was of less interest than one of its strikers. A Uruguayan who had returned to the club with which he had been voted the best player in South America in 1984, shortly before embarking on a European career that included a spell at Marseille. As far as Yazid was concerned, the player in question was a legend: Enzo Francescoli.

At the National Stadium in Tokyo, in the cool Japanese winter, the paths of Zidane and Francescoli finally crossed. Juventus won 1–0. Zizou had won his first title. He also took home an even more precious trophy: a shirt from his hero. He went over to talk to him after the game. Enzo gave him a gift. Back in Turin's *centro storico* at his home, which could have fitted several apartments from La Castellane inside it, Yazid sometimes slept in this present, wearing it like pyjamas. Like a relic.

Life at Juventus was calm. They beat Paris Saint-Germain to win the European Super Cup, played over two legs between the winners of the Champions League – Juve in this case – and those of the UEFA Cup Winners' Cup, a competition doomed to disappear. This success did not inspire much enthusiasm among the 'Bianconeri' because the Super Cup was not a major competition. The scorelines – 6–1 in Paris and 3–1 in Turin – augured well for a spring rich in victories. As at all big clubs accustomed to success, the directors did not stop at this dual achievement, which, as far as they were concerned, merely provided a little added confidence in advance of the two end-of-season objectives: the title of champions of Italy and victory in the Champions League. It would be their second in a row, a feat that had not been achieved in seven seasons, when the cup was still called the European Champion Clubs' Cup. Another Italian club had also distinguished itself: AC Milan. Joining the 'Milanisti' in the recent history of the continent's title-winners was also a question of national pride and northern Italian supremacy.

A year earlier, Juventus had finally returned to the summit of Europe, erasing the sad memory of their previous victory in the Champions' Cup in Brussels in 1985 when, with incomprehensible indecency, justified by a claimed ignorance of the tragedy, the game continued as the death toll rose into the dozens as fans were taken unawares by a crowd surge, powerless to resist and crushed against the fences of the Heysel Stadium. Eleven years on, Juve's renewed success, although won on Italian soil, was hard-fought: in Rome, Ajax of Amsterdam only succumbed in a penalty shootout, with the scoreline locked at 1–1 after extra time.

With Zidane at the helm, Juve's directors wanted a double, and if possible a brilliant one at that. A wonderful success and a wonderful image. The weeks that passed proved them right. Zidane was in full command of his skills. He unsettled opponents, sent his teammates on the path towards the goal and even got on the scoreboard himself. Not often, but when he did it was sumptuous.

The crowd appreciated this imaginative and reliable artist. He imposed himself physically in tough competitions. He never hesitated to try his luck with a strike on goal. From a distance. With his right foot. With his left foot. He was a leader. But certainly not fully-formed yet. He was anything but that, despite the popularity which, especially in France, began increasingly to spread beyond the world of football. His door was always open to his friends.

On one Champions League night in the spring of 1997, he had the Élineau family to stay after watching a game. Their former lodger had become a star after only six years at the highest level; a player whom no decision-makers within the sport could have imagined would ever go on to have such a career.

Lucky had become an engineer. The two friends from Pégomas talked about fate, the past and this unforeseeable adventure called life. At that moment, it was fantastic. They spoke long into the night, until almost 3am. Zinedine was happy in his beautiful apartment. His two families were there. His blood family and the family he had in his heart; the family of his past and the family of his future, intersecting in a happy present. He had not forgotten. Neither the Élineaus nor Monsieur Varraud. Yazid was the only player, among the many dozen, who was sincerely attached to the scout. Some of the best never called, never showed any gratitude by sending even a single photo, shirt or proof of an accomplished career given its start by him.

Nor did the loyal player forget Madame Varraud. She was ill and her condition became increasingly concerning. Yazid was discreetly present, without publicly disclosing his actions. He would go to the clinic where she was being treated as often as his fame would allow. The patients and employees recognised his silhouette and face, popularised by his victories. He was particularly recognisable thanks to his scrutinising and analytical gaze, which could be both suspicious and jubilant. Less evasive than in the past. Harder sometimes. But when you are a star, you have to protect yourself.

Zizou was a star. In France, he was the undisputed director of the national team's play, the man with the sleight of feet loved by football aesthetes, even more respected since he had emerged as the playmaker at a major club with a global reputation. In Turin, he was a centrepiece in the Juventinos' rigorous organisation. A winning machine permitted little failure.

Winning the *scudetto* was almost a minimum. Juve succeeded. Zidane was a hero. Winning a second consecutive Champions League was a priority. Juve did not succeed. Zidane was targeted. As in the previous season with Bordeaux, he lost again in the final to a German side, this time Borussia Dortmund, who won 3–1. His talent was not enough to make a difference, although he almost scored. One of his shots struck the left post but failed to cross the line. His team deserved more.

As in Euro 96 against the Czech Republic, as in the UEFA Cup against Munich, the season came to an end with a feeling of unfinished business.

But from his first league goal, against Inter Milan, to his last in the Champions League, against Ajax – sliding the ball into the goal with the outside of his right foot after bypassing the goalkeeper from the left – Zizou had largely justified his transfer.

The narrowness of the margins, the constant pace of important matches and the ongoing requirement for good results at least had the advantage of exploiting his potential. When constrained and forced, he learned to draw on his mental resources, which were found to be greater than may have been thought, said or written. He liked to dream and he liked to make people dream. But he knew how to remain focused, to think only of victory and to train with the utmost rigour.

The genius of Cannes, the playmaker of Bordeaux and the France team had proved in one season that he could play the same role for Juventus in Turin. He had carved out a place for himself in what was described as the world's toughest league. And a place had been carved out for him in every luxury hotel around the world. Just as it was in Cannes, to which he returned on holiday during the summer of 1997.

Zidane, Zinedine. The receptionist saw his name appear next to the room number on her screen. She knew who the guest was. She also knew that all the hotel's guests were special, but those who stayed in that particular room even more so. The most famous in Cannes: the imperial suite at the Hotel Carlton. When Yazid used to walk past, 'down below', along the Croisette on his way from Mimont, he could never have imagined the service, the luxury interior, the view from the suite beneath one of the city's iconic domes.

The residence was not far away, barely four or five hundred metres. Since he had left Cannes, it had taken five years to travel that distance. The journey from the hotel to a restaurant near the Palais des Festivals was all the sweeter. A short distance but one whose brevity did not guarantee complete tranquillity.

'He'd be better off training than staying there!' Zidane heard a passer-by comment. He smiled, with a clear conscience that so many years of effort had finally paid off. Money, fame and above all sporting success had finally come to him, in ever greater proportions.

Despite the annoyances or admirers, he could still walk down the street in relative peace and quiet.

Soon, however, he would need to guard against the famous pressure, the forms of which would vary almost infinitely as a big event with the potential to crown the coming season loomed on the horizon. A sporting event unprecedented since 1938 in France: the World Cup. An event the media coverage of which, in the 60 intervening years, had multiplied the impact on its fans ... and the pressure on its stars.

7

AN APPOINTMENT WITH THE REST OF THE WORLD

During Zizou's second season in Italy, Juventus remained focused on the dual objective of the Italian league title and the Champions League. Life continued as before: keeping away from the hustle and bustle of press conferences and fleeing microphones to avoid any linguistic misunderstandings. Keeping away but still with plenty of people around him: Véronique and Enzo, Roberto, friends at the club, such as Christian Vieri, whose French mother was very kind, and the Uruguayans Paolo Montero and Daniel Fonseca, through whom he would meet Enzo Francescoli.

Life would become even quieter after a move. The Zidane family later left the apartment to another player, Darko Kovačević. They left the busy streets of the historical centre for Eremo, Turin's most chic neighbourhood, in the hills. The large house gave Enzo the opportunity to run around freely in an important place that had previously been lacking: a garden. This green corner became the first football pitch used by father and son. The duo would soon become a trio: Véronique was pregnant. The baby was due in May 1998. Another deadline in a busy footballing spring, with three events at which Zizou would be judged in accordance with the seriousness befitting his new rank.

In Italy, he reproduced what he had already shown elsewhere. Had the level of the opposition increased? He played brilliantly. His many passes, rare but stunning goals, feints and deviations were lapped up by the fans. Despite almost being jaded connoisseurs, the Italians had rarely seen such a phenomenon! Nor had Martin Djetou. In the semi-final of the Champions League, Zizou was responsible for two decisive moves, resulting in a free kick then a penalty converted by another key player, Alessandro Del Piero. He also scored a symbolic goal: the 500th in Juve's European history. Monaco lost 4–1. Djetou, the Monaco player assigned to mark Zidane, was outsmarted by the accuracy of his opponent.

It now almost seemed normal that Juve had once again won the title of champions of Italy, albeit narrowly this time. Down 1–2, the men in the black and white shirts eventually beat Bologna 3–2. Zizou may have been king of Italy but his European coronation had to wait. It was planned for yet another final in Europe, his third consecutive, the second in the Champions League. But it was not to be. Juventus lost again. This time by a single goal, against Real Madrid, but this was somewhat more expected than it had been the year before. Zidane had still not won a European title. Had still not been decisive. As if he were the only one who could make the decision ... Such accusations failed to take into account that his role was to direct moves more than to conclude them.

The critics did not concern themselves with details: more was expected of Zizou. The World Cup was just around the corner. The first match was to be against South Africa, in Marseille, where, in December, he had led Europe against the 'Rest of the World' at the draw to determine the eight groups for the first round of the competition.

Marseille. His portrait was up on a wall along the Corniche. The advertising photo was accompanied by this proud slogan: 'Made in Marseille'. In February, he returned to his city with the France team, to the renovated Stade Vélodrome. He scored in extraordinary fashion, against Norway. A subtle piece of control, sliding the ball into the net with the outside of his right foot from a position similar to that of the no-less-superb goal scored against Ajax in Europe.

A month earlier, against Spain, he had been the first scorer in the history of the Stade de France, in Saint-Denis. The town where the World Cup final would take place. The town where his father, originally from Kabylie, had come to work on a building site 45 years earlier. Zizou's goals may have been episodic, but they were definitely symbolic. He wanted to be more present at key moments, to rid himself of his reputation, to be ready to recover from any lack of form or substandard performance.

A painful ankle in March did not stop him leading both the play of Juve and the France team. Rumours of competition for his place from Alessandro Del Piero, for Juventus, or Youri Djorkaeff, for France, did not cause him to blow his top. Mentally, he appeared more prepared than ever.

On 13 May, when the build-up to the cup was in full swing, Zinedine told himself he had already achieved his greatest victory: building a family. Enzo would soon be able to play football with his younger brother, Luca. Another Italian name for this son of Marseille of Algerian descent; Zidane rhymed with La Castellane, while for Véronique, from Aveyron but of Spanish descent, Fernandez rhymed with Rodez. They were not necessarily typically

Mediterranean. They were not extroverts. But they were from the South, where children are king. The birth of Luca, well timed before the start of the World Cup, strengthened Zizou's morale. He knew much was expected of him and that he would be forgiven little.

France, the host nation gifted with automatic qualification, were not among the favourites, despite an impressive unbeaten run. But observers, quick to offer analysis, suppositions and statistics, forgot that this was a cup. There was a subtle difference. The best teams didn't necessarily win, as had been the case for Hungary in 1954, the Netherlands in 1974 and Brazil in 1982. Surprises could happen.

Debates held before and after the competition, fuelling conversation and business, overlooked the potentially random nature of the event. Theories cobbled together afterwards proved nothing. They must, they should, they will have to, they should have … It was in vain.

They had to give the best of themselves. And Yazid could be counted upon to do that.

On Marseille's Corniche, passers-by who raised their heads locked eyes with a determined gaze. That of a winner.

Aimé Jacquet, the manager, could also be counted upon to follow through on his ideas. They were not universally supported. They did not repeat his formula of his Girondins' era, 'they don't like us', but that may nevertheless have been the case.

The former factory worker with a strong Loire accent, a dream target for Parisian mockery, had made this World Cup his last professional challenge.

His talent as a leader of men was underestimated. He was sure of his convictions, of the mental strength of his players and the solidity of his defence.

He was convinced of the art of his playmaker. Through the confidence he inspired in his colleagues and the fear he aroused in his opponents, the discreet Zizou, as determined as he seemed in the poster on the Corniche, was the man to take France a very long way indeed. With the friendlies played over the previous two years as the only benchmarks, they began the World Cup in a tense atmosphere. The print media were unrestrained in their doubts, with a degree of exaggeration. The broadcast media, sometimes backed by sponsors and the team's priority partners, were also doubtful, but in a less ostentatious way. Usually away from the microphones.

Aimé Jacquet did not forget his prediction. Two years earlier, after Euro 96, when it came to renewing his contract, he said that France would win the World Cup.

Wednesday 10 June. D-day minus two. In keeping with tradition, the reigning champions – in this case, Brazil – played the opening match. France would make their debut against South Africa, with maximum focus. But however important, facts must not make us forget what is essential in life. The stakes of an event must not consume the lives of men and women. Yazid was waiting for his moment. Sandra was expecting a baby. He had not forgotten. When she picked up the phone in her room at Nice's Saint-Georges maternity clinic, the former secretary of AS Cannes, now at OGC Nice, was pleasantly surprised to hear a familiar voice. Yazid had not forgotten their table-football matches with Amédée in the evenings while they waited for Monsieur Élineau to collect them to go back to Pégomas. He had stayed in touch with her. He had taken the time to phone her. To reassure her.

He wanted to comfort her. He told her about his experience as a father, about the birth of Luca, a few weeks earlier. They said they would see each other soon, without knowing exactly when their young families would be able to meet. One day. When the star was at peace with his schedule. Not now, after four years of preparation. Nor Friday, as the start of a four-week event, if all went well, would begin.

Marseille, again. Here, Zizou was Yazid, more than ever. At home more than anywhere else, in the Stade Vélodrome, where Olympique had never let him play. Not when he was a promising Under-17 nor when he was an experienced professional, in red and white. Yazid from Septèmes, Zinedine from Cannes, Zizou from Bordeaux and Juventus had never worn an Olympique de Marseille shirt. But the fans supported him for what he was: a local boy. Thanks both to this status and that of the playmaker of France's first 11, he had the right to the most memorable of ovations, which swirled like the mistral.

As the match against South Africa began, from the pitch it looked like a human wave, carried by the wind and a flood of emotions, ready to raise up its favourites if all went well. But the rumble also had the potential to cause players to sag under the weight of doubt. Christophe Dugarry, often the crowd scapegoat and as unpopular as the manager, had the look of a player likely to be the target of whistles: he was a forward and was therefore exposed to the risk of missing opportunities; he was also elegant and sensitive, so was consequently vulnerable. On top of that, he was thought to be unlucky; his only piece of luck was said to be that he had a friend named Zidane ... it was even suggested that it was only thanks to him that he had been included in the 22-strong World Cup squad.

South Africa had done little to leave their mark on the history of football. Archivists rightly note that a team from the country came out victorious from the second international match played by the

Brazilians in São Paulo in 1906. A 6–0 win! Since then, nothing significant, until recent performances on their own continent. The Africans were a bit of an unknown quantity. As the minutes ticked by, the French fans began to worry as the scoreline remained unchanged. They wasted no time pointing the finger at Dugarry, who replaced the injured Guivarc'h and miscued the ball on two occasions just before half-time. These two harmless mistakes were seized upon vehemently by many of the spectators, who revealed not only an antipathy towards Duga but also the moderate level of support given to the France team.

It was time for deliverance. And it needed to be quick. Dugarry had come on ten minutes earlier. There were still ten more to be played before the end of the first half. A corner. Zinedine lent a hand. Taking the kick from the left corner, he brushed the ball with a powerful right-footed shot. Following a concave trajectory, it came down towards Christophe's head. He stretched up as high as he could and fired the ball towards the goal. It ended up in the top right-hand corner. Goal! France were leading 1–0. Duga was in a daze. His joy was crazy, almost ecstatic. He ran, pumping his arms up and down along his body and lifting up his knees. Although he could talk the hind legs off a donkey, he said nothing, contenting himself with sticking out his tongue, making it hard to tell whether he was taunting or gloating. He was taunting the critics. Zinedine joined the mass of players who came over to hug their teammate. The duo had done it again.

The bad luck had switched sides. By a quirk of fate, it was Pierre Issa, a South African player with Olympique de Marseille, who unwittingly cemented France's domination by deflecting the ball into his own net. 2–0.

The French finally secured the expected victory with a 3–0 scoreline, banishing any initial doubts. Mathematically, they could afford one mistake, with two games remaining in their group; the knockout challenge of the cup would not begin until the round of 16. But psychologically, the victory was vital. A misstep against such inexperienced opponents would have exacerbated the pressure and controversy over the squad's ability to rise to the level of the world's best teams.

In a single stroke, the concern diminished. It became clear that the French had not remained undefeated for no reason, even during their run of friendlies. The stress receded. The door opened wider. The visitors found a relative serenity. In Mallemort, at the Moulin de Vernègues, the France team's base in Provence, a manager had come to speak to his former protégé: it was Jean Fernandez. He looked back at how far Zinedine had come since his days at La Bocca. He knew that Yaz had long since learned how to turn his back to goal, 'very, very quickly'. He knew that his focus would not waver.

The second game was heralded as the easiest. Although coached by the meticulous Carlos Alberto Parreira, manager of the Brazilian team that had won the World Cup four years earlier in the United States, the Saudi Arabian team was not fancied by many. In his pre-match team talk, Aimé Jacquet mentioned one of the few ways in which they could hurt Les Bleus: there was potential for provocation by the Saudis as a way of compensating for the flagrant difference in standard. It was the classic trap of an anti-game, a hateful feature of so-called modern football, to which some of the French players were also accustomed. Zinedine suffered more often than not.

As had always been the case, since Roanne and Nice, when his vengeful head-butts were not aimed at the ball, he had been familiar with this type of situation. Matches in Italy had made him even more accustomed to it. But the instinct to rebel is not easy to systematically repress. The repetition of aggression or dirty tricks makes a response inevitable. He had already received a yellow card against South Africa. A second would result in suspension.

Saint-Denis. While France were dominating and ahead in the scoreline, the threat of punishment loomed all the more when one of the Saudis was sent off. In such situations, it is not unusual to see a compensatory refereeing decision, whether conscious or not, whether justified or not, to numerically balance out the teams. Such a compensation would mean the sending-off of a French player.

Twenty minutes before the end of the game, badly shaken by a challenge from the opposing captain Fouad Amin, the playmaker, unsettled yet again, stepped on his opponent while he was still on the ground. This time it was a red card. An immediate sending-off, the first for a French player in World Cup history. The punishment was particularly hard to take because it would lead to a one- or two-match suspension. A decision would be made by a committee. Zinedine's eyes were incredulous, then angry. A dark look passed over his face. He said nothing, but it was easy to guess what he was thinking. Every player in the world knew how he was feeling, the insult and profanities that would pass his lips if he let himself go. The sending-off was harsh. At most it deserved a warning, a yellow card. Yazid was well aware of the world as it has been shaped by human beings for millennia. It is unfair. Sport is unfair.

Some great players before him had suffered from aggression that had gone unpunished, even at the World Cup: Pelé, bruised and battered in 1966; Johan Cruyff, who decided he would not play in 1978 – citing increased physicality as one of his reasons; or Diego Maradona and Zico, attacked by the antithesis of a footballer,

Claudio Gentile, in 1982. Zidane, the impulsive, had an easier answer than these champions.

On 23 June, the atmosphere in room 23 was hardly in keeping with the double birthday being celebrated at Clairefontaine, Les Bleus' base. The two friends would not play in the next game, just as they had not played in the first leg of the UEFA Cup final two years earlier. Yazid was suspended for the next two games; the first of these was the last game of the group stage, against Denmark, which would not be too damaging as France had already qualified for the knockout stages. But from then on, Zizou's absence could well become detrimental. He was one of the fundamental elements of Aimé Jacquet's formation. He was the best player in the team; one of the best in the world. An entirely possible elimination – as yet, no one has ever been able to confidently predict the outcome of any match – would not, of course, be simply down to the absence of one of the 22 members of the squad. But he would still get the blame.

Zinedine Zidane, 26 years old, was not master of his destiny. His mood was sullen, despite the obliging smiles as he lent over the cake he shared with Patrick Vieira, who turned 22 on the same day. Yazid needed comfort. He needed the phone.

In Pégomas, he had the phone box next to the *pétanque* ground. At Cannes, there was the office phone. He now had a mobile phone, the use of which has been alleged to cause brain damage. But it does plenty of good to the heart. On the other end of the line were Provence and Aveyron, Smaïl and Malika, Véro and Enzo, and all the friends to whom he did not always have time to talk. During long conversations, his father would constantly remind him of all the things he could do to make people happy, calls and small gestures for those who had not waited until he was famous to love the energetic and mischievous child who had become a discreet champion. The little prince of La Castellane, the baby of the Zidane family, had become a modest king, and would continue to be so for some time longer, more sheltered from the tumult than usual, wandering with his thoughts among the clearings in the grounds of Clairefontaine. Or motionless in his room.

Christophe, on the neighbouring bed, was no more serene than his friend. He was not even sure he would be able to play if they made it to the final. An unfortunate muscle hyperextension against Saudi Arabia had left him with a nasty injury. The companions in misfortune met in the dressing room. For once, they did not say a word. Talking was useless. But they were also thinking about each other, not just about themselves. Zizou was pained by the prospect that Duga would not play in the competition again. Duga was pained by the prospect that Zizou would fall prey to the critics.

They would need both luck and courage if they were to make the walls of room 23 reverberate with joy on the evening of 12 July, after victory in the final, on their return from the Stade de France.

On the end of a cross from the right wing, Zizou had helped Duga to score his first goal for France during qualifying for Euro 96, against Azerbaijan – with his head, just as he had against South Africa. He then also helped him score France's first goal at the World Cup. The last would come in the final. They wanted to believe it.

They had to keep believing it. They had to trust in others and believe in themselves.

In the final game in Group C, Denmark were beaten without them. In the last 16, France faced Paraguay. Still without them. For Zinedine, the only advantage of not playing was that it allowed him to conserve some of his physical strength, some of his nervous energy ... in the hope that it would not be absorbed by waiting and helplessness. He overcame his anger and turned it into positive energy. This was how he worked. Finding out who their opponents would be had also removed some of the guilt. If France lost, even the most extreme critics would struggle to make a case that France needed Zidane to beat Paraguay.

The Paraguayans were well organised but limited up front when it came to getting into their opponents' penalty area, a place where decisions are often made. Limited up front, yes. But not necessarily at the back. Throughout the match and during the first half of an unexpected period of extra time, the South Americans built a wall that was hard to break down, if not impassable.

Sitting on the bench, up on his feet whenever his emotions became too insistent, next to the substitutes who could at least imagine being called upon to support their struggling teammates, Zizou began to have doubts. The France squad, despite not appearing so to external observers, was tremendously tight-knit and very well prepared mentally. But the minutes continued to pass. A perilous situation loomed in the event of a draw at the end of 120 minutes: a penalty shootout, during which the charisma, talent and tricks of Chilavert, the Paraguayan goalkeeper, might well unsettle the French players.

But in the 113th minute, Robert Pires crossed the ball for David Trezeguet, who met it with his head. Laurent Blanc, theoretically the last line of defence but now the first line of attack, picked up the ball and shot from close range. It found the goal! It was over. The sweeper had promised his son a goal. He had kept his promise, after some incredible suspense. The 'golden goal' brought an end to the match, and to any speculation. Zizou would not be blamed. France had qualified for the quarter-final.

Zinedine sprang up, punched his fist in the air, hit the ground twice with his hand and then pulled up a clod of earth. It was a rare moment of jubilation for him, revealing the tension that had built up before and during the game. His penance was over. He could breathe again. As could Véronique. As could Malika, Farid, Lila, Noureddine and Djamel, almost tenser than he was, having envisaged, although without saying so, the worst consequences of an elimination, the terrible end to such a frustrating competition that for Zidane would have only lasted for a match and a half.

The quarter-finals, bringing together eight teams, are the minimum stage to be reached by teams with ambition. From this point on in the competition, a failure by high-level regulars like Germany or Brazil is judged harshly but is not usually considered a humiliation.

Freer mentally and confident of their chances, France were drawn against the most formidable competitors in the world: the Italians. The Brazilians could be brilliant, the Germans powerful, but the Italians were great competitors. Well organised. Wily. Individually solid, technically skilled, elegant and experienced in the drama of knockout games. The year before, during the Tournoi de France at the Parc des Princes in Paris, Zizou had scored a stunning goal against them after controlling the ball with the outside of his right foot, one of the most thrilling features of his game. He was not afraid of the Italians. In addition to their mentality, he also had skills that could be as confusing and subtle as those of the Brazilians. And he was well acquainted with them. In Italy, every Sunday for two seasons now, he had managed to put any thoughts of enjoying himself out of his head to bow to the collective defensive discipline. He knew how to think only of victory.

A victory was not necessary. A draw, followed by a winning penalty shootout, would be enough. The Italians seemed accommodating. But not the French. Zizou was marked tightly by Gianluca Pessotto, one of his Juventus teammates. They had shared champagne in Châtillon in the summer of 1996. Zinedine was celebrating his arrival at the club; Gianluca the birth of his daughter. Of course, feelings meant nothing during the 90 minutes a game usually lasts. Today, it would be two full hours. This time the French could not save themselves with a golden goal.

It would be fate, the lottery of a penalty shootout, that would decide qualification.

Fate was tough on Bixente Lizarazu, the enterprising left-back, vigilant defender and daring striker. An endearing man, respectful of others, simple and intelligent. Zizou and Duga were all the more distressed when they saw him fail in his attempt, having been a part of the Girondins' European adventure alongside him.

In the Stade de France, so dear to him and a reminder of his father's past, Zizou converted his shot. As did all the other French players, while two Italians missed theirs. France had qualified!

Just as in 1990, in the semi-final against Argentina – on Italian soil, in Naples – as in 1994, in the final against Brazil, the 'realism' of *bel paese* football had reached its limits. As in 1986 in the last 16, the Italians were eliminated by their dreaded neighbours, Les Bleus, dressed in white on that occasion.

A roar went up around the country, from windows, in houses and bars. The moral contract made by Aimé *le mal-aimé* (Aimé the unloved) was one step closer to being fulfilled. France were in the semi-final, among the four teams still fighting for the World Cup.

Jacquet savoured it but did not celebrate. He drew the attention of his men, if it were needed, to the quality of the football produced by their next opponents, Croatia. A young nation, a team made up in large part of former Yugoslav internationals, they were often referred to as the Brazilians of Europe. The Croats had qualified with a spectacular 3–0 win over Germany, who had failed to reach the semi-finals for only the third time in nine attempts.

The brilliant and sometimes tricky Croatians were at least as formidable as an inconsistent Brazil, remarkable in extra time against the Netherlands, but somewhat dull prior to that. The Brazilians had only qualified on penalties. Everyone was dreaming of seeing them against France in a final so idealised that the French fans struggled to believe it could become a reality.

But the Croats stood in their way. Jacquet warned his players. He put them on guard. He was concerned when half-time came and went at the Parc des Princes in Paris with the scoreboard still at 0–0. But unlike in the previous rounds, their opponents seemed more comfortable than the Paraguayans or the Italians. Against the Italians, France had applied themselves and dominated. Against Croatia, they were far from flawless. Jacquet was not someone to hold back. In the dressing room at half-time, he got carried away, pointing out their mistakes and shaking up his team. His words were harsh.

Zizou said nothing, as always. He listened. He also analysed the situation. He knew the Croats well. He knew Bokšić, one of the great absentees of the competition, a big weight off the minds of defenders; he knew Aljoša Asanović, someone alongside whom he had been expected to make the most formidable duo ever seen at the Coubertin. Asanović was inconsistent, the nonchalant traveller of world football, the prototype of the gifted dilettante that Zidane, contrary to plenty of unfair judgements, had never been. Zidane had worked hard, made his gifts productive and was conscientious.

But although he had plenty of influence on the game, he was the first to taste potential loss. At the start of the second half, Asanović put Davor Šuker through to open the scoring.

Croatia were ahead! But not for long. Just as Laurent Blanc had against Paraguay, the defender Lilian Thuram found himself in an ideal position in front of goal ... twice. And he scored ... twice! Two signs from above, perhaps, grasped by a footballer full of faith and human warmth, funny and profound, who knew how to put success into perspective and overcome failure. A champion. The Croats paid dearly for their lapses in focus, thinking they had achieved their most difficult task by taking the lead, only to see it last for just a few seconds. Dirty tricks of all kinds changed nothing. France were in the final.

8

TWO GOALS THAT CHANGED A LIFE

France–Brazil. A dream. France–Brazil not Brazil–France. A big difference. France were at home. The whole of France. A wave of jubilation overwhelmed the country. Because of the final. Because of the opponents. Because of the holidays; many French people were already enjoying their summer break. What better distraction than a World Cup final? The purists were hoping to see a return to the quality of the France–Brazil game of the 1986 World Cup in Mexico, when the Brazilians, under the legendary manager Telê Santana, were knocked out in the quarter-final.

Brazil. *Brasil!* A dream. An image conveyed by a song, an anthem almost: '*Aquarela do Brasil*'. Like the other players, directors and managers, Zizou had the melody playing in his head as he went to sit at the back of the coach, just as he always did. As it travelled from Clairefontaine to the Stade de France, the bus ploughed a furrow of joy through the crowds of fans keen to wave to their favourites, amassed on embankments, at the side of roads, along the route marked out long since. The relative indifference to the start of the World Cup had given way to a sudden idolatry, the effects of which were hard to imagine in the event of victory.

The Zidane family had assembled at Yazid's parents' house, where Luca was being looked after. Véronique and Enzo were in the stands. Some friends were there too, some of whom owed their place to a trial as painful as a penalty shootout: a ticket lottery! They were all waiting for Zizou's victory. Football specialists were also expecting him to show what he could do. The sceptics had not been silenced. The France team had played 370 minutes with him and 224 minutes without him. Dugarry had scored; Lizarazu had scored; he had not, with the exception of the penalty shootout against Italy that did not count.

France had found the net 12 times and Brazil 14. But France had only let in two goals, compared with seven for Brazil. At least one in every game. The Brazilians, guaranteed to top their group after two matches, had even lost a game. The defeat against Norway was initially labelled a scandal because of a penalty awarded to the Norwegians. Live on air, a pundit for a national radio station could not restrain himself and attacked the referee with a rarely heard virulence. He displayed an insulting and hasty disregard that proved to be unjustified, when, thanks to shots taken from an angle different to that of the official broadcast, it became clear that the defender Junior Baiano had indeed pulled the shirt of the Norwegian forward Tore André Flo.

Although it made no difference to first place in the group, the defeat proved that the Brazilians were inconsistent.

Les Bleus had no need to worry about complexes; both individually and collectively, their own players had shown plenty of weaknesses. Zizou knew it, just as he knew he was among them, despite, thanks to the variety of options he could call upon, being the most gifted of them all.

The pivotal midfield pairing of Junior Baiano and Aldair had failed to work as well as Márcio Santos and Aldair had at the previous World Cup four years earlier. Left-back Roberto Carlos was intoxicated by his ease and notoriety, largely due to his powerful strikes, such as the one he had scored against the French a year earlier at the Tournoi de France. It was on that occasion that Denilson had been unveiled; the most expensive player in the world since his signing for Betis, he was a deluxe substitute for the Brazil 1998 team, who had several other talents of world football among them. There was no doubt that the right-back Cafu was one of these, as was the midfielder Leonardo, who had made the most appearances since the start of the competition; the playmaker Rivaldo was also a big star, despite the lack of confidence from which he suffered around manager Mario Zagallo. And then there was Ronaldo. An extraordinary player, one of the geniuses of the century. One of few athletes who attract a crowd by their mere presence.

There may have been a lack of serenity around the team, but Brazil were no less impressive. With the most ever World Cup victories, four, already under their belt, by qualifying for their sixth final they had just equalled the record held by Germany since 1990.

Despite the stakes, there was probably less pressure on the French than there had been before their first match, against South Africa, when their value as competitors had been called into question. In the event of a significant loss, there would be no shortage of opportunities to underline their relative inefficiency – their last three goals had been scored by defenders – and the insufficient strength of a deserving but unproductive squad. On the other hand, defeat by one or two goals, provided any terrible mistakes were avoided, would not be a disgrace. A defeat by Brazil is often pardoned. However, these particular Brazilians seemed vulnerable. Their weaknesses were many. At the back and in midfield. Although he had scored three times, Cesar Sampaio had not outshone the volume of play by Mauro Silva, his predecessor in 1994; while the controversial Dunga, a leader of men and captain of the team, seemed physically hampered. The Brazilians had successfully negotiated plenty of set pieces when the whistle was blown in their favour, but seemed lacking in defensive rigour whenever decisions went against them. They lacked focus in marking, whereas focus was one of the France team's strengths, both during and before games. This was evident from the atmosphere in the dressing room. There was an atmosphere of invulnerability similar to that of Bordeaux before the match against Milan in the 1996 UEFA Cup.

Behind the Brazilian scenes, the show was entirely different. Their concentration had long since been disrupted. The big star, the genius Ronaldo, was taken to hospital after feeling unwell. His roommate, Roberto Carlos, said he had found him in their room, motionless. The news sowed fear at the Brazilians' base at the Château de la Grande Romaine in Lésigny, Seine-et-Marne.

Zagallo's style of play lacked variety. He relied too much on Brazil's prowess with set pieces and Ronaldo's huge potential. But would Ronaldo be able to play? Whatever the case, he wanted to. Expectations were high. He had been decisive for his team in qualifying and missing the final would be a personal tragedy. He was keen to play and made this clear as soon as he arrived at the stadium – well after his teammates – even though his name did not appear on the team sheet when it was initially announced. The gifted but whimsical Edmundo replaced him. The rumour of a tactical manoeuvre – a deliberately misleading piece of information leaked to unsettle the France team – began to circulate in the corridors of the Stade de France.

But the illness was clearly real, as proved by the reaction of one former great champion, called in before the World Cup to assist Zagallo as technical coordinator: Zico, who was, on occasion, considered the best player in the world in his day. He called some medical experts he knew for advice. After hearing about Ronaldo's symptoms, their conclusion was clear: at least 48 hours' rest was required.

Zico shared this opinion with the members of the Brazil delegation but Ronaldo insisted on playing. How many of us, in his shoes, would be brave enough to stay in the dressing room? And who, in Zagallo's shoes as sole decision-maker, theoretically at least, would be brave enough to do without such a player, whose presence had a fallout that went well beyond a sporting competition? When the final team sheet was announced, Edmundo's name no longer appeared. Ronaldo would play. Zico said nothing. But he did leave the dressing room, in a clear sign of disapproval. Brazil had already lost in terms of team spirit. Brazil, or at least a team of Brazilians, against a team of French players gaining increasing support from the public. In the grip of frequent internal disagreements, either made public or ignored in silence, Zagallo's squad had lost its cohesion. The players held hands as they came out onto the pitch: a human chain that was simply one final illusion.

The clash was also that of two brands that dominated the sports equipment market. For three whole months, they had almost completely occupied television screens with two advertisements of very different tones. The Nike–Brazil commercial was dreamlike, surrealist, as exhilarating as the melodies of Antonio Carlos Jobim, the great composer after whom the international airport at Galeão in Rio is named. This then led into more light-hearted footage, backed by a famous piece of music by Jorge Ben: '*Mas que nada*'. Its final lyrics were: 'You don't want me to get to the end.' The clip's last image was of Ronaldo, with his head in his hands, after one of his shots hit a makeshift post in the airport that had become an improvised football pitch.

The Adidas–France advert had a more intimate, urban and perhaps even sombre tone. They did not laugh, but were determined. The slogan was: 'Victory is within us'.

On the screen, the Brazilians had fun but failed to win. The French were tight-knit. Zidane the discreet seemed ready to release his power when the time came.

Who knows whether, after months on screen, these images contributed to impregnating the minds of those involved, in a world centred more than ever on media reflections?

Back in sporting reality, the French did not need an advert to stand shoulder to shoulder with their manager. On the pitch, on 12 July 1998, the Brazilians were not as creative or as joyful as they had been for director John Woo's camera. They were less united than their opponents that day. Doubt had set in. In these conditions, how could they withstand an extremely solid, well-prepared France team playing in front of an audience that was, for the most part, behind them? Perhaps a stroke of genius would be enough to resist the blue onslaught. But the genius was called Ronaldo, and he was at his worst. Brazil may have already lost, but France had not yet won. It was only a matter of time. A breakaway by Zizou, punctuated by a one-two with Youri Djorkaeff and concluded with a nutmeg pass to Guivarc'h. A first clear scoring opportunity. A long and impressive run.

It was only a matter of time. The Brazilian defence were even more fragile than usual and their attack seemed to lack potency. The positioning of Zagallo's players was also often questionable.

In the 27th minute, Roberto Carlos attempted the same type of acrobatic gesture that had led to Denmark's equaliser in the quarter-final. He would later claim that he was the victim of a foul. Whatever the case, he was a victim of his imprudence: he had just conceded a corner. A corner kick; a stroke of luck. The kind of luck that leaves its mark on a sporting life: winning the World Cup.

The ball flew up from the right-hand corner. Zizou went in behind Ronaldo, sneaked in front of the defence and jumped up to meet the ball, higher than Leonardo who leapt at the wrong moment. The Stade Chevalier seemed a long time ago. With a headed strike, Yazid slammed the ball into the back of the net a second after jumping up into the sky. One second was all it took to change his career. Goal!

A roar went up in the stadium and across the country.

With narrowed eyes and a tense face, Zizou jumped on an advertising hoarding. He was in a daze: he kept his intense joy inside.

He had to hold on. He had to try to score another goal. The perfect scenario presented itself, just before half-time – 45 seconds after 45 minutes. A fantastic opportunity just a few moments before the end of the first half. Another corner, from the other side of the pitch this time, on the left. Zidane wanted to take it but Djorkaeff told him to let him do it. There was a chance it might achieve what Zinedine had asked of him: let him score, just as he had so often allowed Youri to do.

Djorkaeff's precision corner provided the final nail in Brazil's coffin. Zizou got behind Leonardo, clashed with Dunga, who fell backwards, and, as Thuram was getting out of the way to give him more room, he rushed with determination towards the flight of the ball. It fell lower than it had the first time but the result was identical. Goal!

Another second that would change not only a career but an entire life.

France were 2–0 up at half-time. Zidane had scored two goals! Two goals in the final. Only seven other players had ever achieved that feat in the history of the competition.

Zizou kept on running, towards the fans. He kissed his shirt.

This time he was smiling. He ran towards Djorkaeff. On their knees, the two architects of the goal gave each other a symbolic embrace. Their teammates piled on top of them. In all likelihood they had sealed France's first ever World Cup.

In the second half, Zizou strolled around the pitch, attempting and achieving several daring pieces of dribbling that looked almost Brazilian in style. He ran around in the Saint-Denis night like a genie released from his lamp, lighting up the Stade de France. The two-goal cushion made everything easier. Running, passing, intercepting ... The Brazilians had long since lost. The French had managed to win. Nothing could stop them – even the referee helped, failing to give a foul against Guivarc'h when he held Ronaldo back by the shirt just as Junior Baiano had done to Flo against Norway. No penalty. Few clear threats. No longer any real danger for the French, who were even able to increase the gap. Just as he had promised, Dugarry sped towards the goal. He had scored Les Bleus' first goal; he would score the last on the end of a pass from Zidane. But no. That would be too perfect. Reality, which was already astonishing, would not be able to make that dream come true. Christophe would not score. But when the final whistle blew he was on the pitch to embrace his friend Zinedine. It was over!

It finished 3–0, thanks to Vieira, who provided the last assist, and Emmanuel Petit, who scored. The Brazilians were beaten and deflated. The French fans were euphoric. Who would have thought it possible, a month earlier, when the squad put together by Jacquet had been so disparaged?

A long, very long night of celebration began. The laps of honour went on and on. They only stopped for one final effort, the most long-awaited, the most hoped-for, the least painful: the climb to collect the famous cup, the five kilograms of eighteen carats that were worth all the gold in the world.

Zizou cast his mind back to another cup: a plastic bottle, cut in half and wrapped in tinfoil. This was what had been at stake during the friendly matches played by the kids back in La Castellane.

Listening to cries from both familiar and anonymous voices, the players passed the trophy from one to another, shook hands and bent down to receive their medals. Then they went back down onto the pitch, in a very slow procession.

The focus of everyone's gaze, he suddenly became Yazid again. He saw Véronique and Enzo in front of him. With him. He hugged them tightly, very tightly. He began crying: with joy, of course, not sadness as his son believed before he too started crying! His dad held him in his arms, reassured him, said he would see him soon, then ran off once more, unaware of any fatigue, holding in his hands the precious object, the image of which appeared on the T-shirt he and his teammates had put on. The victory was in them, on them; on the white fabric worn by Les Bleus. Written ... or rather printed.

Zizou clasped the cup to his chest and posed for the photographers, unrestrained but without exhilaration. He took care of the trophy and hugged it like a child. The fruit of an accomplishment, both personal and collective.

As he walked around the pitch, the accolades multiplied. This time, he was not the one crying. It was Christophe. Duga and Zizou, friends for life. Zinedine could not stop hugging Christophe. He jumped with joy. He kept on running.

In Paris, on the Champs-Élysées, the crowd chanted his nickname, which was projected onto the Arc de Triomphe by a laser beneath an image of his face. '*Merci Zizou!*' He was celebrated across France. He ran off again. Suddenly he heard someone shouting at him. Everyone was shouting at him, but this was different. They were calling him Yazid.

He scanned the nearby stand, spotting faces that were dear to his heart: those of his friends. Once again, he saw past the thousands of pairs of eyes looking at him and the millions watching on television. He ran towards them.

They were the only ones he could see. His friends from La Castellane. Up there, in the stand.

After the final lap of honour, in the extraordinary tumult of a crazy night of celebration, Yazid could not wait to meet up with his family. Finally, he would have a short moment of privacy with them at Clairefontaine. Before giving in to the first media requests.

The following day, there would be an afternoon parade down the Champs-Élysées. Like conquering heroes. The winners were given an ovation from one end to the other by a cheering crowd. Zizou smiled, sitting down, while many of Les Bleus stood up to greet the public. He waved in short spells, concerned about those following the procession and fans who might get crushed, oppressed by the heat and risking dehydration. He was astonished by the incredible procession of onlookers, no less numerous than the day before. Zizou was tired but kept on smiling, enjoying the moment that would define his life. He savoured his happiness while Enzo, tired but not understanding the importance of the parade, dozed in his lap. Enzo was sleepy – just as he had been the day before, during the final – and lay down, invisible to those below whose shouts and smiles accompanied the slow progress of the double-decker bus. They would not make it to the Arc de Triomphe, there were so many fans lining the avenue.

That evening, they met up at the Lido. The arrival of Les Bleus was met with an astonishing collective outpouring, rare in French society in which praise for sporting figures is usually restrained and does not give in to hero-worship. Zizou, Véronique and Enzo retreated from this assault to take refuge in one of the venue's control rooms for more than half an hour. They had to let the storm of joy pass. But it would not dissipate immediately, because, high on the summer holiday season, the French wanted to drink in the words of their favourites until they had had their fill. They wanted to admire them, on paper, on TV or better still, for the lucky few, to see them in the flesh, to devour them with their eyes, approach them and touch them.

The World Cup had begun with indifference, mistrust and even hostility towards the France team. It ended with joy and collective euphoria. However, among the throng of painted faces must have been some who were whistling not so long ago. It was not a victory; it was a triumph. Ninety minutes for years of sporting pride. A success that would be dissected at length by football fans. The experts in victory, who had been sarcastic defeatists before the competition, were sure of themselves in the aftermath. The intelligentsia and decision-makers learned to talk about the round ball, cashing their leaden silence into silver words with an alchemy to which only they knew the secret. They were playing catch-up when it came to sport. They were afraid of being submersed by this crazy wave that, they believed, would no doubt profoundly change the country. What then did this overflowing of unexpected and delayed enthusiasm reveal, mobilising energy that had previously been indifferent? Was the population joyful? Sick? Reconciled? Immature? Excessive?

How could you not celebrate when you were the hero? What if you no longer had a reason to stand back and think about the vagaries of life? Or put it into perspective? How could you not think about Monsieur Varraud? Two headed goals! Zinedine Zidane was an idol. Jean Varraud should have been a happy, fulfilled man, knowing that one victory had changed everything, that two successful strikes had done more than all the passes, shots and brilliant goals accumulated by his protégé over the years.

But Monsieur Varraud was unhappy. Despairing. A widower. Seventeen days before the first World Cup game, the end that had been so desperately feared had come. Madame Varraud was not buried in the family vault in Fayence, in the Var, but in the Grand-Jas cemetery in the middle of Cannes. Closer to the man with whom she had shared her life for 60 years. Malika and Smaïl went to the funeral. The tragedy had brought them a little closer to Jean. They were there at the worst of times because they could not forget that he had changed their lives for the better. Smaïl summed it up with a poetic and symbolic phrase: 'An angel passed over the house.'

The recruiter had given much but received little; no transfer commission, few glowing testimonials, just a few interested hellos since Yazid had become Zizou. But his new-found idol status would change nothing. Yazid and Jean would keep in touch. Forever. The watchword was the same for both of them: survive. One would have to survive loneliness; the other fame.

'I Will Survive', suggested by the defender Vincent Candela, was Les Bleus' soundtrack, the song they would burst into in the dressing room after every win. A 20-year-old song, recorded by the American singer Gloria Gaynor in 1978.

'I Will Survive' inundated the airwaves. It was even sung by the Republican Guards to welcome the players to a relaxed garden party at the Élysée Palace. The guests invited by the French president – powerful, high-society elite, artists and athletes – welcomed Zizou with an astonishing 'Zidane for president!'

He would survive. He would not allow himself to be drawn into the quickly absorbing spiral of several of his teammates, who, during a crazy summer, went from romantic or sexual encounters to jet-set receptions and ceremonies of all kinds.

Marbella. It was warm and sunny. There were no fans, apart from a few VIPs asking for photos or autographs. No noise, apart from that of the lapping water in the pool. Silence. Children's laughter, a rubber ball, the occasional breaststroke and some rest. Calm, finally.

In the luxury resort where the Zidane family enjoyed a few days' rest and relaxation, Zizou did not go unnoticed. He realised his days of anonymity were over. All over the world, for at least a few years, and for a very long time in France, no doubt. But, at the hotel, there was peace and quiet at least. He needed it to release the tension that had built up, to piece together the kaleidoscope of memories of a crazy month. He needed it to face a new sporting season and, above all, a new life. Two goals, two seconds, had changed his existence forever.

Nothing would ever be like it was before. Football was no longer just a game, a sport or a competition. At this level, it was a social phenomenon. Elite police officers watched over teams, communications managers and security agents got between the public and their footballers. Goalscorers became legendary heroes. Zizou joined the ranks of Lancelot and Jeanne d'Arc. It may have been a confusion of genres but he would have to get used to it. Zinedine was prepared. His parents ... less so.

'He has done some stupid things in his life ... But scoring those two goals was the worst!'

Malika joked ... partly. For Mme Zidane and her husband, nothing was simple at a time when requests were pouring in from all sides, when ulterior motives lay behind friendly gestures. And this was just the beginning. There was no longer any need to worry about whether the Juventus number 21 had the resources to face a post-World Cup world. There was no longer any doubt as to his supposed lack of efficiency or lack of presence on important occasions. Two goals had swept it all away. He was a hero and would remain a hero, and the advertising executives knew that better than anyone.

However, it was another Bleu who was the first to be contacted about lending his image to a brand: Fabien Barthez, the jovial goalkeeper. A footballer of boundless and spectacular talent and a naturally joyful person whose rustic origins were a guarantee of sincerity, he did not shun social engagements nor did he hesitate to lend his luxury sports car to a trainee at his club. He walked through life with simplicity, willingly demonstrative, even going so far as to spray champagne over France's president and prime minister.

After him, Zizou had an obvious commercial appeal. He was clean-cut and honest, although his image was still a little hazy. He was said to be shy but had evolved in his approach to microphones and lenses. He no longer looked evasive, sometimes a little lost, as he had done during his first years in the sport. He knew how to please, to pose, to show emotion. He was a visceral altruist, who had also learned to love himself, to assume the right dose of ego required to assert himself. He was ready to see his face blown up on photographs, and not just along the Corniche in Marseille.

Launched in January 1999, the campaign for Leader Price, a French supermarket chain, was a great success. The slogan associated with it promised to help customers win. He had become someone who won. A winner. Even of the Ballon d'Or at the end of 1998. And not just a great artist. The brand's recognition rate reached around 70 per cent, delighting those behind the project. While discreetly listening anonymously to the public's reactions to the billboards, they smiled as they heard: 'Look, that's nice. Leader Price picked a handsome guy!' The elderly woman responsible for the comment must have been one of the few who did not recognise the 'model' in question, the mention of whose name was almost superfluous.

Zizou's popularity continued to grow. He tried to manage it. He knew what he did or did not want. They wanted to put his face on supermarket carrier bags. He refused.

'Bags are visible but they sometimes end up on the ground. I don't want people walking on me!'

He was right. He did not want people walking all over him. Every new face, every new person was difficult to analyse. What do they want from me? Who is standing in front of me? Why? Niggling questions, the eternal consequences of fame. They can hurt like poison. But there were antidotes: a rejuvenating trip to La Castellane, arriving at nightfall, or announcing his visit at the last minute, ensuring less chaos; a phone call to a gentleman from Cannes who had not been forgotten.

The higher Yazid climbed, the less he forgot. His unwavering friendship masterfully contradicted the cynicism of the time. Jean Varraud had never needed it so much. Time had lessened neither his pain nor his isolation. Six months after the World Cup, it was a man with a smile that had become sad and fleeting who arrived at the Hôtel Gray d'Albion in Cannes. His discretion, his modest car that had replaced the LN with 250,000 kilometres on the clock, his sober suede jackets and corduroy trousers guaranteed him anonymity, even at a football press conference held to announce the Bellone testimonial due to take place a month later. The charity event had been organised by Didier Roustan, a journalist originally from Cannes. It was he who had given the nickname 'Lucky Luke' to Bruno Bellone, a talented sportsman whose career had been ruined by injury. It was he who, thanks to his way with people, would bring the greatest names in French football of the last 20 years to the Coubertin. It was he who, during the presentation, would give some of the credit to Jean Varraud, to whom a tribute was paid that day.

On 22 February 1999, Jean would smile. And cry, as he allowed his solemn emotions to get the better of him. The participants in the two testimonial games planned for that evening were invited to a lavish lunch in a marquee set up in the grounds of the Villa Domergue, the rooms and gardens of which play host to the city's most important social events. As expected and promised, Cannes' and France's greatest footballers of the past two decades were in attendance. Plus the genius from Cameroon, Roger Milla.

Milla had promised his son he would collect as many autographs as possible and he had plenty of opportunity! He got up from the table and set off around the room on his mission. A few minutes later, the most anticipated guest arrived at the marquee, which was shaking in the wind. As soon as he entered, loud applause rang out. Yet another tribute. One of the most important, from his peers and elders.

The marquee contained footballing royalty, to an extent that may never be matched. Football fans everywhere would have been moved at the sight of Maxime Bossis and Manuel Amoros, former holders of the record number of France caps; Bernard Lacombe and Didier Six, the duo responsible for the fastest ever World Cup goal for France in 1978; Alain Giresse, face of the unforgettable 1982 World Cup in Spain; Dominique Bijotat and Daniel Bravo, symbols of one of the greatest spells in the history of AS Monaco; Joël Bats, the man who knocked out the Brazilians almost single-handedly in 1986; the brilliant referee Robert Wurtz; Dominique Rocheteau and Christian Lopez, the talismans of the exploits achieved by AS Saint-Étienne that allowed French football to lift its head up high once more; Bruno Martini and Pascal Olmeta, two legendary goalkeepers; Johan Micoud and Peter Luccin, jewels in the crown of the Cannes midfield; Christophe Dugarry; Éric Cantona and Jean-Pierre Papin, the two-pronged attack in the years when France did not manage to win a title; Fabien Barthez, Laurent Blanc, Robert Pires and Thierry Henry, figureheads of the France team that finally did do itself justice. Henry even came knowing that he would have to stay on the bench as the directors of his club, Juventus, would allow only one member of their squad to play. Logically, preference was given to Zidane, who, despite the quality of the guests' reputations, was the most widely anticipated.

The cameras were poised once again. Yazid shook hands as he looked for somewhere to sit. Milla's chair was empty but he did not sit in it right away. Just as he would not claim a shirt number that belonged to someone else, he made sure the seat was free first: 'Is anyone sitting here?'

'Roger Milla, but he's gone off somewhere.'

He sat down but did not stay long. Someone was trying to get his attention a few tables further on.

The Élineaus were sitting with Smaïl, Malika and Lila. They were supposed to be having a quiet lunch at Pégomas, but envoys were dispatched by the local council to convince them to come to the Villa Domergue.

Constantly in demand, Yazid had little time to eat. He listened a lot, speaking much less. They wanted to talk to him about his two World Cup goals and the good old days, which were not all that old and not all that good! Some of the praise in Cannes came from those with short memories.

Once most of the guests had left, Jean Varraud and Zinedine were finally left alone to chat. A little earlier, they had received the medal of the City of Cannes, after Bruno Bellone. Monsieur Varraud had cried. Despite the solemnity of the context, a sincere, intense and collective joy began to spread around the marquee. The medals were celebrated, thanks were given and what they had in common was pointed out: generosity and a lack of artifice.

At home, Monsieur Varraud had one of his friends staying with him, Maurice Roche – who worked for the Provence district of the French Football Federation – and his daughter. Anecdotes about Marseille and Cannes could have continued well beyond when the time came to leave for the Coubertin to watch the two testimonial matches. Jean and his friend talked about their greatest regrets in football: the pre-eminence of winning over the game itself; the recruitment of ever younger children, sold on without even playing for the club that bought them; the fouls that ruin matches.

The conversation was interrupted only by the apartment doorbell. Jean went to open the door. Yazid came in. Monsieur Roche's daughter was speechless! She did not know Yazid. Like everyone else, she knew Zizou. From TV, the press and advertising. 'If I'd been there, I would have fainted,' a hostess from AS Cannes was heard to say afterwards.

How many spectators braved the cold just for him that day? The Coubertin was full. The stars were in attendance. The most anticipated of the games was played in three parts ... just like at the Regional Training Centre in Aix, a dozen years earlier. The most anticipated player took part in the final third of the second match. He was, of course, met with an ovation.

He no longer had anything to prove. He just had to avoid becoming as lost as Bruno Bellone, now an insurance broker, with whom Zidane signed a contract. A further guarantee for the future and a gesture towards his former teammate. Zizou was still Yazid. It was his greatest achievement.

A young Zidane (top right) in the line-up for the AS Foresta youth team in the La Castellane neighbourhood of Marseille, wearing the captain's armband.

The AS Cannes team for their match against Montpellier in Division 1 on 27 July 1991. Top row, left to right: François Omam-Biyik, Adick Koot, Michel Dussuyer, Aljoša Asanović, Jean-Luc Sassus, Luis Fernández, Patrick Sébastien. Bottom row, left to right: José Bray, Éric Guérit, Franck Priou, Franck Durix, Zinedine Zidane.

Zidane during his first cap with the French national team on 17 August 1994, coming on as a sub in the 63rd minute against the Czech Republic.

Bayern Munich captain Lothar Matthäus clears from Bordeaux's Zidane during their UEFA Cup final second-leg match in May 1996.

The Juventus team shot for Serie A's 1998–99 season. Top row, left to right: Mark Iuliano, Alessio Tacchinardi, Igor Tudor, Filippo Inzaghi, Angelo Peruzzi, Zinedine Zidane. Bottom row, left to right: Alessandro Birindelli, Alessandro del Piero, Didier Deschamps, Gianluca Pessotto and Edgar Davids.

Zidane gets the better of Manchester United's Roy Keane while playing for Juventus in November 1996.

The French team line up for the 1998 FIFA World Cup final against Brazil. Top row, left to right: Zinedine Zidane, Marcel Desailly, Frank Leboeuf, Lilian Thuram, Stéphane Guivarc'h, Emmanuel Petit. Bottom row, left to right: Christian Karembeu, Youri Djorkaeff, Didier Deschamps, Fabien Barthez, Bixente Lizarazu.

Zidane celebrates
with Djorkaeff,
Petit, Thuram
and Karembeu
after scoring
his second goal
during the final
against Brazil.

Zidane holds aloft the FIFA
World Cup trophy alongside
his teammates following their
victory against Brazil.

Zidane holding the
Ballon d'Or trophy for
European player of the
year in December 1998.

Zidane is presented with his shirt by Real Madrid president Florentino Perez and Di Stefano during a press conference to announce his signing for the club in July 2001.

Zidane vies with Barcelona's Lionel Messi during a Spanish Liga match in Madrid in November 2005.

Roberto Carlos, David Beckham and Zidane wait to take a free kick during Real Madrid's UEFA Champion's League first-leg match against Arsenal at the Bernabeu in February 2006.

Zidane gestures in frustration during Real Madrid's Spanish Copa del Rey match against Athletic Bilbao in San Mamés stadium in January 2006.

Zidane celebrates with Patrick Vieira after Thierry Henry scores the opening goal during the 2006 FIFA World Cup quarter-final match against Brazil.

Zidane is sent off by referee Horacio Elizondo during the 2006 FIFA World Cup final against Italy at the Olympic Stadium in Berlin. This marked the end of Zidane's playing career.

Zidane poses with Real Madrid president Florentino Perez as he is announced as the team's new head coach on 4 January 2016.

Zidane on the touchline during La Liga match between FC Barcelona and Real Madrid at Camp Nou in April 2016.

Zidane looks on alongside Luis Enrique, head coach of FC Barcelona, during that same match.

Zidane celebrates with Real Madrid's Portuguese forward Cristiano Ronaldo after Real Madrid won the UEFA Champion's League final match against Atlético Madrid at the San Siro stadium in Milan on 28 May 2016.

Zidane holds the trophy aloft after his team's Champion's League victory.

Zidane celebrates with his players after being crowned champions of La Liga following the match between Malaga and Real Madrid at La Rosaleda Stadium in Malaga on May 21, 2017.

9

PLAYER OF THE YEAR 2000

Zizou was popular. His fame was unique. Universal and everyday. From now on, no one would dare to point out that he had still not won a European competition. He would not win the Italian league that year either. And he would still take very little real enjoyment in a country where it was only fun when you were winning.

Zinedine had long wanted to play in Spain. He said so himself. Véronique had long wanted to live there as she had family connections in Andalusia, Almeria to be precise. There was talk of Zizou going to Barcelona, Betis or Atlético Madrid. Gianni Agnelli, the Fiat boss and honorary president of Juventus, questioned Zizou about the rumours during a training session. On leaving the pitch, he responded to the journalists who had been watching the discussion with an unusual and clearly calculated frankness. Agnelli gave his version of the remarks made by his star player, implying that the attention paid by Yazid to his wife's wishes was an act of weakness. These treacherous 'revelations' could also be interpreted as the clearest evidence, spoken at a time when Zidane's departure seemed inevitable, of the Piedmontese magnate's fondness for his playmaker.

The Italian press seized upon the controversy with delight, fanning the flames with a declaration made by Filippo Inzaghi, the Juventus forward whose personality did not gel with the rest of the squad. 'When I get married my wife will do what I tell her,' was the comment reportedly made by 'Pippo', brilliant on the pitch but unpopular with his teammates off it. As always, Zinedine said nothing. Neither about possible contracts in Spain for the upcoming season or the one after, nor about his views on married life.

Once again he found himself back in Châtillon during the summer to prepare for the 1999–2000 season after three whole months without football. A knee injury inflicted by a Champions League opponent from Olympiakos, followed by a relapse and surgery, had led to an exceptionally long, unexpected and enforced holiday. Never in his life had Zinedine Zidane enjoyed quite such a long period of rest, without any academic or professional constraints. He had plenty of time to think. Surprisingly, the man whose name was on the lips of football fans everywhere, the winner of popularity contests, the children's idol and someone whom adults aspired to be like, found himself plunged into relative isolation. Sometimes, he fell prey to the doubt inherent in any convalescence. In May, ten months after the World Cup final that had propelled him to the dizzy heights of fame, he was operated on in Strasbourg by surgeon Jean Jaeger. His right knee began to regain mobility. In July, almost a year to the day after France–Brazil, one hundred days after his injury, three months after Agnelli's indiscretions, the Juve playmaker was back on the pitches of the Aosta Valley. David Bettoni returned to Châtillon to enjoy the relative calm of the off-season preparation. He stayed at the hotel and would see his friend between training sessions. He was still playing in Serie C1, for Brescello, a small town known first and foremost as the set for the *Don Camillo* series popularised by the actors Fernandel and Gino Cervi. There was one simple link between David's peaceful career and Yazid's life in the spotlight: they both loved football and appreciated the professionalism of Italian clubs, but much less the exaggeration and polarisation of a sport that often became the centre of the world. It was difficult to escape this passionate environment.

Like almost every player, Zidane had an agent who negotiated his contracts; Alain Migliaccio was his right-hand man who took care of his business affairs. But he also involved his family in managing his promotion. There was no shortage of work for Zidane Diffusion, his company based in Marseille. The success of Leader Price was followed by other campaigns. With a new marketing vehicle – a footballer rather than a couple in love – Christian Dior fragrances refreshed the image of their Eau Sauvage perfume, on the market for 20 years. The CanalSatellite channel package used the presence of Zinedine in a more natural way, with a football angle similar to that of Adidas, whose famous giant poster had loomed over Marseille's Corniche. Volvic mineral water would also later benefit from the moral purity of the champion, whose fans felt it corresponded perfectly with his image. Not fake in any way.

A simple and pure professional. The brand image began to take hold. He was seen as an alien, an incongruity on the celebrity planet. Despite entrusting the decoration of two rooms in their Rodez home to Claude Dalle, a decorator known for his flourishes, the Zidanes preferred neutral tones and a sober, pared-down style.

The tabloid press could get nothing on Zizou. The only rough patch came with creatine, which was hardly the stuff of which celebrity gossip is made. Creatine is a substance that acts on muscle energy. Consumption can be dangerous and its use is controversial. Creatine and the abuse of iron – thought to mask illicit substances and also denounced by medical authorities – can be harmful to the body. Firstly, as an allusion in an account of his own misadventures, then by mentioning the name to Italian investigators who came to question him, a former French professional cyclist claimed to have seen Zinedine in the office of an Italian doctor who became famous for the wrong reasons, issuing prescriptions that were as harmful as they were illegal. Falling under less suspicion than some of his teammates, including the captain of the France team Didier Deschamps, Juventus' number 21 had to answer to the accusations nevertheless, calmly at first then with anger. He did not deny having taken creatine. But he did deny 'doping', something more widespread in the world of football than punishments recognise.

In October 2003, on the Canal+ TV channel, the singer Johnny Hallyday talked about the benefits of his visits to a Swiss clinic, where samples of oxygenated blood were collected then reinjected. He claimed the clinic had been recommended by Zinedine Zidane. Although blood transfusions are certainly a legal but controversial process, this information was poorly understood. It was picked up in June 2006 by *Le Monde*, of whom Zidane was not fond after they had run an interview with him four years earlier promoted on the front page by the headline: 'I stopped using creatine at Real'. Claiming that it unfairly characterised the interview given, this hook, which he complained of roundly and in person to the newspaper's editor, would contribute to his media withdrawal and the minimal communication he established over the years to come.

In April 2005, in the *L'Équipe Magazine* weekly supplement of the sports newspaper, Zinedine would explain that he had 'trusted the medical team' at Juventus. 'I always saw what I was taking [...]. After that, if people with bad intentions try sleights of hand or attempt to manipulate others, then it becomes a criminal act. But my relationship with the Juve doctor was always built on trust. That could not happen.'

In Italy, one coach revealed the extent of the phenomenon with a courage that was sadly isolated. Another 'ZZ' hell-bent on justice. Zdenek Zeman attacked athletes who cheated, with or without the encouragement of their club directors and doctors. The Czech manager of AS Roma became a pariah. Like other brave souls before him, in other sporting disciplines.

The courts continued their investigations, focusing in particular on the medical staff at Juve and several dozen Italian league players. The inquiry would be lengthy.

For Zizou, who no longer talked about leaving Turin, the challenge of the year 2000 was twofold: on a personal level, preserving his serenity and not allowing himself to be caught up in the demands coming from all sides; on a sporting level, removing the last remaining doubts about his value, his ability to win and make his team win. His predictions were optimistic but the 1999–2000 season unfolding in Italy would not prove him right.

After a summer spent recuperating followed by a return to the squad for an Intertoto Cup match against Rennes, played in Cesena, he began the autumn fully fit after four months without competition. Winter passed and the team now managed by Carlo Ancelotti were top of Serie A. For the first time, Zidane had scored four goals in four games.

But the spring was disappointing. For the second consecutive season, Juve failed to win a title: neither cup nor league, losing out to Lazio on the final day of the season. It would, however, be remembered as a good season individually, with some magnificent moves, such as Zizou's left-footed goal against Reggina in Calabria after a string of astonishing pieces of skill.

There was still the summer. Euro 2000, bringing together 16 national teams, was the ideal opportunity for Zidane to demonstrate that he was not just a man with some attractive skills who had scored two timely goals. At the start of the competition, unlike the 1998 World Cup, France were popular with the public and the media. The successor and former deputy of Aimé Jacquet, who had since become the French federation's technical director, was another down-to-earth man. Although more contained and enigmatic than Jacquet, Roger Lemerre turned out to be no less charismatic. His role in the World Cup adventure was primarily focused on physical preparation. He realised that, unlike Euro 96, Zizou was coming into the 2000 edition in good shape.

Lemerre was an attentive and intelligent man. He echoed Jacquet's words: the squad comes first. But he knew his squad included a player unlike any other, whom he knew well, having taken charge of him during his military service nine years earlier. The player was impatient to show off his expertise from start to finish at a major competition.

France were striving for the summit. Before reaching the heights of European football, they set out for the peaks of Savoie. In Tignes – on the Grande-Motte Glacier, in Bourg-Saint Maurice and in Sainte-Foy-en-Tarentaise – Roger Lemerre's Bleus picked up the customs of mountain life so dear to Aimé Jacquet and several of his predecessors. The squad would also occasionally prepare for competitions in the Pyrenees, at Font-Romeu.

Squad. That was the key word, not just a rousing or mobilising formula designed to preserve the collective energy that internal rivalries could blunt. This community of individuals was no longer limited to the starting 11. During matches, the number of substitutions permitted – three, in other words more than a quarter of the team – the variety of team formations and the value of players had rendered the 'Onze de France' formula obsolete. There may have been 11 players on the pitch, but it was rarely the same 11. The boundary between starting player and substitute was clear in some positions, especially in defence, but it was much less obvious than it had been previously. Everyone was likely to play. It was good for morale, which had to be as high as possible, as a repetition of the exploits of the World Cup was expected.

Were Lemerre's Bleus really as good as Jacquet's? After getting their fingers burned by the World Cup, the footballing press did not ask the question so bluntly. Les Bleus' success in 1998, which some had conceitedly doubted despite an unprecedented run of warm-up matches without defeat, had contributed to discrediting them.

Journalistic doubts or not, Roger Lemerre, whose certainties were less visible than those of his predecessor, was firmly convinced that all was well. But he realised that public support, as well as self-interested optimism from the media and partners keen to raise audience figures, could be a double-edged sword. More than anyone, his language was prudent.

Across the country, everyone was affected by the performances of the national side. The footage shot by one TV channel reflected the deeply rooted 'World Cup effect'. Cameras and microphones visited towns and the countryside, urban centres and outlying districts to gather enthusiastic and vibrant images from anonymous people who, without warning, would suddenly see someone creep up behind them ... none other than Zizou himself! The star of Les Bleus sprang out of nowhere to play an almost silent prank, smiling like a Buster Keaton impersonator. Open-mouthed and wide-eyed with disbelief, they screamed like teenagers; the surprise was touching. Zizou was standing right beside them. They were in shock!

This trailer was uplifting. It may have been encouraging, but it hinted at the difficult road ahead. The nation was expecting a result and plenty of style. As the hierarchy of events is dominated by the World Cup, only victory in the final and a more attractive, dominant performance would allow them to reach greater heights. The objective was ambitious.

For Zizou, the pre-competition debate in France, which fuelled the economy and conversations, was nothing but gentle folklore compared with the lyrical flourishes of Italian-style melodrama. The undisputed playmaker at Juve, recognised by *calcio* experts as one of the greatest players ever seen in their stadiums, was getting close to reaching his target: asserting his all-round skill for the France team.

He had always had a gift for moving around in space. He had retained and refined his ball control since his days in Marseille and Septèmes. He had also remembered the precepts learned in Cannes. He had improved his physicality since Bordeaux and had acquired the Italian reflex of a mindset focused on victory.

Nothing could stop him. Not even a clash during a game against AC Milan on 19 March 2000 that forced him to leave the pitch on a stretcher. Four years after his car accident, there were concerns about an injury as disabling as the one that had tarnished his performance at Euro 96. But the fear was quickly dispelled. It was instead a Zizou in full strength who arrived in Belgium, joint co-hosts of Euro 2000 with the Netherlands, whose team was one of the two favourites for the event. If the Dutch made it to the final, they would play in front of their home fans in Rotterdam.

Les Bleus were based at the Château de Genval, in the Brussels suburbs. For the competition, Zinedine had hired a friend who would help his taste buds feel right at home: Roberto! The chef from Da Angelino received plenty of compliments from those who were yet to be introduced to his dishes. Members of the French delegation were also especially flattered when he claimed he would be supporting France even if they were drawn against Italy.

Zizou was at ease. Calm, on the shores of the Lac de Genval, the perfect spot for the moments of spirituality he needed in order to escape; at ease within the squad where he was loved and respected. The team were strong, well prepared and had the right people around them. Beyond appearances, the World Cup had topped off an environment of perfectionism. Perfection, a pipe dream that motivates progression, can sometimes be achieved. When it comes to medical treatment, for example. Whenever a joint or muscle has suffered a trauma, the most important thing is to take away the pain. Thanks to a state-of-the-art procedure, one that was almost exclusive to the French medical team, this had been possible since the World Cup. The injection of a gas – at a temperature never previously used in equipment intended for use in sports, a temperature so low that it not only removed discomfort but real pain – allowed the injured player to put their best foot forward.

The French were sharp. Prepared to win. Prepared to overcome challenges.

Their difficult first game against Denmark in Bruges proved helpful. Les Bleus reacted well and imposed themselves firmly. Also in Bruges, they beat the Czech Republic, a symbolic revenge for their elimination in 1996. Because their qualification for the quarter-finals was guaranteed, they could afford a defeat against the Netherlands. Zizou was on the bench. This time, the playmaker was Johan Micoud, who had trained at AS Cannes. One January afternoon, in a Coupe Gambardella game ten years earlier, they had knocked out Saint-Rémy-de-Provence together. Zidane and Micoud ... They were all grown up now.

Zizou had become great, dominating against the Spanish in the quarter-final in Brussels. He ran, he passed, he went one way and his opponent the other. He performed conjuring tricks that only TV viewers could understand through slow-motion replays, so quick and complex were his movements. After three group games, the tension of the knockout rounds hit. Every shot was potentially decisive. A set piece, for example. France had one on the edge of the penalty area, left to His Majesty Zidane, king of free kicks. He shot. He scored! The strike was unstoppable, precise and powerful, identical to those he had unleashed at the beginning of the year with Juve against Perugia, or for the national team against Poland. Well before that he had shown he had mastered the exercise, especially at Bordeaux, with the unforgettable memory of a goal in the UEFA Cup that had mystified the Karlsruhe goalkeeper Oliver Kahn in 1993.

Despite this, the opposition were vigorous and threatening, applying themselves fully. And unlucky, when Raúl, star of the national team and idol of Real Madrid, missed a penalty just before the final whistle that would have seen the Spanish equalise. The scoreline remained unchanged: 2–1. France had qualified. There was no longer any talk of chance. Just as they had been in 1996 and 1998, France were in the semi-final. They were a 'cup team', whose mental strength gave their technical and physical foundation the added edge when it came to getting past opponents.

Portugal believed – just as Croatia had in another semi-final two years earlier in Paris – they held the key to victory by scoring first, cleverly occupying the Bruges pitch. The Portuguese, like the Croats, were skilful technically. As was Zidane. He was in the midfield, at the centre of the sporting world watching on. He was the elegant strategist, bringing forth daring moves. He got around opponents and turned compromised situations on their heads. He was a tower of strength at the peak of his ability, dishing out a single-handed lesson in football.

Despite this, the Portuguese were vigorous and threatening, applying themselves fully. And unlucky, when, just before the end of a period of extra time of an intensity worthy of France–Paraguay, they conceded a strongly disputed penalty for a handball. The Portuguese were furious, arguing that the penalty would never have been given if the opposition had been anyone but France. There was some honour in this recognition of a status that France had taken a century to obtain: that of a dominant team in world football, like a Brazil, a Germany, an Argentina or an Italy.

Of course, the referee did not go back on his decision.

Penalty. If the ball went in, the French were in the final. If it did not cross the line, a likely and dramatic penalty shootout would bring plenty of other decisive moments just a few minutes later. Zidane was called forward to convert the kick. He had not missed against the Czechs in 1996. Nor against the Italians in 1998. He was a man sure of his strength, a champion sure of his talent. But even the greatest champions can sometimes be off target. A successful strike would be greeted with the satisfaction it deserved. A failure could jeopardise qualification and bring the penalty's taker in for criticism, or even hasty scorn about his worth, despite the fact that he had just demonstrated the almost insurmountable standard his current performances were reaching.

Zizou began his run-up. The shot was accurate. Clean. Victorious! Goal. Golden goal!

The same score as the quarter-final: 2–1. Zinedine Zidane had taken France through. In the final in Rotterdam they would not find the Netherlands, but some familiar faces who had knocked out the bumbling Dutch players on their home turf – after missing two penalties, the Netherlands went down in a shootout against a team reduced to ten men after the first half following a sending-off. But this was not just any team. It was Italy.

Everyone dreaded the Italians. They were great technicians and peerless competitors. They were the very definition of a 'cup team'. Unfortunately, Italian football was more inclined to bad habits than other teams. Some managers, mostly foreigners, such as the Swede Niels Liedholm with AS Roma in the 1980s, had tried to take the system apart. But the classic arguments – namely, pressure and financial stakes – made it easy to impede any evolution towards more spontaneity.

Often well placed at international level, Italian clubs had been largely dominated by the English until the latter were suspended from all competition following the events at Heysel. From that point on, European domination shifted to the south. But the national team had not won anything since the 1982 World Cup, a distressing memory for all those who love fair play and morality in sport. The Italians had begun with three draws and come within a hair's breadth of elimination after a valid goal scored by Cameroon's Roger Milla was disallowed. But their tournament ended with an unjust apotheosis. One symbolic image of their feat would remain: Gentile, with a raised fist, triumphing over Germany after giving in to the antithesis of the game from start to finish against Argentina then Telê Santana's Brazil.

In this final, in Rotterdam, the Italians presented a rather more pleasant face. Zidane stood firm like a rock. He offered a lesson in football … less obvious than in the previous games but with a rich vocabulary. The footballers from the Italian peninsula listened and responded. They marked their territory. It became clear they might pull off a surprise, just as they had done in 1982. They missed opportunities but scored a fine goal. A wonderful goal. The only one of the game it would seem… until the very last seconds. Just as it had against Spain and Portugal, the end of the match turned in France's favour. A few moments before the final whistle, Sylvain Wiltord scored with his left foot from a very tight angle. France were saved by pinpoint accuracy!

The Italians, who for once had not been able to capitalise on other opportunities, found it equally impossible to play for time to gain precious seconds, seeing the title vanish from their grasp. Their morale was shattered. There was no way back for them when, a few minutes later, David Trezeguet brought an end to extra time by pulling off a stunning volley, also with his left foot, on the end of some remarkable work by Robert Pires down the left wing. A golden goal!

France, a team of realists, had won the Euros! Multicoloured confetti rained down on the French players as they received their second consecutive trophy. Gathered in small groups on a pitch they did not want to leave, the players enjoyed a victory with an Italian flavour ... not just because of Roberto's dishes. For Lemerre's squad, the Euros had been a confirmation: they were indeed a cup team and they knew how to force destiny's hand. The manager collected himself inwardly as no one dared to trouble him. He was thinking about his father, who had died during the competition. A dignified emotion, another memory, a sad one, of the journey Les Bleus had been on.

For Roger Lemerre, the tournament had been a masterly personal success. His squad had won with panache. Two years after the World Cup, success at the Euros was another part of the legacy owed to Fernand Sastre, the late president of the French Football Federation to whom Jacquet had dedicated their win in 1998. For Lemerre, it was also a stepping stone to the next World Cup. Although not an experienced manager, he had succeeded in retaining the cohesion of a group rich in personalities. Some cryptic remarks nevertheless suggested that he would not continue in his role, something that he had 'never asked for'. In the microcosm of football, teeming with unspoken and unacknowledged ambitions, speculation often gives in to rumours. But Lemerre would stay. The breathless 2–1 win over Italy was worth the same as 3–0 over Brazil. These two victories marked the beginning of an era, one of confidence, but also the end of another, that of the building of a tight-knit team, several pillars of which would soon be gone.

For Yazid, this tournament was not just a response to doubts about his supposed lack of impact on the game. Above all, it was a tournament that highlighted his individual supremacy, thanks to his brilliance put at the service of the team. A delight to watch and influential on the pitch, he had become the prototype of a team sport champion. It seemed as if he had never been flying so high. He knew it. His behaviour stayed closer to the straight and narrow than ever.

He remained defiant in the face of praise that put him in a different category. He simply aspired to be human, to be someone with a genuine humanity. Red carpets were not for him.

The day after the celebrations in the Netherlands, the players were invited to greet the assembled crowd in Paris, as well as all their other fans through the medium of television. The Zidane family then had a holiday in the Balearics planned. But Véronique left on her own on Monday morning. Zizou would join them that evening, once Yazid has visited Marseille. And Septèmes-les-Vallons.

Noureddine Zidane had received a call from Fernand Boix, the director of SOS. Three letters that unfortunately symbolised the urgency of the request: Robert Centenero, the man who had brought Yazid to SO Septèmes, was ill. Seriously ill. He had told his wife that he would like to see Yazid again, for one last time, perhaps. Fernande Boix wanted to make him happy. Noureddine understood and reacted quickly: 'I'll call you back in half an hour.' Yazid had no hesitation. He responded favourably to the request that had come through his brother. Noureddine and Fernand set up a meeting.

At the agreed time, a Mercedes with tinted windows pulled up in Septèmes. Fernand opened the door and got into the back of the vehicle, next to a child seat. Noureddine was driving; Yazid was in the front. The star footballer and the volunteer director drove along a route of loyalty and friendship.

Robert Centenero had not been told about the visit. The door of his apartment opened with astonishment. Amazement. The following scenes, gestures and words are strictly private. Those of simple men finally reunited, away from prying eyes, long after their first meeting.

They would not see each other again. Yazid's time was precious. His body needed rest, but his heart beat only to the rhythm of his feelings. What was a little more time given when a life is almost over? His presence was hoped for. And he came.

Five o'clock. Time to go on holiday. His flight left from Marseille's Marignane airport. Destination: Ibiza. Spain, where he had always said he would have liked to play. Monsieur Boix, who was originally from the Iberian peninsula, brought up the subject spontaneously. He would have liked to have seen his former protégé play at Valencia, in the region of his ancestors.

'You'd love it if you went to Spain. You'd see that the people are genuine, not fake.'

Spain. Yes, he was thinking about it, but he had extended his contract in Italy. He had not expected to see out its original term, the end of the 2002–03 season, yet here he was tied to Juve until 2005. Despite this extension, the probability of an early departure was high. He would have liked to have won a title during the 2000–01 season while he was still with the Bianconeri. If possible, a European title – after the European Championship had eventually turned the season that had just come to an end into a great one, including in terms of results. It was also the season in which he had matched his highest number of international caps: 14, as in 1995–96, another great season, his last at Bordeaux.

Les Bleus were Zizou's greatest pleasure. The ideal canvas on which to express his genius. Especially whenever he was back in Marseille.

On 16 August 2000, during a friendly against the 'Rest of the World', Laurent Blanc, known as 'The President', was about to retire from the team. But the context was far from ideal: in the corridors of the Stade Vélodrome, he was one of those who railed most openly at the attitude shown by the fans. He was scandalised by the whistles that rang out every time Nicolas Anelka and Christophe Dugarry touched the ball. The former was paying for his allegiance to Paris Saint-Germain, Olympique de Marseille's great rivals, while the latter, who had left the club a few months earlier, had never been unanimously popular.

Duga's exasperation reached its peak. As did Zizou's. The former Septèmes player may have been a local boy but his pleas did not succeed in calming the vehemence of the crowd. He did have experience of this kind of situation, although slightly further east than Provence.

Zinedine lost his temper. He was furious that this pleasant friendly between France and an international team should have been turned into an irrational opportunity for score settling. All the more so because it was in aid of a humanitarian cause. As the minutes passed, the mood became significantly heavier than it had been two weeks earlier in the same stadium, when he took part in the testimonial for the ebullient Pascal Olmeta. On 16 August, at a time of the year when summer storms are common, the whirlwind just kept swirling.

Zidane was angry and, to express it, kicked the ball out into touch. The message had not been heard by everyone but was clearly understood by some. Zidane was still Yazid. A brave and honest man; someone who was kind and courageous.

The superstar did not stay on his pedestal. He would go out on a limb for others. He was not someone who refused to get his hands dirty, nor someone who would let others get one over on him. As Guy Lacombe had said: 'If one day you stop getting hit, you'll know you aren't as good any more!' Zizou played well. He took hits. Plenty of them. But he sometimes saw red, like the card he received in a game against La Coruña in the Champions League. He also saw red against Hamburg on 24 October 2000. Once again, he sought revenge for an attack with a head-butt. The referee did not hesitate. Zizou, Yazid once more, understood. While the man in black's arm was still outstretched, brandishing the card in his hand, he clenched his jaw and turned towards the dressing room.

The suspension would be harsh: five games. Zizou admitted he had been at fault, apologised to the fans and said he was keen to regain the league title. The Champions League would have to wait. He would have to watch on impatiently as his teammates qualified for the second round, for the quarter-final and for the semi-final before he could rejoin them. But it was not to be. They failed to get past the first round. That year, the third in a row, he would not manage to add a trophy to his cabinet. Juventus were eliminated. Yet again, Zizou would have to postpone his hopes for victory in the Champions League until the following season.

On 11 December, despite the early elimination and his lapses in behaviour, FIFA, the highest authority in football, chose him as their footballer of the year. This award honoured a footballer who had not only shown what he could do over the previous 12 months, but was also the player of the year 2000: a modern era in which technique began to play a greater role than ever before.

For children and footballers of the dawning 21st century, Zidane was a formidable role model. Proof that the game had never lost its virtues of aesthetics and elegance. Proof that this discipline, like all sports requiring an ever-increasing physical conditioning, was not simply the domain of those with pace.

Player of the year 2000. It was a fine reward. A fine recognition for Yazid and a hope for those keen to emulate him. It meant that in the year 2000 football could still be a game.

10

THE GALAXY OF SUPERSTARS

The player of the year 2000 no longer had anything to prove. Just a few awards still to be won or empty spaces to be filled in his trophy cabinet. A few lines to be added to his list of achievements, on the basis of which those with a fondness for figures would determine the place granted to him by posterity.

Zinedine, a quiet father, aspired above all to become the anonymous face he may never be again. He knew how to say no, but still agreed to link his name to that of a car manufacturer. On the first day of the first year of the first century of the new millennium, at peak viewing time, just before the eight o'clock news, his face appeared on the screen. He did not utter a word but made the advertiser's slogan his own: 'The important thing is not what we say but what we do.' The sobriety of this message was as noticeable as the brand: Ford. A competitor of Fiat, a company with close links to Juventus!

The club's management had not opposed the partnership, however. They did not cross Zizou, whose reputation was continuing to grow. In Geneva, he received an important passport with a red cover. Like the Brazilian Ronaldo, he became a Goodwill Ambassador for the United Nations in an effort to combat worldwide poverty.

Juve could not be ungrateful to Zizou. And nor could he to them. He had won the Intercontinental Cup, the European Super Cup and two league titles in his first two seasons at the Turin club. But nothing in 1999 or 2000. As for the 2000–01 season, hopes of a Champions League victory had already vanished. Added to this the prospect of ongoing clashes with little entertainment value to speak of and systems of play that were too hermetically sealed to fan the flames of passion.

A break for his advertising commitments provided some welcome peace and was conducive to reflection. Zizou was pensive. Unlike the image portrayed in the commercial, he was not feeling serene. He wanted to leave. He did not say so out loud but he was sure the prospect would make him happy.

Well-placed but not dominating in the league, the Turin team had received a moderate welcome from their fans after the Champions League elimination. The target of abuse, Zizou calmed the rumours by declaring that he wanted to give his all to win the league. These comments were somewhat hastily interpreted as a clear desire to stay in Turin. But that was not what he said. He said something else in Monaco, secretly.

Pelé or Maradona? At the annual UEFA gala in the principality, on the eve of the European Super Cup between Real Madrid and Galatasaray, discussions were rife as to who would be voted the player of the century. Zidane voted for his idol, Enzo Francescoli.

The award-winners of the season were also revealed. Player of the season: Redondo, a Real player who had gone to AC Milan. Striker of the season: Raúl, at Real Madrid. Goal of the Euros: David Trezeguet. Player of the Euros: Zinedine Zidane, for whom the 1999–2000 season had undoubtedly been one of the best of his career.

UEFA loves congratulating itself and it had its sights set high that year. Football's elite were in attendance, including all of Real Madrid's stars, who had won the Champions League, beating Valencia in the final.

Zidane was well acquainted with these somewhat awkward ceremonies, for which players, club directors, journalists and beautiful women all don their finery. He was never really comfortable at them. He knew how to smile and pat some of his acquaintances on the back, but often felt on edge in the presence of unknown faces, or sometimes even friends. He was his usual discreet self, whereas some of his more exuberant teammates liked to draw attention to themselves with extravagant outfits or flashy comments.

Despite this, he was one of the stars of the evening. 'It is always nice to win these sorts of trophies. It means I've done my job well and my work's been recognised by others,' he admitted humbly during a press conference before the ceremony. In a good mood, he answered questions, looked back on his past and talked about his aspirations: 'I'm still missing the Champions League.'

It was around this time that Zidane became aware that there might be interest in him from Real Madrid. One of the dominant forces in La Liga, the club had won the Champions League in 1998 and 2000, so Zidane knew that they could offer him a new challenge. Once the wheels were set in motion, it would become the most expensive transfer in the history of football.

Zidane, who had joined Juventus in 1996, examined the question from all sides. Without realising it, he had grown tired of the club at which he had won everything, except the Champions League. He had lost two finals, in 1997 and 1998. He had also lost the last Serie A title in 2000 on the final day of the season. He did not know it yet, but he would also lose the 2001 league title.

He had grown tired of *calcio* and its rough defenders. He thought about his future. He wanted to experience something else. France? That was no longer really an option because of the media phenomenon his return would provoke. Not to mention the lack of quality in the French league for a player of his level ...

Another Italian club? That really would be a betrayal of Juve and he would encounter the same problems. That left England and Spain.

Spain was the ideal destination for him, both as an athlete and a person. The Spanish league was more attacking, with patterns of play that were less rigid than in Italy. The game was much more developed than in the Premier League. When it came to his family, it would allow Véronique the opportunity to reconnect with her roots.

But nothing is easy. His contract did not allow for a transfer and Juventus, who had put their trust in him by recruiting him from Bordeaux – quite a gamble at the time – would not facilitate his departure. Juve had turned into a gilded cage. A big club, a great team, a beautiful house, a good salary ...

But Florentino Perez was not dreaming. He was thinking it over, constructing a plan to snatch Zidane from Juventus. But firstly, he had to keep it secret. There was no question of the Italians finding out, or his Spanish and English competitors.

Perez was well aware that anything is possible in football. As president of the largest public-works company in Spain, ACS, he was convinced that all he needed to do was apply methods similar to those of the market economy to the often conservative world of football. You also had to know how to grasp opportunities, how not to hesitate when it came to investing in potential benefits and, most importantly, how not to consider any situation as set in stone. In the construction industry, the best deals go to the highest bidder. Why should football be any different? Perez was convinced, and Luis Figo was the living proof.

To get himself elected president of Real Madrid the year before, he had promised during his electoral campaign that he would 'pinch' the Portuguese star from Barcelona, Madrid's hated rivals.

'It doesn't work like that in football. Perez doesn't know anything about the sport,' sneered his adversary, Lorenzo Sanz, the president of Real at the time and a connoisseur of the ins and outs of the Madrid club. What Sanz thought was a boast turned out to be a masterstroke. Perez was careful neither to reveal his methods nor the secret contract agreed with Figo's agent, whom he had paid in exchange for a firm commitment that his player would sign for Real. For an almost unbelievable salary: €6 million a year ... if Perez was elected president, of course. The agent believed he had banked a risk-free cheque, given that Perez was languishing a long way behind Sanz in the presidential race if the polls were to be believed. But he was wrong.

Since his election and the Figo 'coup', Perez was surfing a wave of positivity among the club's *socios,* or members. But he had promised them 'a star a year'.

'As far as I was concerned, Zidane was the best player in the world. He had to play for Real. So I did everything I could to get him to come here.'

A consummate tactician, Perez knew it would not be easy. Zidane was a well-known footballer. He had a considerable salary, played at a big club and had adapted well to Italy. Most importantly, he was under contract. But the insatiable entrepreneur would pay the price required.

While ensuring the economic viability of his plan, in September 2000, he set a lengthy undermining process in motion, about which even Zidane knew nothing. He enquired as to the player's contracts, made financial projections based on the expected revenue of his arrival and studied the legal details of his transfer ...

In May 2001, a number of leaks, presumably organised by the president himself, rocked the world of football. 'Zidane is close to signing for Real.' Juventus issued a denial. As did Real, despite continuing to fuel the rumour. The Italian fans, and the club's directors in particular, were more than a little annoyed, not to mention concerned when Real made their initial approach, officially, simply to enquire about the price of a transfer. Zizou was 'not for sale', came the answer from Turin. But doubt had already been placed in their minds.

A dialogue between two parties who were not listening to each other continued for several weeks. As did the manoeuvring. Florentino Perez made a very 'honourable' offer. But Juventus refused again. On a daily basis, the press reported rumours and what it believed to be the direction the negotiations were taking. Real's chances of snatching Zidane from the club at which he had made his global reputation, well before the 1998 World Cup, were not rated highly.

'Why Zidane won't go to Real', was the headline in *L'Équipe*, usually very well informed about transfers and with a well-established network in Turin. But the newspaper had got it wrong. Very wrong. They were simply relaying the atmosphere at the Italian club, which did not give any credence to Real's ambitions. Juventus were determined to keep Zidane, convinced even that it would be impossible to nab him.

But Lorenzo Sanz, *L'Équipe* and Juventus had all underestimated the 'newcomer' Perez, who was already one step ahead. At the same time as his representatives were negotiating with the directors at Juventus, he was asking the player to take an official position. 'I want to play in Spain,' Zizou announced immediately. His agent, Alain Migliaccio, who was in daily contact with the Juventus directors, increased the pressure.

The situation was no longer tenable. There was now a gulf between Zidane and the Italian club, which seemed to be in a difficult position. The *tifosi* were restless: 'What if Zidane leaves?'

It was the start of a power struggle. The Juventus directors Luciano Moggi and Roberto Bettega stood firm but they had begun to understand that the French player was by then lost to them. It was now a question of making the Madrid club pay a heavy price. 'Didn't they pay €62 million for Luis Figo? Zidane is better and therefore more expensive,' reasoned the Italians, thinking to the future. 'If we sell Zidane, we'll have to give the fans a decent team,' was a comment heard behind the scenes.

The Czech player Pavel Nedved was already in their sights. They also enquired about strikers and defenders. With the windfall they were about to come in for, they would have something to take to the transfer market.

He was going to leave. That was certain. He was going to leave after a third season without a title, but with some individual reward: he had been voted the best player in Italy by his peers. After Lazio had done the same the previous year, it was the turn of the Italian capital's other team, AS Roma, to get one over on Juventus on the last day of the season.

Zizou could leave, on holiday at first, discreetly allowing the clubs to negotiate. On 23 June, his 29th birthday, he broke his silence and unambiguously answered the questions asked by *La Repubblica*: 'If it were up to me, I would already be at Real Madrid.'

The major players then began to engage in the usual negotiations dance: revelations, information, counter-information and denials, which no longer surprised anyone. But even the most naive of football fans has learned that lies are often told face to face without so much as an eyelid being batted.

Although denied at first, except by the person concerned, the transfer was eventually confirmed.

On 7 July 2001, the negotiations came to an end. Although not yet official, the transfer was no longer a secret. The following day, the media picked up on the news: Zinedine Zidane was about to sign a four-year contract with Real Madrid, a contract that would eventually be extended.

Kept secret by the two clubs, the fee would vary between €73 and €76 million, depending on the methods of calculation. It was eventually rounded up to €75 million for posterity. It was the most expensive transfer in the history of football. Forget Maradona or the Brazilians, Ronaldo and Denilson. Forget Figo.

The teenager the scouts had not wanted, the apprentice who had almost begun his professional career in Division 2, had been signed for a fee the equivalent of 500 million French francs!

In just two years, Florentino Perez had walked away with the two most expensive players in the world. But although he presented himself as a financial miracle worker, many in Spain doubted the real profitability of his operations and the transparency of his accounts.

According to certain audits, the club practised what is known as 'cheque kiting', using part of its structural revenues – the sale of its training ground – for short-term ends, in other words, for transfer fees. Real also had a significant and long-standing track record ...

Zidane refused to be drawn into economic considerations. 'We are always surprised by the figures. I don't look at them any more. The sums of money are enormous. I'm not worth it. No player in the world is worth it, but that's the way things are. It represents a lot, an awful lot of money. I'm aware of that,' he confessed. He then went on to analyse the strategy of his former club: 'At 29, it was Juve's last opportunity to get a good price for my transfer. After that, it would have been hard to sell me for a fee like that. And they can use the money to rebuild.'

It was a supreme luxury: the creative midfielder, whose decisive impact on the game had been called into question by those who demanded proof of his genius, arrived in Spain on a pedestal when he had won nothing at club level for three years. He left a Juventus that seemed powerless to regain the Serie A title and had been knocked out of the UEFA Cup in the last 16 and in the first round of the Champions League in the previous two seasons.

Despite the praise he heaped on his now former club, the Italians were somewhat peeved. 'Zidane was more entertaining than useful,' said Gionni Agnelli. The honorary president of Fiat and boss of Juve, a shrewd businessmen, could be delighted with the profitable transfer. But he could not stop himself from adding another phrase, which may well have unsettled the minds of the Madrid fans: 'After five years he wanted a change. His wife was keen to go to Barcelona at first before choosing Madrid.'

Always a gentleman, the player pretended not to hear these jibes. Two years later, he even went to Turin to attend the funeral of Agnelli, the 'Avvocato'.

In the evening of Sunday 8 July 2001, after a family holiday in the Polynesian atolls and a few days on the west coast of the United States, from where he had been able to follow the negotiations,

Zinedine arrived in Madrid … at a military airbase in Torrejon, in the suburbs, aboard a private jet hired secretly by Real. It was a guarantee of peace and quiet.

Jorge Valdano, who had won the World Cup with Argentina in 1986 and was Real's general manager, welcomed him and took him, still incognito, to a large hotel in the Spanish capital, near the Santiago-Bernabeu stadium. An establishment of which the new recruit would not only have happy memories.

In the morning of Monday 9 July, 'Zizoumania' began. Radio stations, television channels and newspapers could talk of nothing but Zidane. Zizou – pronounced 'Sissou' by the Spanish – was on everyone's lips. If the transfer had attracted a lot of attention in Italy and France, it was nothing compared to the joy of the Madrid supporters.

Real launched a major communications campaign around their new star. Zidane was sucked into a media whirlwind. He was due to be officially presented at a ceremony funded by a sponsor, broadcast live on Spanish TV and radio at around 1pm. Two hundred journalists were in attendance. Hundreds of fans were waiting outside to catch a glimpse.

Driven from the hotel to a gym, Zizou, wearing a black suit and a white shirt, was uncomfortable. He was guided between banks of people he did not know. He found himself on stage for the ceremony. Alfredo Di Stefano – a legend at the club and of the history of football – and the president Florentino Perez were waiting for him there. 'Some players are born to play for Real Madrid. The best club must have the best players,' said Perez, as dozens of cameras recorded Zidane's every move.

'It is an honour to come to Madrid. I've been looking forward to this moment,' said the Frenchman, visibly embarrassed. Five minutes later, the ceremony was over. Zidane was back in a car, on his way back to his hotel.

'Real is a universal club and Zidane corresponds to that message of universality,' explained Perez. But even he had underestimated the extent of the phenomenon.

From the first few days following the arrival of the latest wearer of the famous white strip, shirts with his name and number were selling in their hundreds! Printed in secret as the transfer had still to be concluded, three hundred shirts were sold on the day of the signing.

As had been the case in Turin, the number 10 was unavailable. But the number 5 – usually given to a defender and previously worn by Manuel Sanchis, a big name at the club, now in retirement – was to be his. Five: the number Zinedine had worn at Saint-Raphaël 14½ years earlier, with Septèmes, during the last match he played before leaving for Cannes. Fourteen and a half years, already! Half his life. A life with a regal destiny and a staggering salary of around €6 million a year, equivalent to that of the club's other two stars, Raúl and Figo.

The new hero could not go out without attracting a crowd. Shopping was out of the question, unless the store was asked to close for his visit. He found himself a prisoner in his hotel, forced to stay in his room watching television or a DVD.

The first few days were difficult. Zizou could not yet speak Spanish and the club, which had organised his transfer so smoothly, had not thought at all about his arrival, which seemed much more complex than that of Figo. The player was almost left to drift for several days, before being taken in hand and shown around the city to visit properties for sale; he did not want to rent.

Then came another Zizoumania ceremony: he was to be presented at the Santiago-Bernabeu, where he would be the new star, but in which he had yet to set foot. He discovered this mythical ground that bears the name of a legendary former president of the club; with 75,000 seats, it is in the heart of the city, in the business district. He also discovered the huge media interest he aroused. Again, dozens of journalists and hundreds of fans were in attendance. '*Encantado, Madrid!*' he said to the fans, before continuing in French at a press conference. He smiled, but inside he was waiting impatiently for the frenzy to die down.

The hotel where he was staying, the luxurious Eurobuilding next to the Santiago-Bernabeu, had been designed primarily for business travellers. Its soulless rooms did not make it easy for the Zidane family to join him. The player was holed up there, almost distressed by the magnitude of the phenomenon he was causing.

His compatriot and teammate Claude Makelele, who had stayed in the same hotel and often made appointments in its lounges, immediately realised the problem and alerted the club's directors. A few days later, Zidane left for the Santo Mauro, a luxury hotel with a much more welcoming ambience.

The press was on high alert. Where was Zidane? What was he doing? What was he eating? What was he thinking? It was not a craze, it was a tsunami. But Real Madrid had welcomed some great players, including another Frenchman, Raymond Kopa, who had won three European Champion Clubs' Cups. Real was the club of the legendary Di Stefano, and more recently the versatile Bernd Schuster and Fernando Redondo. But Zizou's aura seemed to blow them all away. His style, his physical and moral elegance, his impressive discretion that could suddenly be broken by a charming smile all contributed to a phenomenon that would not stop at the gates of the Ciudad Deportiva, Real's training centre, where the sale of the pitches to the city council had allowed Real to erase its colossal €300 million debt.

Just as they had been doing for a decade, the Madrid players prepared for the upcoming season in Nyon, near Lake Geneva. Autograph hunters, local Swiss and holidaymakers alike, were no less enthusiastic than the people of Madrid. They wanted to see Zizou, talk to him and touch him. He agreed to the many requests with good grace, as always.

Overall, the atmosphere at pre-season training was peaceful. Finally, after a long period of telephone silence enforced by his tumultuous arrival in Madrid, Yazid once again had time to call the man who had discovered him. They spoke with the same friendship as ever. They talked about the many demands on his time, such as a trip with the Prime Minister to Moscow, three years to the day after the World Cup final, to promote Paris's candidacy for the Olympic Games. Jean Varraud was kindly concerned: 'Stop saying yes to everyone! Look where doing that has got me.' They were talking about football, but not only about football.

Zizou's settling-in, which had already been disrupted by the excitement his arrival had created, was not made any easier by a challenging schedule: after training in Switzerland came a whirlwind trip to Egypt that seemed to fly in the face of common sense. Egypt was a country where the club earned plenty of money through its players, including Zidane, who was particularly popular in Arab countries. He would then return to Spain to play in some friendlies, including one against Montpellier in Alicante.

Wherever he went, the crowd only had eyes for Zizou. On the pitch, however, he had yet to find harmony with his teammates because of the constant change in training location, incessant travelling and perhaps especially because of the pressure of the media coverage surrounding him.

Real Madrid were also overtaken by the event and the enthusiasm it generated. They thought they were used to stars, but the addition of Zidane had resulted in an almost unexpected madness. The club was forced to hastily employ bodyguards for team travel. The club shop was out of stock of postcards of Zidane. Shirts were selling hand over fist. Fans laid siege to training sessions and lay in wait for their idol's every move.

One example of Zizoumania: shortly after his arrival, Zidane and his friend Malek decided to visit a shopping centre. In Italy, they would have come across nothing more than a few autograph hunters. Here, the arrival of Zidane provoked a riot. The two men were forced to leave immediately.

It was against this backdrop that Zizou made his official competitive debut for Real in the first game of the league season on 26 August 2001. In Valencia, at the Mestalla stadium, where the atmosphere can often be lively.

The transfer had heightened passions. The Madrid fans now thought they had an invincible team that would stroll to victory everywhere. They believed they were about to recreate the team of the 1950s, with Di Stefano, Puskás, Kopa, Gento et al. Dozens of foreign journalists were now following Real. Talk began of a 'galactic' team made up of '*galacticos*', the supermen of the footballing world.

At other clubs, Madrid's policy made people cringe. Anti-Madridism was exacerbated. Real were now considered the enemy to be beaten at all costs, an opponent too rich and above all too pretentious that needed to be brought back down to earth. The atmosphere was electric. The day before the game in Valencia, the Real team bus – empty at the time – had been pelted with stones.

The Valencia supporters had also wound up their players. As well as their manager. With only 15 minutes gone, Zidane had already been the victim of four fouls. He was on the receiving end of some shock treatment and extremely tight marking. Targeted by the rough Argentine Roberto Ayala and the experienced Miroslav Đukić, he was also fouled by two defensive midfielders, the Uruguayan Gonzalo de Los Santos and particularly the Spaniard David Albelda, guilty of several nasty tackles. The result was an inevitable defeat, 3–1.

Zidane had failed to shine. Valencia's French defender Jocelyn Angloma, who had played with him at Euro 96 in particular, tried to comfort him and issued a warning: 'When it comes to football, there is no doubt about Zizou's quality. But all of the demands on him make it hard for him as a person. He's an uncomplicated and intelligent guy, but he's shy. Someone needs to pay attention to all the stress caused by this hullaballoo.' Having also played in Italy, Angloma went on to point out: 'In Spain, everything to do with Real is important. To a much greater extent than in Italy. So when the best player in the world arrives, it's crazy!'

The press did not wait: 'It's not enough to spend millions and walk around on tiptoes if you want to win. In Spain, we strike blows and fight to the death. There is no respect for names here,' said the newspaper *AS*.

Zizou became the subject of a national debate, especially in the famous radio and television *tertulias*, improvised discussions between well-known people not necessarily from the footballing world.

Variety singers of varying popularity, well- or lesser-known actresses, politicians, economists or simply the ex-partners of stars voiced their opinions. 'Zizou isn't doing this enough', 'isn't doing that' or 'he'll get there' …

The Bulgarian Hristo Stoichkov, the effervescent former Barcelona player of whom the whole of France would forever have bad memories – he was in the team that had prevented Les Bleus reaching the World Cup in 1994 – tried to add fuel to the fire: 'Zidane will end up like Anelka.' The French striker Nicolas Anelka had left Real through the back door after a year in which he had often been substituted, and, most importantly, had failed to integrate into the squad or maintain a cordial relationship with the club's directors.

But Zidane stood up and reminded everyone that he had come from the Italian league, 'where the game is much more defensive', where he had been subjected to 'plenty of tight marking'.

However, the pressure was mounting and, unfortunately for him, results did not help. After the defeat in Valencia, Real were whistled following a lacklustre draw at home against Malaga (1–1).

Zidane scored his first goal against Betis in the third game of the season in early September. But his team once again lost the game and found themselves off the pace in the league from mid-September, just a few months after winning the previous season's La Liga and reaching the semi-finals of the Champions League.

The worst was that Real were racking up good performances in the Champions League, in which Zinedine was not able to take part temporarily, due to a suspension following his sending-off for a head-butt while playing for Juve against Deportivo de la Coruña the previous season.

He was sometimes made a scapegoat for bad results as a newcomer who was struggling to fit into the system of play. The fact that his arrival had cost €75 million also went against him among those often quick to turn to demagogy. The press now pointed out every time he lost the ball rather than his pieces of skill; his failed passes rather than those that were on target. Some supporters even thought the Frenchman had come to Madrid to retire. The policy of Florentino Perez, guilty of paying too high a price for the star, was widely criticised: 'Too many stars in a team cannot work.'

A joke began doing the rounds: 'Do you know why Zidane plays in the number 5 for Madrid but in the number 10 for France? Because he plays half as well!'

The player still had the support of his club, however. His teammates and the manager Vicente Del Bosque defended him as much as they could. But the critical breakthrough would soon sweep it all away.

11

THE 'BEST PLAYER IN THE WORLD' GETS BETTER AND BETTER

The interviews, sponsor events, TV and radio programmes were over. In mid-September 2001, Zinedine began devoting himself solely to his sport. To the game.

'It's never nice to be criticised, but they're not giving me any time to adapt. I need to be allowed some time to adapt. I understand the fans' expectations, but I've only been here for two months. I signed for four years, not two months.'

With humanity, he called for some peace and quiet: 'I want to be calm in my life when I go home, just like you do. Except I play for Real Madrid. There are even more demands here than in Italy. The important thing is to focus on the pitch and get back to full fitness,' he promised, announcing a media blackout.

Although he did not admit it, he was full of doubts, something he would recognise some months later: 'It wasn't easy. In fact, it was very hard. Not so much in terms of the football, but everything else that goes with it. There was a lot expected of me. But that's normal given the context. And I have to know how to accept criticism.'

As well as the need to focus, there was another imperative: work as hard as you can. 'When you're tired and games are building up, that's when you think you need to rest; but that's exactly when you have to put even more work in. Work harder! I have to work hard to adapt. I didn't arrive in Spain at the peak of my form.' So he worked tirelessly at the Ciudad Deportivo, Real Madrid's training centre to the north of the capital, at the end of the famous Castellana Avenue.

The site may have been sold off by the club, but Real's players were still training there. It boasted a dozen pitches, the medical centre, car park and the players' dressing rooms. They would sometimes meet at the cafeteria in the neighbouring Raimundo-Saporta Pavilion, home to Real's basketball team. Zidane would often have a coffee with Luis Figo or Fernando Hierro because he regularly arrived early for training.

Particularly diligent, he took advantage of his Champions League suspension to train on his own in the middle of the week, when Real were playing without him.

Normally watched for his every move, on those days the Ciudad Deportivo was a haven of peace and quiet that brought him a little serenity.

He was also more serene in his private life, having finally found a house he liked in the upscale neighbourhood of Conde de Orgaz, where his neighbours included his teammates Luis Figo and Raúl.

Green and relatively cool in summer compared with the rest of the city, the neighbourhood was also close to the Ciudad Deportivo and the Santiago-Bernabeu stadium. Above all, it had the advantage of being right next to Madrid's French high school, which the Zidane family's children attended.

Of course, taking Luca and Enzo to school every day without attracting attention was not easy. It was quite a challenge as Zizoumania had become even bigger. But, little by little, Zinedine became familiar with Spain, while at the same time making progress with his fitness. His Spanish was no longer hesitant but he did mix in a lot of Italian words. From time to time, he hesitated, but his efforts were appreciated, especially by his teammates.

'He's a great guy, very down-to-earth. Even though he's Zidane,' said Ivan Helguera, Real's defender-cum-midfielder who was a good friend of Claude Makelele, known as 'Make', responsible for showing his compatriot the ropes despite explaining that 'Zidane doesn't need anyone.'

He just needed the support of his friends and family, which he had always had and would always continue to have. This support was invaluable, particularly on this morning unlike any other at the Ciudad Deportivo.

Sitting at a table in the almost deserted cafeteria, Zinedine looked as if he had got out of bed on the wrong side. His wife and his father were there. Everyone appeared to be in a state of shock.

He had just returned from the France–Algeria game. It had been a complete disaster.

It was the first time France and Algeria had met on a football pitch; never had a France game been abandoned before the end. But this was exactly what happened at the Stade de France on Saturday 6 October 2001.

It was supposed to be a big party, supposed to be played, according to the media, in the same spirit as the *France Black-Blanc-Beur*' (France Black-White-North African) slogans and 'Zidane for President' after the 1998 World Cup.

Zidane was delighted to be playing in the match, admitting a few days beforehand that he would feel 'a twinge in his heart'. Originally from the small village of Aguemoune in the heart of the Babor Mountains in Kabylie, his family were very much looking forward to the event.

The match was symbolic for Smaïl Zidane. However, instead of the anticipated party, it quickly went far beyond a friendly game between sportsmen.

On a political level, right-wing parties were calling for the match to be cancelled for security reasons. The Renseignements Généraux, the French police intelligence service, reported a possible influx of youths from deprived areas supporting Osama bin Laden, leader of the nebulous Islamic terrorist network Al Qaeda, whose name was already familiar to all: three weeks earlier, on 11 September, a series of attacks in the United States were to have yet incalculable consequences.

The mayor of Saint-Denis, who belonged to the Communist Party, a member of the ruling left-wing coalition, denounced the rumours, while Marie-George Buffet, the Sports Minister, came under scrutiny.

Zidane was careful not to interfere in the debate so as not to stir up passions.

A particularly imposing police presence was brought in for the match. The atmosphere was very tense. Two weeks after the match, the president of the French Football Federation, Claude Simonet, would acknowledge having received a bomb threat judged to be credible by the police: 'We went around twice with sniffer dogs. Since they found nothing, we decided not to change anything. But you can imagine how concerned I was at kick-off.'

Before the start of the game, the tension was palpable. A standing ovation was given for the Algerian national anthem, *Kassaman*, while *La Marseillaise* was booed and whistled. When the teams were announced, most of the French players were greeted with whistles from the spectators. Apart from one: Zidane, whose tightly drawn face showed no signs that he had heard these misdemeanours.

Missiles were thrown from the stands as the officials were targeted and shouted at. This was widely reported by the foreign press … more so than in the French media. In the 76th minute, when the score was 4–1 to France, one, then ten, then a hundred young spectators began invading the pitch. Although there was little real violence, they prevented the match from finishing.

Zidane left the stadium without saying anything to the waiting journalists, but he was furious. He was sickened by the turn of events. It was the first time that his adventure with Les Bleus had turned into a nightmare.

His return to playing in a white shirt might help him get over it, on one condition: he needed to impose himself in Madrid. By dint of talent and hard work, he succeeded.

Imperceptibly, he became more integrated into the Madrid squad. On the pitch, Raúl looked after the defenders, Figo helped take charge of the play, and Zizou made the most of the dynamic to score goals. Some beautiful goals, as always.

He had rediscovered the fun, far from the padlocked defences of the Italian league. He was playing well and playing with his opponents. The spectators got out of their seats to salute his genius. But the demanding fans would have to wait a little longer, as those at Juve had five years earlier, before seeing him in his best form, finally able to exploit the full extent of his repertoire consistently.

He was more comfortable with Real's style of football than with Juventus's, and he said so: 'I'm free here, and it's a lot more fun.' Free and more serene, despite the pressure of celebrity increased by publicity.

Shirts printed with the number 5 were now selling in the tens of thousands. The car manufacturer Ford launched a competition that boasted a meeting with Zidane as its second prize. The fee for Zizou was like a 'dream'. It was a convenient argument for those who had paid €75 million to buy a man. The debate became endless. Why was €75 million any worse than €50 or €25 million?

The Madrid directors wanted panache at all costs. They were driven by the desire to have the greatest players. By lust for the most beautiful football. Dream football.

And Zizou was the stuff of which dreams are made. He came to Madrid for fun, for his own happiness and that of the fans. Once again he was talking about the beautiful game, 14½ years after leaving Septèmes. The passes, feints, flicks and nutmegs brought his passion back to life, taking him back to when he was a child running on other pitches, with an urgency to share his emotions, as if he was christening a new ball every time. A sphere, whose magical rotation is understood only by children, dreamers and astronomers.

He kept at it and eventually imposed himself. As Monsieur Boix had predicted, there were plenty of cheers, cries, shrieks, collective exclamations from a single breath, in praise, from a crowd that had finally been won over.

'Zidane is now fully integrated into the squad. It took him a while, but that's normal,' said Vicente Del Bosque.

'It's clear that he is a different kind of footballer: the best in the world,' wrote the biggest Spanish daily *El País*, mentioning a stunning assist against the Greek team Panathinaikos.

Zidane's rise in power corresponded with that of his team. After a difficult start, Real began to string together wins in the Champions League, the domestic league and the Spanish Cup. The club had become 'unstoppable', conducted by Zidane in a team composed of talented soloists.

'Apart from the France team, Real is the best team I've ever played in. There are so many quality players. It's the team of my dreams. I wanted to play a happier kind of football and I've found it,' the now popular number 5 confirmed.

On 1 December 2001, following the draw for the World Cup at which France would defend their title, Zizou was once again in a good mood. Les Bleus had drawn Senegal, Uruguay and Denmark. Confidence reigned: 'At any rate, to win the World Cup, you have to win all your matches. We will do our best to top the group.'

But the France team, champions of the world and Europe, were not all that reassuring. Apart from the abandoned victory against the weak Algeria, they had posted two poor performances.

France had lost to Chile (2–1). Zizou seemed more popular with the Santiago crowd than Ivan Zamorano, the huge Chilean star who was playing his last match for the national side! France had then only been able to manage a draw in Australia (1–1) after an unusual trip: the federation had paid a great deal to kit out a special plane, installing beds and massage tables so Les Bleus could rest on the 30-hour journey.

Zizou remained confident: 'Australia played their matches the wrong way round (they had lost another much more important one against Uruguay in the World Cup play-offs). Losing warm-up games is not important. [...] We know what we have to do. [...] We can raise our level of play. I'm not concerned. [...] We will defend our title to the end. We can become world champions again,' he repeated at his various appearances, in front of a press becoming increasingly sceptical about Les Bleus' form. But they also remembered their mediocre results before the win in 1998.

An important year was about to begin. With a bang. With fireworks. On 5 January 2002, in the 19th game of the Spanish league season, the 2000 champions, Deportivo de la Coruña, were playing Real, their successors in 2001: the two strongest teams of recent seasons.

Some 75,000 fans had travelled to see what they believed would be the title decider.

Zidane was on another level. In the ninth minute, while the stadium was already cheering after goals from two of the most well-respected centre-forwards in the world – Fernando Morientes (sixth minute) and an equaliser from Roy Makaay (seventh minute) – Zidane received the ball from Luis Figo. To the left of the box, he pretended to go deeper towards the corner before drifting back to the right and setting off again to the left immediately, with the ball stuck to his foot. He unleashed a cannonball, impossible for the Spanish national-team goalkeeper Molina to save. The three 'Depor' defenders charged with stopping him could do nothing.

'Even if you're playing against him, you can only applaud a goal like that,' admitted Noureddine Naybet, La Coruña's Moroccan international, sportingly.

Throughout the game, won 3–1 with a final goal from Raúl, Zidane distilled some extraordinary passes, including a flick that sent Solari towards the goal. Almost all his dribbling came off.

Once again, he had lived up to the big occasion. To pay tribute to his performance and allow him to receive a predictable ovation when he left the field, Del Bosque substituted him in the last minute of normal time. The ovation came and the fans screamed: 'Zizou! Zizou!' A love story between the Madrid public and the champion had begun.

The guest of honour, the basketball player Magic Johnson, a former member of the famous American dream team of 1992, on a gala tour with a team of other ex-stars, had nothing but praise: 'Zidane is both Magic and Jordan in a single player,' an allusion to Michael Jordan, the other great basketball player of his generation.

The following day, the front page of Spain's biggest sports daily, *Marca*, was eloquent: an enormous Z, an allusion to Zorro, took over the entire page. Compliments, praise and enthusiasm had replaced the doubts. And it would stay that way for a long time.

The victory against Depor saw Real top the table at exactly halfway through the season, something that was particularly welcome during the club's centenary year.

In the Champions League, Real had won its group ahead of AS Roma, Lokomotiv Moscow and Anderlecht, and was in first place in the second group phase, ahead of Porto, Panathinaikos and Sparta Prague. The club was also among the last eight still in the running for the Copa del Rey. They were euphoric. The media was full of excitement at the prospect that Real could pull off an unprecedented treble: the European Cup, La Liga and the Copa del Rey. The talk in Madrid was increasingly about trebles, trefoils and *galaticos*.

Zidane tried to play it down: 'We haven't won anything yet. It's no good playing well if you lose games at the end of the season.'

Real were, in fact, far from dominant, although two or three flashes of genius were enough to subdue an opponent in a tight match.

Television amplified everything. The team's goals, often masterpieces combining individual feats and collective mastery, were seen all over the world. By definition, TV viewers often only see highlights of a match. Reality is distorted: an impression was created that Real had played 90 minutes with ease, when in fact they had to fight hard to win.

On 6 March 2002, relatively early in the season, the final of the Copa del Rey was held at the Santiago-Bernabeu stadium. President Florentino Perez had managed to convince the Spanish Federation to agree to the match taking place on this unusual date ... the club's centenary.

Real were in the final after knocking out Rayo Vallecano and Athletic Bilbao among others. There they met Deportivo de la Coruña.

No one, except the Galicians themselves, thought Depor would win. Yet they were victorious with a scoreline of 2–1 and a demonstration of football. The Madrid team's unexpected defeat was compared to that of Brazil in the 1950 World Cup in Rio at the Maracanã, a loss known as the 'Maracanazo'. It was a hammer blow to both players and fans. A huge blow to Zidane, who was beginning to collect lost finals at club level.

Two months later, Real faced Bayer Leverkusen in the Champions League final in Glasgow. The Madrid team seemed tired – with a sub-par Luis Figo in particular, because of a knee problem – and not incisive enough after a long season. The stakes were huge for Real who, after having been top of the league for two-thirds of the season, had let the title slip in the last five games to the benefit of Valencia, who were back in the lead after a catastrophic start.

Real had dreamed of a treble in their centenary year. They might now finish the season without a title. Many pundits thought the Germans offered a game that was both more attractive and better as a team than Real, who were exhausted and out of ideas.

But with eight victories behind them already since the event was founded in the 1955–56 season, Real were the standard bearers for the competition, Europe's most prestigious cup, previously the European Champion Clubs' Cup and now the Champions League.

In the quarter-final, Real had knocked out Bayern Munich, their bogey team, after two legs brimming with tension and suspense. A defeat in Germany (2–1) but a fine return to the Santiago-Bernabeu (2–0) had opened the way to the last four.

In the semi-final, Real had to dig deep against their hated rivals Barcelona. In the first leg, the Madrid team scored their first victory at Barcelona's Camp Nou in 19 years, 2–0. It was Zinedine Zidane who opened the scoring. In the 55th minute, on the end of a magnificent pass from Raúl after a 40-metre sprint, he was thinking clearly enough to pull off a wonderful lob.

The return leg was overshadowed by a car-bomb attack claimed by ETA four hours before kick-off. Seventeen people were injured – a relatively low number thanks to a warning from a representative of the Basque separatist organisation a few minutes before the explosion. The importance of a football match, even one between fierce rivals, was put back in its rightful place.

'I have the inner strength to win this game and won't accept anything else,' said Zizou in Glasgow just before the final. He would keep his word. As against Deportivo de la Coruña in the final of the Copa del Rey, Real opened the scoring but were caught immediately (Raúl scored in the eighth minute; Lucio equalised in the 13th). The two teams were tense and did not offer much in the way of entertainment until a fabulous left-footed volley from Zidane in the 45th minute. The winning goal! A Champions League title at last.

A moment of magic at Hampden Park. Roberto Carlos ran down the left wing but appeared to hesitate. The trajectory of the ball, which flew up a little too vertically, almost floating, did not look as if it would amount to anything. But as it fell back down to earth, Zidane fired the ball into the top corner, a perfect left-footed volley under the dumbfounded gaze of the brilliant young Michael Ballack.

'I followed Roberto Carlos' run and saw the cross come in. I kept my eye on the ball and struck it on the volley without thinking. It was just intuition,' explained the hero of the hour. His role was as decisive in Glasgow as it had been four years earlier against Brazil in the World Cup final.

'A real gem' (*Nacion*); 'Perfect!' (*AFP*); 'A moment of magic' (*Westdeutsche Allgemeine*); 'Magic foot' (*Bild*); 'Goal of the year' (*Gazzetta dello Sport*); 'Extraordinary' (*Corriere dello Sport*); 'A beautiful explosion' (Jorge Valdano); 'I was speechless' (Del Piero); 'A piece of exceptional technique' (Thierry Henry): the media and players all over the world paid tribute to Zidane's shot.

With a reference to El Cid, the Spanish hero of the Reconquista, *Marca* ran with the headline 'El Zid!' with a photo of Zidane on the cover. Despite Raúl's opener and heroics from the goalkeeper Casillas, Zizou's volley, more than his performances during the season, would forever make him the 'man of the ninth [cup]', just as Mijatović was the 'man of the seventh', thanks to his much less impressive goal against Zidane's Juventus in 1998.

Logically voted man of the match in the final, Zizou remained as modest as ever. 'I don't know what's going on or what I'm feeling.

I was missing this title ... But I didn't win it on my own. The whole team won it together.' It was his title, his cup. But Yazid did not celebrate on his own but with Malek, whom he spotted and literally dragged out of the stands to invite him to join him in the dressing room.

The following day, the players were greeted by thousands of jubilant fans at Madrid airport and driven to the venerable Cibeles Fountain, built in 1782, where Real always celebrate their titles. Its players would climb onto the historical monument to hang a scarf in the club's colours.

'It's amazing. There have been people everywhere since we arrived at the airport. It's really fantastic! It reminds me of the atmosphere at the World Cup in 1998. It's just like that. It's a great joy! I'm really happy to have won, and to have had this welcome for my first year in Spain and my first Champions League. It's really great!' said Zizou as the fans chanted: 'Who's the best player in the world? Zizou, Zizou!' and 'What a goal! What a goal! Olé, Olé! Zidane, Zidane!'

More so than ever, Zidane was the most highly anticipated player at the World Cup in the Far East, where he arrived with important news in his personal life: the birth of his third son, Théo.

The time had come to dream of a double. A wave of sweet euphoria swept across France. In an advertising campaign, a second star – although still far from being won – was imprudently printed on a Bleus shirt next to the one representing their 1998 victory.

The manager Roger Lemerre, who had brilliantly taken Les Bleus to a difficult and unprecedented World Cup-Euros double, was criticised for being locked into a rigid system. He was also reproached for failing to properly control his squad. His players may have been more experienced, but they were also older. In addition, several influential players had left, including Didier Deschamps and Laurent Blanc.

The French coaching team committed rookie errors at the World Cup: picking tired players for friendlies; not taking into account local weather conditions; choosing a hotel in an urban area, an argument that was rejected on the assumption that the location was more convenient for match venues; failing to check out the stadiums in advance; not imposing strict rules for squad life . . .

The misjudgements piled up. Thierry Henry was playing with only one fit leg and Zizou picked up a right-thigh injury during a run-of-the-mill friendly against South Korea in Suwon on 26 May 2002. It was serious.

'I made myself available for the game, so I take responsibility for it,' he said, not wanting anyone to be blamed. But there was one question on everyone's lips: why did he play that day?

A race against time began. A treatment plan was implemented to achieve a miracle: to get Zizou ready, if possible, for the second World Cup game against Uruguay. The medical team had already ruled him out of playing against Senegal.

During the opening match, Zidane watched France's defeat from the bench.

The fact that he was not on the pitch implied that Les Bleus were at a disadvantage, but also gave their opponents confidence. In addition, he was taking very little part in squad life, imprisoned as he was by his treatment. He trained on a separate pitch, far from his teammates, and went to the pool at the Sheraton hotel to swim laps under the watchful eye of osteopath Philippe Boixel and security chief François Vidal. He braved Seoul's congested traffic to visit private local clinics with state-of-the-art equipment.

'The presence of Zidane is important to the squad. He is reassuring. We only saw him every now and then. It was as if he wasn't there,' explained Claude Makelele, who was not picked by Roger Lemerre until the last game. He was forced to watch the tense game helplessly alongside Zizou, who did not play against Uruguay either. France resisted, despite going down to ten men after Thierry Henry was sent off. The final score was 0–0. 'It's very frustrating,' recognised Zizou at the time, without criticising his teammates.

To qualify, they had to beat Denmark by a two-goal margin or better. 'We'll do it,' promised Zidane, who made his return, despite being far from 100 per cent fit. Regardless, Les Bleus believed in him, although he was lacking match fitness and playing with strapping around his thigh to cover the wound that had not yet healed properly.

The miracle did not happen. There was total disappointment. After arguably letting it go to their heads, Les Bleus left with their heads lowered. Out in the first round, without even scoring a single goal! France were the first world champions since Brazil in 1966 to be eliminated at this stage of the competition, without showing either a performance or a team spirit worthy of their title.

Despite the bitterness, Zidane did not openly attack anyone; he did not betray his teammates. Even those who had shown a certain apathy on the pitch, those who had failed to maintain a lifestyle compatible with that of a major competition, drinking or staying up late the night before a game, almost indifferent to an 'unspeakable organisational mess', to use the words of someone close to the team.

'We were missing someone to bang their fist down on the table. We should've torn ourselves to shreds out there, been harder on ourselves on the pitch,' Zizou would later regret, although still without taking pot-shots at anyone in particular.

He had given everything he had to save the France team from disaster, but they had not paid him back. He felt as if some of his teammates had betrayed him. After France–Algeria, it came as a second disappointment with the national side. The 'World Champions', a title that had been repeated to excess for four years, were disparaged by their fans. The sponsors quickly packed away shirts and campaigns hastily prepared for victory.

Once again, it was the Brazilians who were celebrating. Their team spirit, unlike that of France and their own behaviour four years earlier, was decisive in their World Cup win. Their fifth.

'I'm tied with Zizou at one-one!' said Roberto Carlos, laughing, when training resumed at Real. Four years after losing to Zidane's France, this time he had been on the winning side in the final against Germany.

For the rest of Real's squad, the Asian World Cup offered anything but happy memories. The Spaniards Raúl – injured in his last game – Casillas, Salgado, Helguera and Morientes felt as if they had been hard done by thanks to a refereeing decision that went the way of South Korea in their quarter-final.

But no one would be able to forget the World Cup entirely once its biggest star and top scorer arrived in Madrid: Ronaldo, who had left Inter Milan and their manager Hector Cuper, with whom he had fallen out. Ronaldo, an unexpected hero, had returned from injury to score eight goals, something no one had done since Germany's Gerd Müller in 1970.

The arrival of the Brazilian striker, like that of Zidane a year earlier, whipped the fans and press into a frenzy. With him at the peak of his powers on the pitch alongside Zizou – with four

FIFA 'Player of the Year' titles between them – Real would be unbeatable, they said.

The two men got on well off the pitch, comparing experiences in Italy. 'Zizou came to visit me in hospital in Paris when I had knee surgery. Some of my Inter teammates didn't bother,' explained Ronaldo.

As for Zidane, he was happy with this media-hyped reinforcement: 'It's a relief: almost all the attention has been on him since he arrived. Now I can get on with things quietly!' he said, happily. For once, he would depart from his usual caution: 'It will be very difficult to stop us if everyone is 100 per cent fit. I can only see AC Milan being at a level comparable to ours in terms of big players. But, unlike Milan, we're more of a team, a squad.'

Behind the scenes at the club, the smiles were nervous. The 'Spanish clan' were rather reluctant about the arrival of the Brazilian, who was no doubt going to 'pinch' Fernando Morientes' place. Not only was Morientes popular in the squad, he had also proven himself on the pitch, scoring important goals. Fortunately, the manager Vicente Del Bosque, a master in diplomacy and psychology, succeeded in calming the various tensions.

Early December saw the first big match of the season: the Intercontinental Cup against Olimpia Asunción of Paraguay in Yokohama. In Japan, Zizou was hoping to go at least some way to erasing his bad memories of the Asian World Cup.

In front of 69,000 fans, Real won more easily than expected, by 2–0 thanks to goals from Ronaldo and Guti.

When victory seemed assured, Zidane came off in the 86th minute to allow Solari to enjoy a few moments of the game. He received a memorable ovation. His 2002 ended as well as it had started, with recognition from the fans.

One month later, Real played host to Valencia for what had been billed as a Liga 'final' between the incumbent champions and those of the previous year.

The result was a lesson in football, a symphony given by Madrid's virtuosos, with Zinedine Zidane conducting with a magic wand. It was one of his best, if not his absolute best match in a white shirt.

With one goal, two assists and an extraordinary performance, he set the crowd, his teammates and journalists on fire. The *Marca* headline read 'One of the Three Kings' on 5 January, the day before the Epiphany. 'Zizou's finest piece of football in a Madrid shirt,' wrote a journalist in the newspaper about the fourth goal, scored by the young 20-year-old Portillo.

This textbook goal owed much to Zidane: after a genius piece of control in the centre circle, some unstoppable dribbling and a 30-metre run, he wrong-footed the entire defence before gifting Portillo a perfect pass.

'As far as I'm concerned, he's the best player in the world. A magician with the ball. He did all the hard work and then said to me, "Go get it, kid,"' Portillo remembered. 'He picked up the ball in midfield and got past two players with step-overs. I stuck close to Ayala [Valencia's Argentine international defender], but couldn't see any space. So I moved over towards the left wing. It's not easy to understand Zidane, because he's so good he can do anything … I thought he was going to pass to the right, to Figo, but then he pulled out a brilliant pass from under his hat. It was the best Epiphany gift he could have given me!'

The praise continued to rain down. Roberto Carlos summed it up: 'If you send Zidane a potato, he'll send you back a caress.' Ronaldo added: 'I'm in love with Zizou.'

With this victory, Real climbed to within three points of the leaders, Real Sociedad from San Sebastián. They had also done well in the first phase of the Champions League, qualified for the quarter-final of the Copa del Rey and won the club world title. But then the machinery began to seize up.

The humiliating 4–0 defeat inflicted by Mallorca in the Copa del Rey was interpreted as a blip at the time. Particularly because everything was going well for Real in La Liga and in the Champions League especially. They had beaten Borussia Dortmund (2–1) and AC Milan (3–1) before offering up a thrilling double-header against Manchester United in the quarter-final: a 3–1 victory in the first leg; a 4–3 defeat in the second. Ronaldo's efficiency and Zidane's mastery enabled Real to come away from Old Trafford with an aggregate win. Roy Keane, not someone to often give compliments, acknowledged: 'The best player I've ever come up against would have to be Zidane. It seems so easy for him. He works hard on his game, he is a physically strong player, he's got a great attitude and has all the attributes. He would have to be the best, and he is still probably improving, which is the frightening thing for all of us!'

But Zizou's genius would not be enough to avoid another beating from Mallorca: 5–1 at home! And just before the second leg against Juventus in the European semi-final.

Winners by 2–1 in the first leg, Real did not go into the clash in the best possible state, deprived in particular of Makelele, the linchpin of the midfield.

It was awkward for Zidane. He would be playing his former teammates and setting foot in the away-team dressing room at the Stadio delle Alpi.

There was also plenty of motivation for Pavel Nedved, who had replaced Zidane at Juve and did not want to come off second best in any comparison.

Zizou tried to play down the emotional aspect of his return: 'It's very moving coming back to the Delle Alpi. I spent five great years here and I hope the fans enjoyed them as much as I did. I want to tell myself that it's a match like any other. That I'm going to come out on the pitch trying to play as well as I can and win. Without thinking that I'm going to play Juventus or against my friends. It might bother me, but this is not the time to lose focus.'

The match turned into a nightmare. The Madrid team were outplayed to an astonishing degree. They strolled from one end of the pitch to the other and hardly saw the ball. Although a penalty miss by Figo could have changed plenty, the 3–1 scoreline was almost flattering, given that Zidane had pulled one back just before the final whistle.

The match was a real shock back in Spain, where the realisation that Real were not the best team in the world suddenly dawned. Quite the contrary, it even appeared as if there was a gulf between them and Juve. All of a sudden, the 'blips' of recent weeks were seen in a different light. The atmosphere was no longer serene. Inside the club as well as outside. Real tried to right the ship in La Liga and began chasing the surprising Real Sociedad, managed by the Frenchman Raynald Denoueix. The former Nantes player had transformed a club that had narrowly escaped relegation in the final game of the previous season into title contenders.

In second place behind the Basques going into the 34th game, Real Madrid had to win all their matches and hope for a Sociedad slip-up if they wanted to finish at the top.

Real Sociedad cracked in the penultimate game. They lost to Celta Vigo and handed the lead to Real, who saved their season by beating Athletic Bilbao (3–1) in the final game. They were champions of Spain for the 29th time in their history. A first for Zidane.

'We lost to the great Real. A team of stars: Zidane, Ronaldo, Raúl, Roberto Carlos, Makelele ... With the number of points we had, we would have been champions in most other years. That just goes to show the level at which both we and they performed. They were too good, we just didn't have enough to beat them,' Denoueix would remember.

When the final whistle blew against Bilbao, the Madrid players celebrated, taking a lap of honour of the stadium but not staying for the fireworks. This absence was interpreted in a variety of ways.

Wearing shirts freshly printed with the number 29, the players once again returned to the Cibeles Fountain by open-top bus. More than 100,000 people were waiting for them. But they were greeted by a surprise on their arrival: the fountain was cordoned off by police, who refused to let the players climb the goddess statue.

The police had received strict orders from the town hall, tired of the constant repairs the municipal services were forced to make almost every year to this symbol of the city, photographed by millions of tourists.

As far as the players were concerned, it was a capital offence. They were being deprived of their traditional celebration. But there were more serious things to worry about.

Gathering at around midnight in a large Madrid hotel, the players and directors looked glum at a meal that was supposed to be a celebration. Things that had been unspoken were voiced:

Jorge Valdano, the club's general manager, was criticised for his double-talk, just as Florentino Perez was for his policy, particularly his attitude towards Morientes and his authoritarian approach. The club was accused of not respecting the lives of its players. The veteran and captain Fernando Hierro almost came to blows with Valdano. A revolt was simmering; the players even talked about boycotting the official celebrations scheduled for the following day.

At around 4am, Florentino Perez had to bang his fist on the table. With a microphone in his hand, he appealed to everyone for calm, promised fines for those who would not comply and reminded everyone that they were supposed to be celebrating the title. With the exception of Steve McManaman, who was excused, and Ronaldo, who claimed he had overslept, all the players were at the event.

Punishments were dished out the following day: at the same time as he announced the dismissal of manager Vicente Del Bosque, made a scapegoat for the debacle against Juventus, Perez revealed that Hierro's contract would not be extended.

'I was told that my behaviour on Sunday was unacceptable, but I think my fate had been sealed for a long time,' said the former captain.

During the holidays, Real announced the recruitment of the Portuguese manager Carlos Queiroz. Other plans were afoot: once again, the president tried to transfer Morientes – this time successfully – sending him out on loan to Monaco. Most importantly, he refused to raise the salary of Claude Makelele, the club linchpin, who thought he deserved greater rewards. Supported by Zidane, Makelele had obtained a verbal promise from Valdano in return for not requesting a salary increase during the season. He felt betrayed. An uncompromising confrontation led to his transfer to Chelsea. Florentino Perez thought he had got rid of an easily replaceable troublemaker. But after the side-lining of Del Bosque, it seemed as if he had made a huge mistake. One of the biggest of his mandate.

12

THE UNBELIEVABLE COMEBACK

Real may have been a great club but did they still have a great team? Was the right person at the helm?

After the turmoil of the end of the 2002–03 season, in Queiroz, Sir Alex Ferguson's former deputy at Manchester United, Zizou and Real found themselves working under someone who had never managed a big team on his own before. Somewhat paradoxical, given that he was now in charge of the most prestigious team in the world!

The atmosphere appeared to have calmed down but appearances can be deceptive. The players were still unhappy with Jorge Valdano and Florentino Perez due to their past behaviour. They were also struggling increasingly to understand the policy at the club, which had just recruited David Beckham – undoubtedly a brilliant player and one with considerable off-the-pitch appeal – but had refused to raise the salary of the extremely valuable Claude Makelele.

A defensive midfielder with an extraordinarily high work rate, Makelele had been very popular in the dressing room. Zidane intervened to try to influence the position taken by the club's directors, but Florentino Perez stood his ground, showing his limitations in terms of his knowledge of the game. In his eyes, Makelele was neither a star who sold lots of replica shirts nor a technically brilliant player, so he believed he was someone who could be easily replaced.

Real began the season with one more *galactico*, Beckham, the star, and one less 'grafter', the worker bee Makelele, who would bestow plenty of happiness on Chelsea.

Zidane felt as if the mistakes of the previous year were being repeated . . . with the addition of a few more. One particular example was the tour to China and Japan, which used up precious resources when the players should have been saving energy. 'It's a real screw-up!' said Zizou, sadly, away from the microphones. In public, he formulated his criticism with a little more diplomacy, such as this terse but clear phrase: 'It's not the best possible preparation.'

Like his teammates, he was upset but did not let it show too conspicuously: 'Perez is the president. He's the one who decides,' he reminded everyone with a mixture of irony and disappointment.

However, the initial results of the 2003–04 season failed to prove the president wrong. With Beckham surprisingly transformed into a defensive midfielder, Zidane on the left, Figo on the right and Raúl behind Ronaldo, manager Carlos Queiroz could hardly have been accused of using his players to the max, but the machine was functioning well.

Real had been camped out at the top of the league table since the beginning of the season, including a notable demonstration against Valladolid with a 7–2 scoreline that was a reminder of the 1950s and the days of Di Stefano et al.

In the Champions League, they won brilliantly at Porto, 3–1, before facing . . . Marseille. Zidane's home town.

'There's much more talk about the game on the Canebière than here in Madrid,' said the man who would once again be known as Yazid for an evening. 'Of course, it's special for me. It's the club I supported as a child. I would go to matches at the Vélodrome. I used to get so excited. I was and am still an Olympique fan. But it won't be the first time I've played against them. It's the game in Marseille that will be particularly special, with my friends and family.'

On 26 November, in Marseille, Real had already qualified for the quarter-finals, but needed to secure first place in the group. Welcomed by applause as well as the odd whistle whenever he touched the ball, Zizou played a serious professional game. Real won 2–1. Their French star remained on top.

'Nijinsky with a ball,' Zidane 'handles the ball like a Stradivarius', reported the Spanish daily *El País* on 17 December, the day after Zizou was voted FIFA Player of 2003 for the third time.

The fans at the Santiago-Bernabeu had their eyes peeled for every piece of ball control, every exceptional demonstration of skill or sequence of dribbling from the footballer-cum-dancer-cum-virtuoso, making him their darling ahead of Spaniard and local boy Raúl. In January 2004, Zidane was offered both the opportunity to become a 'lifetime ambassador' for the club and a contract extension until 2007. 'It feels as if I arrived only yesterday. I still want to play for Real for a long time,' he said.

The dream of the famous Champions League – Liga – Copa del Rey treble was in their sights once again. 'Every competition is a priority!' announced Perez.

'We've been through this before. You have to be very careful about getting carried away. We could lose them all as well as win them all,' said Zidane, playing it down.

At the end of January, the Madrid team swept Valencia away in the quarter-final of the Copa del Rey. At the end of February, they were leading La Liga by eight points, ahead of Valencia again. In the Champions League, they had struggled past the obstacle of Bayern Munich (1–1, 1–0).

But on 17 March, the only Spanish title Zidane was lacking, the Copa del Rey, escaped him again after a defeat against Zaragoza. 'We were playing well until then. After eight months at a high level, we made it to the Copa del Rey final, were top of La Liga and in the quarter-finals of the Champions League. Everything was going well,' he remembered. 'We cracked a bit physically, and then we took a blow to the head. We fell behind in La Liga.' Then in Europe, in Monaco, in the quarter-final, pitifully.

At half-time in the Stade Louis II, Real were still in a strong position: with the score at 1–1, they were still two goals ahead on aggregate. The Monaco player Ludovic Giuly was unaware of the full extent of Real's problems. In the tunnel at half-time, he spoke to Zizou, his teammate for France: 'Be nice, go easy on us in the second half!' Was he being candid or was it a joke? Zidane did not have time to analyse the comment and, without knowing that his response would be reported and then publicly discussed, retorted with lucid sincerity: 'Can't you see we're done for?'

Real let in two goals in the second half, one from Giuly and the other from Fernando Morientes, who was delighted to be getting one over on President Perez, whose club were paying half the player's salary while he was on loan to the principality. They were eliminated on the away-goals rule.

Back in Spain, despite recognition of Monaco's superiority over both legs, it was unacceptable that the 'great Real' had got themselves knocked out by a club that was not of the stature of

Juventus, Manchester United or Bayern. It was seen as proof that something had been organised badly or done wrong. They were right: the tired *galacticos* ended the 2003–04 season without glory, making qualification for the preliminary round of the Champions League by the skin of their teeth.

'It was the worst time I've had at Real. Physically, we couldn't do it any more. We'd lost everything in a month and a half. These are the moments you need to know how to get through. Luckily my family were there for me. But even so, it's not depressing, it's just football,' said Zizou, trying to put it into perspective.

Fortunately, the national side had the potential to help him forget his club worries.

France and Zidane were dreaming once more ahead of Euro 2004 in Portugal. Les Bleus, now managed by Jacques Santini, had qualified without losing a game. They would rediscover the spirit of 1998, some observers wanted to believe.

The players appeared confident. The coaching team claimed to have learned from the mistakes made in Korea. In Portugal, they were also on more familiar ground than in the mysterious East.

Zidane had 'wiped the slate clean' and even accepted sacrifice: he would play slightly further over to the right to allow Robert Pires to take his place in a tactical formation in which Santini firmly believed.

On 13 June 2004, the first game was played in Lisbon's Estádio da Luz against a valiant England team containing Beckham, Lampard, Gerrard, Owen and the 18-year-old Rooney. With Barthez, Gallas, Thuram, Vieira, Makelele, Henry and Trezeguet, France were also looking good. But straight after kick-off, it was clear that their system of play was not working. The French were jostled and somewhat inevitably let in a free kick by Lampard in the

38th minute. In the 73rd minute, still under the cosh, they even conceded a penalty. It was taken by Beckham, whom Barthez knew well from their days together at Manchester United. But the French keeper saved his shot. The English luck had turned.

With 90 minutes gone, France were still 1–0 down. But in the 91st minute, in stoppage time, they were awarded a free kick at an ideal distance from the English goal on the edge of the box. Zidane, who took fewer free kicks at Real than he had at Juventus, particularly since the arrival of a certain David Beckham, picked up the ball confidently. His powerful brushed shot ended up in the top left-hand corner. There was nothing James, the England goalkeeper, could do.

At 1–1, the scoreline almost flattered the French.

Two minutes later, Henry was brought down by the England keeper and Zidane remorselessly converted the penalty. Les Bleus had won. Three points for France and none for England; the press described the match as a 'hold-up', and an 'undeserved victory', but also talked of Zidane, whom they portrayed in the guise of its saviour.

Logically voted man of the match by UEFA, the hero remained modest. And lucid, paying tribute to Barthez and Henry.

'The good Lord helped us,' said Patrick Vieira, without making it clear whether or not he was talking about Zidane … Whatever the case, France had showed more weaknesses than strengths. Santini made changes for the clash with Croatia. But again the quality was not up to scratch and the game in Leiria ended in a lacklustre 2–2 draw. One highlight of the match for sports psychology enthusiasts was the sermon delivered abruptly by Zizou to his teammates after they had just conceded the goal to make it 1–2. He picked up the ball and had everyone gather around him for a brief but unusual plea not to let themselves be beaten. This unexpected uprising was interpreted as evidence of an urgent need to react, as a change in the behaviour of the playmaker; the star player now realised he was playing the role of leader on the pitch, just as Didier Deschamps and Laurent Blanc had done.

'It was a miracle we didn't lose,' said Barthez.

'The Croatians played well. It wasn't a physical problem on our part,' said Zidane.

For the last group game against Switzerland in Coimbra, Santini returned to his system, with Zizou on the right. He scored the first goal with his head on the end of a corner from Pires. The French only needed a draw, but won 3–1 despite remaining unconvincing. The result was flattering. 'It was not perfect, but we qualified and did what we had to do. We stand together and we all want to go as far as we can. That's the most important thing,' said Zizou after the game.

Were his comments intended to create a unity of which there were few signs? Whatever the case, it would be in vain. Four days later, in the quarter-final in Lisbon, France were knocked out 1–0 by Greece, the eventual winners of the competition, who played with a hermetically sealed defence and developed a boring but effective and lucky game.

Zidane was once again disappointed by the attitude of some of his teammates when it came to commitment. 'We didn't play at our usual level and we didn't play enough. We could only do it after conceding the goal. We weren't all pushing in the same direction. It's disappointing. We could have played differently but there was a lack of harmony. Is it a sign that a cycle is coming to an end? We'll see. We all lost together,' he said on the evening of the match, when even his inclusion in the team was being discussed here and there for the first time ever.

The *Le Parisien-Aujourd'hui en France* newspaper even mentioned an anti-Zidane plot hatched by Arsenal's French players. Thierry Henry and Robert Pires were named. The media reported that Henry was annoyed: 'Zidane doesn't pass me the ball!' But what team doesn't experience this kind of discussion, outburst or internal debate?

Accentuated by the bitterness of public opinion, these rumours would not pierce the impenetrable silence that cloaked the Portuguese misadventure. Neither the meetings between Santini and his players, nor the states of mind of some would be officially mentioned, thus inviting a wide range of interpretations.

For Zidane, this third big disappointment with Les Bleus in less than three years would no doubt force a decision that was brewing within him: his retirement from the French national side.

As announced before the departure for Portugal in strange circumstances – while his contract was awaiting renewal, or so he believed – Jacques Santini would not continue as the French manager. On 12 July, he was replaced by his counterpart from the Under-21 team, Raymond Domenech, a decision that failed to win unanimous support; the appointment of Blanc or Deschamps would likely have prompted Zizou to extend his adventure with the France team.

At every press conference or public appearance when he was asked to give an opinion, there was a feeling he was getting ready to hang up his blue tracksuit. The message left on his answering machine by the new manager would change nothing. And it would perhaps even be interpreted as a lack of respect compared with a face-to-face meeting.

It was not until Wednesday 11 August, almost a month after the appointment of the new manager, that the two men met in Madrid. Raymond Domenech told Zidane he was going to change some of the France team's lifestyle rules: forbidding the use of mobile phones in the massage or meeting rooms, more rigorous controls over night-time outings and strict observance of punctuality. The French playmaker was not hostile to this change within the squad, where the egos of certain players had often exceeded acceptable levels for community life. But Domenech, who was a fan of Zidane's game and told him so, did not offer any guarantees for the future – in short, no promises would be made because of his reputation, if not privileged status, which had become somewhat less 'comfortable'.

Part of Zidane would have liked to stay. But part of him no longer wanted to, despite the opinions of his friends and family, who would have liked to see him keep playing while he still had the passion. The inner turmoil was therefore solved to a certain extent by a majority vote: two against one. There was life after the blue shirt, sons to watch grow up. Since leaving his home in Marseille before turning 15, the boy from La Castellane had spent relatively little time – compared with ordinary mortals – with his parents, sister and brothers. Then with his wife and children.

Seventeen years of football had brought fabulous joys but few real relaxed family breaks without pressure.

Tired of the constraints and atmosphere in the team, Zizou chose not to rise to what appeared to be a new challenge. He confirmed the latent desire within him: to retire from international football.

However, federation rules require a player to attend if they are called up, subject to sanctions. But who would dare to punish an idol? And who would even dare to bring up this point? A handful of observers, including the legendary Auxerre manager Guy Roux, did so openly when France was shaken by a meticulously staged announcement in the middle of the summer holidays.

On 12 August, Zizou issued the following statement on his website: 'I believe that at some point you have to know how to say stop. I have thought about it carefully. It is not a whim. Regardless of the Euro result, I had planned to stop. It's hard to tell yourself that it's all going to come to an end, but at some point you have to know how to do it. It was time, it is my time.'

On Canal+, his sponsor channel, he appeared as a relieved icon, seemingly relaxed, wearing unlaced trainers and gently delivering the abrupt message his admirers so regretted.

Before the media stir caused by this announcement, a radio station on the Côte d'Azur had already leaked the information, revealed unwittingly by an old man already let in on the secret and taken by surprise during a telephone call: Jean Varraud, of course, aware of a desire to leave that dated from before the Euros in Portugal.

At aged 32 with 93 caps to his name, Zinedine Zidane thought he had drawn a definitive line under an adventure that had brought him his greatest joys, as well as some recent disappointments.

His decision was not only openly criticised by Guy Roux but also by Aimé Jacquet, according to whom his former protégé had a duty to serve as a link with subsequent generations. Zizou was disappointed by these comments. A debate, one that was carried out in hushed tones given the huge popularity of the person in question, emerged: the concessions made for the profession of footballer, the service of an international player, however brilliant they are, could they be assimilated to a sacrifice for others, or even for the nation?

If the polls were to be believed, the majority of the French people nevertheless understood the decision made by their most popular citizen. 'He has brought so much to the France team that he can be forgiven,' they said. He also had to get used to the unfamiliar atmosphere during international matches: Zizou was no longer involved. He stayed in Madrid, where the club facilities were deserted by the many players on international duty.

'It's weird. For years, I've lived to the rhythm of international matches. Being here while everyone is at Clairefontaine is a strange sensation. But it's good! I can rest and see my family more. It's a good thing.'

He refused to comment on the performance of Les Bleus. 'I didn't see it,' 'It wasn't broadcast,' and even 'I was at a Madonna concert,' he answered when questioned.

Each time, he was asked if he would return to the team. Each time, he would answer that 'it was not a decision taken lightly'. In October 2004, he even lost his temper: 'I'm no longer answering that question. I'm going to stop coming to press conferences if you keep asking me!' Observers had to admit that the page had been turned, that the story of Zizou in blue was over once and for all.

At Real, they thought they would be able to take advantage of the situation, believing they would have a more relaxed player with more nervous energy, something that was often required in abundance in the electric atmosphere of the *galacticos*.

To give his players, and the fans in particular, a shock expected to be beneficial, Florentino Perez, who had just experienced his first season without a title, hired José Antonio Camacho.

A former player at the club and still one of its most legendary figures, this ex-defender had led the Spanish national team to the quarter-finals of the 2002 World Cup and Euro 2000. But his appointment turned out to be a monumental mistake.

Unlike Queiroz, who never managed to earn respect, Camacho's sin was authoritarianism. His understanding of football had little in common with his team of stars. He asked them to play more physically, imposing technical training sessions that were difficult to understand.

'Zizou, you're good, all right! I respect you, but, and I'm telling you this for your own good and for that of the team, you have to stop all this fussing about and play one-touch football. No more Marseille turns or all those bits of ball control!' Zidane did not respond. He spoke to the journalists who asked him about it without taking offence: 'Sometimes it's good if someone takes things in hand and speaks to us a little bit more harshly.'

In terms of the team, Zizou was convinced that Real needed more rigour. Now that they were without Makelele, there was no longer anyone to cover runs made down either wing. A man like Camacho could remedy this weakness. But from there to asking Zidane to simplify his game or Ronaldo to cover Roberto Carlos when he came forward was quite a leap. A very big leap.

Zizou had hoped to start the new season off on the right foot. But here he was caught up in a new storm. He and his teammates posted a run of subpar performances until the humiliating Champions League defeat on 15 September 2004: 3–0 against Bayer in Leverkusen. Completely outplayed, Real had delivered a game that was close to ridicule.

Less than three months after his arrival, Camacho left, saying he was acting for 'the good of the club'. Privately, he said: 'The players won't listen to me any more. They won't do what I tell them. There's no point in staying.'

Zizou was not necessarily unhappy at the departure of Camacho but he knew plenty of time had been lost. 'Camacho or no Camacho, it was the players who were on the pitch. We have to react. We have a great team and we have to prove it,' he said.

With new manager Mariano Garcia Rémon at the helm, the atmosphere within the team began to relax and results improved slightly. Real did what they had to do, qualifying for the last 16 of the Champions League 2004–05.

To relieve some of the pressure, Zidane sought refuge in Réunion for the winter holidays. The calm before a busy return, with two new arrivals. Garcia Rémon had already been replaced by the Brazilian manager Wanderlei Luxemburgo. The Danish midfielder Thomas Gravesen was given a mission to fill the hole in the midfield, still gaping since the departure of Claude Makelele.

A joker, Gravesen brought some humour and lightness to a squad in crisis. On entering the Real dressing room for the first time, he had a few words to say that made him instantly likeable: 'Hello Figo, Raúl, Zidane, Ronaldo, Beckham ... I'm Gravesen and I'm here to save you!' Unfortunately, his performances were not always as effective as his quips.

However, the change of manager was more reassuring: unlike Garcia Rémon, Luxemburgo was used to managing stars and had precise tactical ideas. In addition, he was particularly fond of Zizou's game. He wanted to move him into a more central position which, in his opinion, would suit him better.

Although Real were still not reigning supreme, results were up to scratch, with victories piling up week after week. The team were at their best in the second half of the La Liga season but still did not manage to win it. Another failure.

'It's a bit like the previous season in reverse. We played well in the second half, but by then it was too late. If you want to win titles, you have to play well all season,' said Zidane, also disappointed by another elimination at the hands of Juventus in the Champions League after an extra-time goal scored by Zalayeta.

Once again, spring came and went without a single title. It was during the summer heat that the biggest news of 2005 broke.

'God is back!' The phrase, reported by the daily *Le Parisien*, was spoken by Thierry Henry after an announcement from Zizou. On 3 August 2005, almost a year after announcing his retirement, the most prestigious player in French football revealed on his website that he would be putting the famous blue shirt on again after all. As much as his departure from the team had seemed possible, or even probable, his return was equally unexpected. Almost unbelievable!

'I've decided to come back to Les Bleus. One year on, I'm going back on a decision I was categorical about. For the first time in my life, I'm changing my mind about something very important. When I made my decision, I didn't make it lightly, I had thought about it carefully.'

The announcement was such a surprise that some thought his website had been hacked. A few hours later, a confirmation from the federation removed any room for doubt: 'Zidane will be making his return to the France team.'

Discussions had been going on for several weeks. 'The manager told me he was counting on me. He came to see me several times in Madrid,' said Zidane.

'I've always been in favour of him playing. I never burned my bridges and that's why I always refused to let the France team play a match in honour of its former world champions who were leaving. It would have been like rubber-stamping their retirement. Personally, I never accepted it,' said Domenech.

The contribution of captain Patrick Vieira to Zidane's return to the France team was also underlined. He had also facilitated the return of Lilian Thuram – not the most enthusiastic – and Claude Makelele.

'I know Zizou well and saw Thu-Thu every day at Juventus, where I had just arrived,' he said about a comeback that would cost him the captaincy; Zizou was also taking back the armband.

During the negotiations, both Zidane and Domenech made their terms clear. The player would only play in his preferred area of the pitch, in the centre or on the left, but not on the right. He wanted Claude Makelele, with whom his understanding on the pitch was clear, to play alongside him. He also agreed to do whatever he could to convince Thuram to return. As for Domenech, he wanted the new arrivals to comply with the rules introduced when he took over.

An agreement was reached, including the way in which news of the return would be released to the media: Zizou would announce it first, before Domenech revealed his team for the next match, a friendly against Côte d'Ivoire.

This communication strategy generated commercial spin-offs. The initial announcement was made on the zidane.fr website. An interview could then be accessed for a fee by calling the Orange telephone service provider, with whom the player was under contract. Before Zizou spoke openly to the media – the following day at Irdning in Austria, where Real's pre-season training was taking place – an interview was granted to Canal+, to whom he had entrusted the announcement of his departure the year before. Zizou was also under contract with the channel. This unusual process and its carefully handled steps gave rise to a certain amount of suspicion.

For all those announcing Zidane's news, the presence of France and the player in question at the 2006 World Cup was a guarantee of revenue. For his equipment supplier, Adidas, which had already struggled to come to terms with Zidane's international retirement, the elimination of the France team, which they also sponsored, would be a disaster. For the money-makers in French football, TV-station advertising bosses (TF1, M6, Canal+) and even a newspaper such as *L'Équipe*, it would be very damaging if Les Bleus failed to qualify.

The question was inevitably asked: had Zizou been pressured by his sponsors?

'Absolutely not,' he insisted. 'I would never have come back for that. It's a decision I took on my own. No one has influenced me. Of course, there may have been requests and pressures on some fronts, but I made this decision alone. I've rediscovered my motivation and am more rested.' He added that he had received his parents' 'blessing'. This detail was not insignificant to those who knew the importance of the small circle of people, mainly family members, with whom he felt at ease. A circle he trusted. A circle unconstrained by other interests of any kind.

His loved ones had not wanted him to leave the team so, logically, they were happy about his comeback. Above all, Zinedine Yazid Zidane is a man of feelings, thoughts and impulses that are sometimes contrary but never stifled by material concerns. He did not despise money, however. He knew how much his fame could help his nearest and dearest, more than himself, given that it had been a long time since he had had any financial worries.

To everyone's surprise, this time without anybody accusing him of being calculating, he made a revelation that generated plenty of comment. It came in the form of an esoteric enigma.

During an interview, a journalist from *France Football*, whom he knew well and who knew him well, recounted the following comments:

It was pretty mystical and I'm not sure I understand it completely. It was almost irrational. One night, at 3am, I woke up suddenly and spoke to someone. Someone you will never meet. I can't explain it myself. During the hours that followed, I was on my own with that person, and I made the decision to come back. It was as if I was powerless in the face of this force telling me what to do.

Zinedine had probably not thought about the impact of these remarks. Was that exactly what he had said? Had they been 'rewritten', as is often the case for better readability, by the journalist or some of his colleagues? Contacted by a radio station for a special programme, the interviewer chose to keep his silence. His reputation, as well as the trusted relationship he had had with Zidane since his time in Bordeaux, went in his favour. If not about all the wording, at least about the substance of the comments.

For once Zizou had opened up, in such a profound way, but been caricatured. It was easy to mock him for 'hearing voices like Joan of Arc'.

Who has never 'spoken' with someone, consciously or unconsciously? And what if that communication was just an entirely unremarkable night-time thought?

The public and the media were troubled by this puzzle. The identity of the person with whom Zinedine could have communicated was the subject of several questions: did they really exist? Was it Zidane resorting to his childhood? Was it Jean Varraud?

What about a former teammate? An old friend from Marseille? A member of his family? Someone who, according to Zizou, was linked to the time when he was learning the game?

The affair got so blown out of proportion that Zidane made a second announcement on his website: 'I want to let people know they have misinterpreted things. I have always been clear. If you read the article, you'll see that I'm clearly talking about a person, not about religion or anything mystical. That person was my brother. It was something personal. I didn't want to say who the person was, but I'm going to reveal it now to stop everyone talking.'

His brother? Which one? Farid? Noureddine? Djamel? Why? This detail did not necessarily solve the puzzle, and even mystified those who had found Zinedine's initial remarks more touching than unlikely. He would not be trusting the media any more, announcing that thanks to 'these painful reactions', he would not be speaking in public other than to say 'the bare minimum'.

To understand the conditions of his return to the national team, it was also important to understand the conditions of his departure.

In August 2004, Zizou had just finished a mentally exhausting Euros at which he had given plenty of himself and received nothing in return. The tense relations within Jacques Santini's squad had demotivated him somewhat. The appointment of Raymond Domenech, instead of Blanc or Deschamps, whom he would have preferred, had confirmed his decision. The initial approach of the new manager, which questioned everyone's status, had undoubtedly also weighed in the balance. Added to this, he had just finished a challenging season without a title win of any kind.

In August 2005, he had been able to take a step back from Les Bleus and put the internal conflict into perspective. With

Real, he began the season in a huge squad, to which Wanderlei Luxemburgo had promised rotations to keep everyone satisfied. He accepted the principle that from time to time, he would stand down for the young Brazilian striker Robinho. This would allow him to keep a better handle on his stress at club level and be more available for the France team.

Above all, he had the desire, strong and renewed by a period of abstinence, to play in blue once again. 'The France team has brought me the best moments of my playing career.'

The comeback was risky. Les Bleus would have a fight on their hands to qualify for the World Cup. Elimination would inevitably affect opinions on Zizou, who had more to lose than to win on the footballing front. 'I needed the France team. It's not about calculations. I worked on my desire, my soul, and what's deep within me.' His words struck the right note.

The announcement of his comeback made the front page of every newspaper. He was returning because he did not want to have any regrets. Because for some months, like everyone who loved Les Bleus, he had been suffering in front of his TV screen, watching them play like shadows of their former selves and struggling against second-rate teams.

'Who could have forgotten in less than a year that Zidane is a genius? Even with his 33-year-old legs [...] He strikes fear into his opponents, like the Z of Zorro,' wrote the daily *L'Alsace*.

The first stop for his comeback was the friendly against Côte d'Ivoire in Montpellier. Zidanemania was in full swing. The organisers recorded a last-minute surge of interest and the few remaining tickets were snapped up in a matter of hours.

The same was true in Lens, where the following match would take place, a World Cup qualifier against the Faroe Islands.

Two days after his announcement, a survey showed that 79 per cent of French people were satisfied with this comeback, with 73 per cent saying – although it was not clear whether the two percentages were linked – that Les Bleus would qualify for the World Cup.

With 9.7 million spectators, Zidane's comeback coincided with the highest television audience during the month of August for 11 years. 'France says thank you,' wrote one Montpellier fan on a banner.

As he came out onto the pitch at the Stade de la Masson, wearing a blue shirt, Zidane said he was 'almost more emotional' than he had been on winning his first cap against the Czech Republic in August 1994. 'When I pulled on the shirt and stepped out onto the turf, I remembered that moment. It was like I'd gone back 11 years.' There was almost talk of a renaissance.

The France team shone that night in Montpellier. With chants of 'Zizou! Zizou!' as the soundtrack, France with their magical number 10 at the helm were reassuring when it came to their level of play, scoring three goals without conceding. The second goal came courtesy of ... Zinedine Zidane, who scored with the inside of his left foot, picking up a corner from the left.

'I tried to get involved as I would have done in the past. I tried to talk to my teammates during the warm-up and in the dressing room, to say something to everyone, so it all went well. The most important thing is winning our World Cup qualifying games. But beating Côte d'Ivoire is good for our confidence,' said Captain Zidane.

Two weeks later, there were two games in quick succession: one not expected to be difficult against the Faroe Islands, then a more concerning visit to Lansdowne Road, where France had never won, against the Republic of Ireland, one of their biggest rivals in the group.

The formality against the Faroe Islands was navigated successfully (3–0). At the same time, Switzerland and Israel could manage only a draw that put Les Bleus in a stronger position. The same could be said of the media chiefs: TF1 had increased its advertising rates by 10 per cent. In other words, depending on the time of broadcast, from €77,000 to €89,000 for 30 seconds, before the match or during half-time.

Yazid returned to Ireland more than 18 years after his first call-up, for the Under-19s, in a delegation led by someone who had since become president of the French Football Federation: Jean-Pierre Escalettes. It was yet another important marker in a very long journey in blue. This time, in a blue tracksuit.

On 7 September, the match in Dublin was far from enjoyable. 'You have to be physically present when you play in Ireland because they really take it to you,' Zidane had rightly judged. From the start of the game, in the inferno of Lansdowne Road, better known by rugby players than footballers, Roy Keane, the side's bad boy, went in on Zizou hard with both feet. 'I saw him coming and said to myself: I'm going to take a hit, but I won't move and we'll win the game.'

Having proved himself physically, he did win that clash but then picked up an injury shortly afterwards, to his thigh and right adductors.

Thanks to the 1–0 win – with a magnificent goal from Thierry Henry – the outlook was getting clearer for Les Bleus and that was the most important thing.

The only shadow on the horizon, besides the injury, was an unwanted hoax. A few hours before the Republic of Ireland–France kick-off, a press officer from the French Football Federation handed his mobile to Zidane and told him the President of France was on the line. Somewhat surprised, Zidane took the call and heard the voice of the head of state enquire as to the team's form. Zizou was astonished. He knew the president was convalescing and still in hospital following a stroke. But he appreciated the concern.

'All is well, Mr President. We're going to try to win.' 'Chirac' then asked him for a 'small favour' for himself and for France; he asked that all the players put their right hand on their chest during *La Marseillaise*. Zidane promised: 'We'll do it.' Before the game, he got his teammates together in the dressing room and told them about this conversation with the president. They all agreed to comply.

A few moments later, on the pitch at Lansdowne Road for the decisive game, France's starting 11, as well as the substitutes and coaching staff, all placed their right hand over their heart. It was quite remarkable, so much so that *Agence France Presse* immediately issued a report.

It was revealed the following day, however, that the call had been a prank carried out by a radio station. The president himself had never called. Amid a political storm, the radio station proudly claimed its questionable 'coup'. 'I just dialled the number of the French Federation and I kept getting put through,' confirmed the impersonator.

The players were embarrassed. 'It's a bit unethical to take advantage of the president's health. It would have been fantastic if it hadn't been for that,' said Jean-Alain Boumsong. 'I don't think it's all that great. It shows a lack of respect towards us and the president,' said Djibril Cissé, adding, however, that the president would have taken it 'as a bit of fun'.

Zinedine Zidane, the primary victim of the joke, failed to see the funny side. He refused to talk about the subject but told his teammates that he did not like the 'commercial aspect' of the call. Once again, once too often, his sincerity had been abused and mockery had ensued, even if he eventually came out of it more popular than ever. He felt as if closing himself off even further was the only option, committing more than ever to his media silence.

Before Switzerland–France, their penultimate qualifying match for the World Cup in Germany, the question was asked: should the France team repeat a gesture that was in itself powerful and binding, even if it had originally been the result of a joke? In the press conference, the captain Zidane refused to answer before discussing it with his teammates. 'We'll see,' he said, while the decision was almost certain. It had already been made: it was a no, so as not to show support for the hoax.

For the decisive game in Bern, Zizou took to the pitch having played barely 30 minutes for Real since his injury.

If they won, France would qualify. They would still be in with a chance if they drew, but would no longer be masters of their own destiny. Defeat would consign them, at best, to the play-offs.

Zidane confirmed he was 100 per cent fit. 'I've only played for half an hour, but when you have the desire and the mindset, it's not necessarily the most important thing to have lots of training sessions and games in your legs. I didn't train with the squad but I'll be there. We're ready to win!' The French coaching team were not necessarily keen on seeing Zidane in the starting 11: there was some concern that he may not be able to stand up to the physicality of the Swiss and that it might be better to change the system by playing without him. After all, in the home match, Les Bleus had dominated Switzerland before his return, even if the result had been a goalless draw.

In the end, he played. In the absence of Henry and Trezeguet, he was one of the few players capable of changing the course of the game. The psychological impact on his teammates, even on his opponents, was taken into account, as well as his physical fitness. The result was a lacklustre 1–1 draw. France would need to win their final match against Cyprus and hope Switzerland did not beat the Republic of Ireland in Dublin.

On 12 October, against Cyprus at the Stade de France, Les Bleus kept banging their heads against a consolidated defence. Neither Cissé, Wiltord nor Govou could break the deadlock. It would be down to Zidane. On the end of a cross from Sagnol, he opened the scoring in the 29th minute after a fine piece of control and a shot from the left of the box.

Les Bleus won 4–0, one goal less than the gap required for qualification regardless of other results that evening. But Switzerland could only manage a draw with the Republic of Ireland.

France had qualified for the World Cup! For the first time in 20 years, they had emerged from the qualifying phase victorious. The last two times they had played, in 1998 and 2002, had been thanks to their successive status as host country then as previous champions. In both 1990 and 1994, they had failed to qualify.

Curiously, Zizou stood on his own in the centre circle after the game, with his head lowered and no apparent sign of celebration. He left the ground and flew back to Madrid. Without saying a word to the press.

A few days later, he admitted he was still struggling with the media criticism he had received after the game against Switzerland. He also pointed out that the important win had come against the

Republic of Ireland, and that there was no reason to get overexcited after beating Cyprus at home. But he neglected to say that he also had bad memories of his last visits to the Stade de France, of the match against the Czech Republic in particular. France had lost 2–0 on 12 February 2003. Unusually, Zidane had not been spared by the whistles that day. A reminder that the fickleness of fans could even affect a player of his stature, a living legend.

The next objective was the World Cup in Germany. He was thinking about it optimistically: 'We can win it. We have the means to do it.' He also answered with a joke when asked about his return to the France team: 'It's like I never left!'

13

TIME TO LEAVE

1.88 metres (6 feet 2 inches) tall, in shoes; 68 centimetres (27 inches) along the folded arms; 46 centimetres (18 inches) from shoulder to shoulder; 106 centimetres (42 inches) around the waist; 104 centimetres (41 inches) around the chest: these are the vital statistics of the Madrid Wax Museum's version of Zinedine Zidane. Immortalised as a statue during his lifetime.

Already a star at Juventus, he entered a new dimension during his stint at Real. He not only added to his title record, with one Spanish championship and one Champions League, but, most importantly, he entered the imaginary and almost impenetrable club of legendary players, objects of fascination for fans and advertising agencies alike.

Prior to 2001, his fame was at its height in France, but he had now become a worldwide star of the round-ball game. If he wanted to avoid being assailed by autograph hunters or onlookers keen to take photos or simply to give him a friendly pat on the back, he now had to take his holidays in far-flung destinations, or in the United States, where football's popularity was still limited.

He was not all that comfortable with this level of fame, to which he had never aspired: 'There are good and bad things about celebrity. When it comes down to it, I never forget where I've come from and I always think about what's really important.'

Enjoying an annual income estimated at around €12 million – €6 million in wages from Real, plus €6 million from advertising revenue – he had achieved relative control over commercial, media and advertising demands, showing himself to be generous, where necessary, either by making donations or paying from his own pocket.

An ambassador, alongside Ronaldo, for the United Nations Development Programme (UNDP), he had visited children in hospital during his Christmas holidays in Réunion. He continued to sponsor the European Leukodystrophies Association and the struggle against poverty, and participated in charity matches to benefit flood victims, against drugs or for those affected by both the explosion of the AZF factory in France and earthquakes in Algeria.

Sometimes insecure in the company of adults, he becomes affable and spontaneous around children. He knows how to find the right words when talking to those who are ill. More than in albeit necessary marketing campaigns, his generosity is practised on a daily basis, far from the cameras.

After one particular Real Madrid defeat, the club's players and coaching staff marched past stern-faced without stopping to speak to the waiting journalists or club guests, insufficiently important for the VIP room but still influential enough to get past certain barriers.

When a couple with a Down's syndrome child tried timidly to call out to the players, only three of them noticed and stopped to speak to them: Raúl, Roberto Carlos and Zidane. Zinedine smiled, signed the boy's shirt, shook his hand and agreed to be photographed with his hand on the boy's shoulder.

Another young French Zidane fan suffering from a degenerative disease dreamed of seeing Real play. His father made the journey with him to attend the game. He also tried unsuccessfully to contact Zidane to find out if he would sign an autograph for him after the match. But some journalists got word to Zizou, who went one better than an autograph. He invited the boy and his father to attend a Real training session, took the time to chat with them a little and even came out of the dressing room with a gift: a Real shirt, signed by him and all his teammates. Before agreeing to meet the child, he only had one condition: no cameras or media coverage. This was the logical consequence of a behaviour that had remained unchanged since his days in Cannes and his very first pay cheques; since the first markers of fame, even if he was now better at managing a world populated by those who were often not what they claimed to be. 'I try to remember that I was a kid once too. I remember I would have loved to have had autographs or shirts signed by Francescoli. If I can give some of that, then I have to do it,' explained the star, who never refuses an autograph to a child.

Unfortunately for the media and fans who would have loved to see him appear on talk shows, read interviews in the papers every day or find out the slightest detail about his sporting and private life, Zidane built a shell around himself to avoid unnecessary demands and, most importantly, the fatigue and pressure that resulted from them. Too bad for the 50 or so interview requests that arrived every month at Real; too bad for his popularity with reporters trying to snatch meetings; too bad for the businessmen or companies without sufficient economic weight, or in an industry with which he preferred not to associate his image.

This scene witnessed at the Ciudad Deportiva provides a good example:

'Zinedine, can you give me a quick half-hour?'

'No, as I've already said, I only do press conferences now.'

'I've come all the way from Paris just to see you.'

'Like I said, no interviews.'

'That's really not cool, man.'

'What gives you the right to speak to me like that? We don't know each other. I don't owe you anything. I never promised you anything. You have no right to demand things and then insult me.'

Exchanges with journalists from France, Italy and beyond who came to see Zidane at Real could sometimes be tense. It was as if most of them had yet to understand the extent of the Zizou phenomenon.

The time he devoted to the media was extremely limited, except for a small circle of journalists, most of whom had known him for a long time, and except of course for Canal+, a channel with which he was under contract.

He would attend a press conference for Spanish journalists once a month or every two months. As soon as the date came, a crowd would form. It was always an event. Zinedine would see to it that the few French correspondents living in Madrid were not disappointed, without making more appearances than he needed to, however.

In the same way, he did not like to talk publicly about politics. Whenever a question on that subject was asked, he would be elusive or answer that it was not his place to talk about such things.

Despite his status as a superstar, Zidane did not live in an ivory tower on the outskirts of Madrid. He would regularly visit restaurants but had to take care every time to not cause a riot. He loved life in Madrid: 'I think I'll stay in Madrid after I've retired from the sport,' he said, in line with something he had remembered humorously during an interview with teammate Ivan Helguera: 'In Italy, I was in my pyjamas by 7pm, then in bed by 11pm. We live very well in Madrid. We live very well in Spain. I like seeing shows or going to the cinema. I also like flamenco. There are lots of things about Madrid that appeal to me.'

Castile was also where two of his four children had been born: Théo in May 2002; Elyaz, a Christmas present, on 26 December 2005. Elyaz? 'The Yaz' in Spanish?

On 15 January 2006, it was the turn of Zizou to give a gift: three of them. Three goals in one game for the first time in his very long career. Scored in the 19th match of La Liga season, against Sevilla, the best defence in the league. Despite this, Real's players were not happy as they returned from their Christmas break. Results were not good. Juan Ramon Lopez Caro, the manager called upon to replace Wanderlei Luxemburgo, was not a charismatic leader and the season began to look like the previous one: devoid of a title. On 15 January, Real welcomed Sevilla to a full stadium, however. It was a heavyweight clash: Sevilla were a big club with a good team; they would even go on to win the UEFA Cup later that year. The Madrid team got off to a lively start and opened the scoring in the seventh minute through Guti, on the end of a left-footed pass from Zinedine Zidane. Sevilla equalised, but in the 58th minute, Real's former Sevilla player Julio Baptista was fouled in the box. Zidane converted the penalty to hand the advantage back to the Madrid team. Less than two minutes later, after a wonderful backheel from Guti, Zidane once again got the better of Palop. Sevilla came back to 3–2 in the 84th minute and began to lay siege to Real's goal, consequentially stripping their own of its back line. Zidane took advantage in injury time to round off an exceptional performance.

Despite this individual effort, the atmosphere at Real continued to deteriorate. Barely a month later, the president Florentino Perez announced his resignation and was replaced by Fernando Martin. The news caught everyone off-guard, including Zidane, who was with France at Clairefontaine preparing for a friendly against Slovakia that ended in a 2–1 defeat, his only setback between his Bleus comeback and his last official match. 'First of all, it's a big surprise and no one was expecting it. I'm obviously surprised, but it's a decision he must have thought about carefully. Signing for Real is one of the best things that's ever happened to me. And without him I wouldn't have been able to, so I've got great memories of that,' said Zidane. Nonetheless, he did not forget that the president had once had an unfortunate formula: '*Zidanes y Pavones*' (Zidanes and Pavons), to differentiate the stars from young players trained by the club, Francisco Pavon being one of them.

'It's a shame he said that because there's no doubt it divided us within the squad. Our problem came from the fact that there were a lot of different personalities and some players with big personalities as well; it's possible there was a lack of communication.' However, he did say he was not yet thinking about retirement: 'I still have a year and three months left on my contract. Let's get through these three months, prepare for a great World Cup and then we'll see.'

Two weeks later, Real, who had lost 1–0 to Arsenal in the last 16 of the Champions League at the Santiago-Bernabeu, were unable to reverse the deficit in London. Lopez Caro had left all the young players on the bench and the newspapers took pot-shots at the 'old guard'. 'The kilos and the years are weighing them down,' said *Marca*, while all the newspapers criticised the older players: Ronaldo, Beckham and Zidane. Zinedine began to draw his own conclusions from this oppressive atmosphere.

Top of La Liga was out of reach, given that Barça were showing no signs of weakness.

Zizou was regularly carrying injuries and struggled increasingly to motivate himself for training sessions, especially when he was not enjoying his time on the pitch.

On 25 April, the Cadena Ser radio station broke a scoop: Zidane was reported to have told Real Madrid's president, coaches and team captains (Raúl, Guti and Roberto Carlos) that he was going to 'hang up his boots' after the World Cup. He would give up the last year of his contract. As had become his habit, the following day, Zizou announced his retirement from the sport on Canal+: 'I'm going to stop playing football after the World Cup. It might seem a bit strange to announce it now, two weeks from the end of the league season and 53 days before the World Cup, but it's a decision I've been thinking about carefully and I had to take it before the World Cup. It's something that's been in my head for a while and I wanted to get it off my mind,' he explained. 'I can't come to the end of the World Cup knowing that there will be three weeks of holiday and say: "OK, I'm done. I'm stopping playing and you've got to look for someone else now." It was an important thing that I wanted to do for the club, so they can find a player. Most of all, I think it's my body. I told myself I cannot carry on for another year,' he continued, with another argument. 'It's been two years now that the results haven't been there. Everyone knows the importance of results at a club like Madrid. Once you have objectives that are not reached, you ask yourself the question. I don't want to start a third year knowing that I won't be able to do better than I've done in the past. I'm getting to an age where it's getting harder and harder. I don't want to start another year and for it to be like this one, or even two years ago.'

Zidane would now focus on 'his' last World Cup: 'I needed to say it, so I could focus on this World Cup and only that. It's my last objective and the only thing I want to think about. This is a final decision. Although I decided a year ago to come back to the France team, the context was different. I was still playing for Real Madrid. Now, I'm stopping for good and I'm stopping everything. I might get an amateur licence, but that's up to me. But professionally and at the top level, that's my decision[…]. It feels like a weight off my mind. It feels as if I'm saying to myself: "There you go, you've still got the World Cup." I wanted everyone to know beforehand so they don't ask me the thousands of questions you ask when there are doubts. When I'm at the World Cup, now I'll only be asked questions about the World Cup, about the France team and what we need to do, not about what I'm going to do next season. I couldn't do it any more.'

A few days later, he attended a packed press conference. Journalists from all over the world were in attendance. He underlined how tired he was feeling:

There are five or six titles to be won every year and it's not possible to win them all. But it hurts when you don't win any. It's better to stop. It's been two years now that I haven't been playing like I want to. And I'm not 25 any more. Every day, it's a bit tougher. And I don't want to be there just for the sake of it. When I signed my contract extension, I only wanted to sign for one more year. But Florentino Perez told me he wanted me to sign for two years. Football has given me everything. There are two main things in my life: my family and football. I've done my best to make people happy. For me, football is everything. My teammates asked me not to stop, to stay at least another year. I felt a bit bad. I have three matches left to play with Real Madrid. They're important matches for the club because we're still playing for second place. Let's hope I'll get to play in ten more matches!

Ten matches? Three with Real and seven with the France team … provided they reached the World Cup final.

What would Zidane do after his retirement? Manage? 'Never say never, but for the time being, it's a no.' However, he did not hide his interest in young people, children. 'I've spoken with the president and we have a plan to do something with children. I'm giving up football but I would like to continue my relationship with Real Madrid. It's something we're discussing. I'd like to give back to kids what football has given me. I'd like to stay in Spain; maybe not for the rest of my life, but for now.'

Reactions flooded in from around the world. Zico, who shared perspective, collective and individual genius with Zidane, said that it was a 'great loss to football because he is such an important player. I admire him enormously. We always want players like him to continue playing as long as they can to inspire future generations.' The Real manager, Juan Ramon Lopez Caro, said that he was 'without a doubt the best player in the world. Zizou is an example to be followed, even down to the way he walks.'

Diego Maradona even hoped to convince him to reconsider his decision: 'I will see him at the World Cup and I'll talk to him. I'll ask him to keep playing, not to retire, because we don't love him for the cups he's won but because of how he plays and how he has made us enjoy football. I respect his decision but I can't agree with him. Seeing someone who has given so much joy to the world of football retire makes all those who love the round ball sad. Zidane is a master. Watching him control the ball with his long body is the most amazing thing. Zidane is one of those players who make people happy.'

Real Madrid's fans respected his decision: they appreciated the dignity of Zidane, who had given up €6 million not to play one season too many. They preferred to remember the joy he had brought them during his years in Madrid. They gave him a triumphal farewell at the Santiago-Bernabeu. He had undoubtedly given these fans his finest years, pieces of control and passes that would linger long in the collective memory.

A week after being hailed by Racing's fans in Santander, Zizou bid farewell to Real Madrid's home fans on 7 May against Villareal, who were in a tussle with Real for a Champions League place. Giant screens broadcast the Frenchman's finest moves in a white shirt before the game. The montage ended with his volley against Leverkusen in the Champions League final ... given an ovation by 80,000 fans!

When he came out onto the pitch, the crowd held up huge photos of him that had been distributed by the club. Applauded every time he touched the ball at the start of the game, both he and his teammates still had to endure the whistles of dissatisfied fans at half-time. But in the 66th minute, it was he who scored a goal to appease them, with his head, as seemed to be the case on so many big occasions. Despite the final score, 3–3, he was given an ovation.

In front of his family, in front of Malek, in front of the fans chanting 'Zizou! Zizou!' and holding up posters saying '*Gracias Zizou!*' he began to sob. Too moved to speak, he applauded and refused to talk to any journalists.

His final professional club game came the following week on 16 May in Seville. It was not a gala match there either as Real were not yet assured of second place in La Liga or automatic Champions League qualification. They were under threat from Valencia. Sevilla could also still qualify, provided Osasuna lost. The atmosphere was tense in the Sanchez-Pizjuan stadium. The Andalusian fans had no qualms about whistling Zidane, just as they whistled every star who came to play in Seville.

Was Zizou's head already elsewhere? 'Distracted, Real's playmaker almost missed his final pre-match photograph with his teammates, who had already scattered across the pitch when he showed up a little late. On protests from the assembled photographers, Zidane called the *galacticos* back for a second picture with the whole team,' reported the *Agence France Presse* correspondent.

Zizou's 506th league game ended in a 4–3 defeat and a somewhat unspectacular goal in the 66th minute. His ninth of the season. His last at club level.

Those who wanted to see Zidane play football in a Real Madrid shirt for a little while longer would have to go to the cinema. *Zidane: a 21st Century Portrait*, by the visual artists Philippe Parreno and Douglas Gordon, followed the player in real time over the course of a single match against Villareal in 2005. Seventeen cameras focused only on him ... until his sending-off. Among them, two unique ultramodern zooms used by the American army. The film was selected for the Cannes Film Festival in 2016, where it would be screened alongside another documentary in which Zidane appeared: *Une équipe de rêve* (A Dream Team).

This second feature film did not focus on the player but had been shot with his participation and was still of sufficient interest to a wider public, film fans included. *Une équipe de rêve* previewed during Critics' Week, a longer-established selection running parallel to the Cannes Film Festival. However, it was *Zidane: a 21st Century Portrait* – screened out of competition and promoted by the player – that was the Zidane event most highly anticipated by movie-goers. But not necessarily by football enthusiasts.

An aesthetic and technological feat, the film provided an interesting insight into the life of a star footballer. However, many spectators were disappointed, confused by an unexpectedly conceptual approach.

With a smaller budget but more feeling, *Une équipe de rêve* did not only feature one body, but 11 souls, those of Zinedine and ten men reunited 15 years after their lives together as apprentice footballers at the Logis des Jeunes in Cannes. Unswervingly linked to them all, Yazid – whom none of them addressed other than by his diminutive, Yaz – agreed to take part in the filming, which retraced destinies light years away from his own and implicitly suggested the star system had its limits and could be cruel. The former trainees were filmed one by one for two years as they went about their daily lives, far removed from the world of professional football, with which some of them had had brushes. Frédéric Dufau had become a caretaker at a municipal swimming pool; Éric Giacopino ran an ambulance company and Fabrice Monachino a security firm. Denis Armbruster worked in a perfumery; Jojot Moussa-Madi was a paramedic after having been a policeman and Gilles Hampartzoumian was experiencing a period of transition.

At each of the film's three screenings in Cannes, the reaction was the same: rapt attention to Yazid's words; silence when Franck Gomez talked about his regrets; tenderness when Noureddine Mouka described his disappointments with successive clubs; and spontaneous affection for the touching story of Michel Almandoz, the goalkeeper who had suffered a serious injury.

The audience applauded. *Une équipe de rêve* was seen as a film in the image of Zidane, full of sincere emotions and simplicity.

Symbolically, it was screened one final time at La Bocca. Jean Fernandez was in hospital and could not attend. But Guy Lacombe was there, loyal to his former trainees. After the film, David Bettoni had some strong words to say: 'Football is good. But an education is better.' Many are called upon but few are chosen. The 'chosen one' was getting ready to leave for a training camp with Les Bleus at Tignes and had warned them he would not be able to make it to the festival.

For the filming of some of the scenes in *Une équipe de rêve*, Zizou had met with his ten friends in Madrid two and a half months earlier, in March. The film crew and its cast stayed in the hotel where Real's players would meet before their matches. Immersed in the heart of top-flight football, the luxury hotel was bustling with Real's stars at a time when there was plenty going on at the club, including Fernando Martin's installation as president.

In the muted atmosphere of the lobby, Gilles Hampartzoumian, the last of the 11 friends to arrive, livened things up by shouting: 'Where's Beckham?! Tell him we're here!'

Eleven friends together for the first time in 15 years. The reunion was emotional. Despite the Madrid derby against Atlético, Yazid generously made himself available. For a moment the Madrid star became the carefree kid of the Foyer Mimont once more. He was delighted, as well as visibly moved: 'It's like going back in time.'

14

ONE FINAL CHALLENGE

'*Allez les vieux!*' (Come on, old guys!) was used to encourage Les Bleus in the weeks leading up to the Germany World Cup. The joyless and goalless elimination in 2002 had made people wary of getting overexcited. This memory was now paired with a number of additional factors that included the team's struggle to qualify – despite the return of the supposed saviours Zizou, Thuram and Makelele – the albeit not unusual criticism of the squad of 23 players, their above-average age, and their manager, the much-maligned Raymond Domenech.

Despite his past achievements, the press voiced doubts about Zidane's ability to play again at the highest level. Thanks to the niggling injuries he was carrying, his final performances at Real Madrid had not been sharp. Had he been taking it easy over recent months in order to give himself the best possible farewell? Had he cruised through his final matches in Spain to be fully fit for the World Cup and avoid the problems he had faced in 2002? It would have been understandable. In 2002, after a marathon season of more than 70 matches, topped off by the Champions League, he had arrived at the World Cup in Asia tired, picking up an injury against South Korea just before the start of the competition.

The 2006 World Cup adventure began on 19 May at the ski resort of Tignes, with a training camp for the players called up. It was there that Zidane and his teammates had come together in 1998 and the atmosphere was somewhat similar. Like Aimé Jacquet, Raymond Domenech was criticised by the press and the 'silent majority' thought Les Bleus' performances had been mediocre.

The 23 featured the surprise presence of Pascal Chimbonda – with no previous caps to his credit but an excellent season in England with Wigan that had earned him the official title of best right-back in the Premier League – but, most importantly, the absence of Ludovic Giuly, Nicolas Anelka, Johan Micoud, Robert Pires and Olivier Dacourt. The most widely discussed choice did not concern a specific call-up but the role of Barthez as first-choice keeper.

Close to Barthez, this was something Zidane had lobbied for. Despite performances over previous seasons that had sometimes been judged as not up to scratch, he still considered him, at a tournament at least, to be the best goalkeeper in the world. The question of his place in the starting 11 despite the all-encompassing media coverage of Grégory Coupet – the remarkable goalkeeper for French champions Olympique Lyonnais – would not have been asked, or at least not so often, had Barthez not been banned for six months for spitting at a referee during a friendly for Olympique de Marseille in Morocco.

The coaching staff had planned a roped ascent of the Grande-Motte Glacier to help with team bonding. They were attached to each other, literally. In the event of a fall, those left standing would hold up their fallen teammate. It was symbolic, even if the glacier was hardly a Himalayan or even an Alpine peak.

But the atmosphere was far from idyllic. Fabien Barthez, who was not in the physical shape of his teammates, dropped out during the climb. He was late for lunch. It was all too much for Grégory Coupet. The Lyon keeper thought Barthez was being given special treatment and showed no respect for the rules with which the rest of the squad had to comply.

Coupet left. He even took the same route back, with his wife and children! Robert Duverne, the Olympique Lyonnais physical trainer then also with the France team, called his mobile and convinced him to backtrack.

Zidane commented soberly on the incident: 'It's good that it happened then and not later on.' The group could have imploded, but ultimately it brought them closer together. This unity would become even stronger in the days that followed. France–Mexico was played two weeks before the start of the World Cup. The stage was familiar, the Stade de France, where Zizou had scored the goal in the stadium's inaugural match, where he had performed so many exhilarating and memorable feats, and where he had played his last game. His hundredth cap for France.

But anniversaries and celebrations were put on the back burner. He was there to prepare. Substituted in the 52nd minute by Vikash Dhorasoo, he delivered an average, no-frills performance. Although he was given an ovation as he came off, several players were whistled by certain sections of the fans for various reasons: Vikash Dhorasoo, Djibril Cissé and, above all, Fabien Barthez. The whole team, Zidane in particular, was hurt by this. The darling of the Stade de France, who had quietly left the field after the qualifying match against Cyprus, had hoped for a reconciliation between the Parisian fans and Les Bleus.

In the dressing room, the whistles hit home. Les Bleus, who had been criticised, and perhaps rightly so, by the press for not signing enough autographs in Tignes, turned inward. The outside world was hostile; solidarity was starting to emerge within the squad. Just as it had in 1998.

'Live together, die together,' the phrase that had been Les Bleus' rallying call throughout the 1998 World Cup, was resurrected. It was of prime importance because, at least in terms of results, France were still unconvincing: 2–0 against Denmark in Lens; 3–1 against China in Saint-Étienne, a match that also had plenty of drama. Cissé was brought down, grimacing in pain, with a broken right leg and was eventually replaced in the squad by the Olympique Lyonnais player Sydney Govou. And something else happened. Something more anecdotal but previously unheard of: Zidane missed a penalty, slipping just as he was about to kick the ball!

The following day, the French delegation left for their World Cup base, a five-star hotel in a late 16th-century castle: the Schlosshotel Münchhausen in Hameln, near Hanover. This village in north-western Germany owes its fame to a legend: in the Middle Ages, the Pied Piper is said to have bewitched and drowned the town's rats before doing the same with Hameln's – or Hamelin's – children when its villagers refused to honour their debts. Sceptical journalists and pundits had a field day with this story, as well as the name Münchhausen – reminiscent of the adventures of the wacky fictional baron of the same name – and the presence of an 18-hole golf course at the hotel. Zidane and France had booked their rooms until 8 July, the night before the final in Berlin. FIFA required teams to spend the night before a game in the city where the match would take place.

The objective was 9 July, the day of the final. Raymond Domenech repeated this over and over, to general incredulity, sometimes even sarcasm.

In the meantime, they had to get out of Group G, which also included Switzerland, South Korea and Togo.

Les Bleus were working hard, on tactics and fitness in particular. They had learned physical lessons from the disaster of 2002. For the first time in the history of French football, a physical trainer was hired for the World Cup. Another new component, he was not part of the 'inner circle', namely the National Technical Direction (DTN).

Robert Duverne, an Olympique Lyonnais employee, was at the top of his profession. 'We worked hard, under the guidance of the trainer,' explained Zizou. 'He took the risk of getting us in shape for the last 16,' and not for the group matches, although France had not even managed to get that far in 2002.

Tactically, the issue was more complex. Relations between Domenech and Zizou were not good. The captain had never publicly criticised his manager, but he did not think much of him. As for Domenech, he admired the player but was not fond of the fact that certain individuals, including the stars, were given priority at the expense of the group. But they had to work together, communicating and exchanging views.

Domenech listened to Zidane on certain topics, but he also took decisions that went against what the player wanted. Barthez would play in goal, but the two strikers the captain wanted, Henry and Trezeguet, did not feature in the manager's plans.

Domenech felt that France had never played its best football with its two stars up front. At the same time, he was mulling over the idea of Ribéry, the Marseille player who was aggressive, quick and attacking. He could take up a position in midfield, coming forward to offer solutions in space opened up by Henry.

'We needed to be more defensive, so we could be more confident,' Zidane said afterwards on Canal+.

When it came to communication, the manager gave carte blanche to the leaders of his squad and its star. What if Zizou did not want to talk to the media? There was no obligation, Domenech said.

The players appeared very rarely in front of the press, creating a certain resentment towards them on the part of the journalists.

What happened in the dressing room was also considered secret. Nothing was supposed to filter out. Most of the players respected these instructions. And the squad continued to bond.

On the pitch, Zidane and Henry even took on defensive tasks, putting their past differences behind them, especially those of Euro 2004.

In Portugal – where he only took on the captaincy when Marcel Desailly was not playing – Zizou had gathered the players around him during the France–Croatia game. In Germany, his role as a leader would be less visible, less spectacular, but more consistent and important. Before every game, he would make a speech in the dressing room. On the pitch, he did not hesitate to scold the defenders William Gallas or even Lilian Thuram, to put Franck Ribéry and Florent Malouda in their place or to discuss positioning with his friend Claude Makelele.

France finally began their World Cup on 13 June, after following four days of unbridled competition on television. The Tricolores' first game, in Stuttgart, had a look of déjà vu: Switzerland, their main rivals in qualification, stood in their way once again.

The priority was not to concede. Against a Swiss team even more defensively minded than Les Bleus – playing in white, a colour they would use through most of the tournament – the game was far from a festival of football.

France dominated but were unconvincing, with a Zidane who, although not at his worst, was not decisive. But he could have been, with two high-quality passes and a looping flick to Ribéry with the tip of his foot.

However, Les Bleus' performance was nothing to be ashamed of. Lilian Thuram explained: 'The team showed a responsible attitude on the pitch. Just look at how tight our defensive substitutes were. It was nothing like Euro 2004.'

But the French press were not convinced and could see the spectre of 2002 looming. 'Zinedine Zidane and his team missed their cue at the World Cup,' wrote *L'Équipe*, which was far from being the only newspaper to be pessimistic, some much more so. There was talk elsewhere of 'mediocrity', 'a lack of play', 'collapse', and 'non-existent inspiration'.

The players were unhappy with this criticism, which they considered unfair. But confidence grew within the squad. Zidane and Thuram, thanks to their experience in both 1998 and 2002, calmed the nerves of some of their teammates, who were already overwhelmed by worry.

They had to look forward to their next matches. All of which, from now on, would have a particular connotation for Zinedine Zidane.

The game against South Korea, on 18 June in Leipzig, was top of the list. It was in Korea that Zizou had been injured in 2002, before a World Cup that was all about suffering and helplessness as far as he was concerned.

It started well, with a goal from Thierry Henry in the ninth minute. But somewhat disconcerted by the disallowing of a valid goal scored by Vieira – the referee thought the ball had not crossed the line – Les Bleus wanted to guarantee all three points but failed to take the initiative.

Park exploited their inefficiency to equalise in the 81st minute. Although superior, the French then began to work hard at regaining their advantage. Zidane demonstrated the depth of his determination by winning the ball and slipping it to Henry. It was a great chance, but Henry tripped over the keeper Lee Woon-Jae, who was then brought down by Zidane as he went after the ball on the rebound. It was a foul. Yellow card.

'If the second goal had been given as it should have, it would have been 2–0 and we would have been in a good position. After that, we were always at risk of conceding a goal and when we did in the end, it knocked us a little. We didn't play as well in the second half. We stopped pressing, stopped doing what we'd been doing well in the first half because our fitness had dropped a bit,' was the analysis of the captain, who would not stay on the pitch until the final whistle.

After this second card, more justified than the first – received against Switzerland for having taken a free kick too quickly – Zidane knew he would be suspended for the next game: France–Togo.

Domenech added insult to injury by substituting him two minutes from the end with Trezeguet, who also took the captain's armband. It was astonishing.

Zinedine left the pitch with a face like thunder, refused to look at his bench and threw the sweatband he was wearing around his wrist to the ground.

One Leipzig stadium official even went so far as to attempt a 'publicity stunt' that drew as much attention as the much-discussed substitution. He claimed Zidane had damaged a door by kicking it in anger; the door would apparently be kept as it was 'as a memory of one of the greatest footballers of all time', but, according to several witnesses, the kick never happened and the door had already been in a terrible state before the game!

This anecdote speaks volumes about the scrutiny forced upon the superstar of world football for almost ten years.

More seriously, the tension was mounting between the manager and his captain, who, since his return to the French team, had never mentioned his name in public. But Domenech would attempt to explain the controversial substitution by claiming he was 'looking to the next game' – without Zidane – while pretending not to have noticed the player's icy stare.

For his part, Zizou kept his cool. Despite being upset, he did not let himself get carried away and put forward a credible argument: 'I was sad and annoyed because we needed to win all three points. I wasn't going to come off with a smile on my face, high-fiving my teammates like it was a good result. I'm fine.'

The media had a field day after this result. *Le Parisien-Aujourd'hui en France* summed up the general feeling with a huge '*Nul*' (meaning both 'drawn' and 'rubbish') on the front page, referring both to the draw and the quality of their team's football.

Zidane was suspended against Togo. Some quarters of the press even went so far as to describe it as 'lucky', saying he would not be missed and that it was an opportunity to build without him. Forgetting a little too quickly that two of his passes could have, or should have, proved decisive.

Abroad, there was talk that Zidane's career might come to an end in a farce.

9 July? Domenech had still not forgotten the final in Berlin, but his comments were roundly mocked.

The players remained united. Florent Malouda said Les Bleus would give 'Zidane qualification as a present', as the France–Togo game would be played on his 34th birthday. Willy Sagnol, a close friend of Zizou, recalled: 'Zidane was suspended in

1998 as well and France went all the way.' Zinedine himself was convinced: 'The whole team is looking further ahead. We're going to suffer in the first round but after that we still have a long way to go. We're convinced of it. I have faith in my teammates.'

Faith in them? Maybe. Faith in the coaching team? That was less certain. All the players, and only the players, had a meeting to talk for several hours. To bond around a rallying call: 'We live together, we die together.' The scene took place outside the castle. A band of knights outside an inn: it was the stuff of movies and heroes, chosen by fate. They did not yet know the surprises the script of life had in store for them.

Zidane apologised to his teammates. Before France–Togo, he behaved like a leader and, despite being suspended, met his teammates in the dressing room to give his usual pre-match speech. Was he shy or expansive? Had he metamorphosed or did he stay faithful to himself? Had he rediscovered the 'talkative' side so criticised by one of his teachers back in Cannes? When he was comfortable with his arguments and surroundings, was he capable, at least in the short term, of being a rousing speaker?

In front of the cameras for *Une équipe de rêve*, the late Robert Centenero from Septèmes-les-Vallons had said that the boy had a 'more forceful personality'. Discreet but strong. In 2006, experience, self-confidence and success finally allowed him to show who he really is: a leader.

As the France team came out onto the pitch, the media were searching desperately for Zidane, for whom every match could now potentially be his last. He was not in the stands, nor on the bench, something that is normally prohibited in the case of a suspension, except in the event of a special dispensation.

In the company of Éric Abidal, who was also suspended, he chose to watch the game on television in the dressing room as a way of being close to his teammates and far from the media. At half-time, he congratulated his teammates, with the scoreline still at 0–0, and reiterated his faith in them. The chances were there, they just needed to improve their finishing. During the first half, there had been plenty of low-flying missiles, thrown in frustration by the two watching players at every missed opportunity.

Forty-five minutes later, France, victorious by 2–0, returned to the dressing room with the best of birthday presents for Zizou: qualification. Patrick Vieira, who had played a key part in the victory, could also celebrate his 30th birthday in style.

They had needed to beat the decidedly non-threatening Togo by two goals. They had done it, indirectly helped by the Swiss who had beaten South Korea, robbing them of first place in the group in the process.

Nonetheless, Les Bleus' objective had been achieved. Their objective and perhaps something extra for the soul of the team: 'Something happened at half-time,' said Sagnol.

Once again, Raymond Domenech mentioned 9 July. It still seemed a long way off.

France's football-watching public were relieved. One man would not see qualification, however: Jean Varraud, whose life was coming to an end. He died in the early morning, the day after the match.

As one man passed away, another was coming to the end of his career. It was the end of an era. This symbolism had not escaped Madame Zidane, Yazid's mother, when she had learned that the scout from Cannes had been taken ill. She did not want to tell her son about it straight away, just as he had not told her about the tears he had cried into his pillow in Pégomas.

None of his relatives told Zizou the news. They did not want to upset him. But despite the players' isolation, it was hard to imagine that the information, picked up on quickly by the media, would not reach him soon. He found out the following day from a former Cannes teammate. Zidane said nothing in public as to his thoughts or glances up to the sky, which some observers thought were not entirely aimed at the stadium's big screen.

After finishing second in their group, France would play Spain in the last 16. Spain, where Zidane lived and had been playing for five years. Spain, where he wanted to stay. Spain, the nation of his Real teammates: Sergio Ramos, Casillas, Michel Salgado and especially Raúl.

For Les Bleus, it was double or quits. Elimination and the World Cup would have been a failure; qualification and they might face a pressure-free quarter-final. It was likely the winners would play Brazil, the logical favourites for the competition having won four years earlier and now facing a Ghana without their suspended key player, Michael Essien, in their last-16 game.

The France team returned to Hameln with a conquering mindset. Zidane, Makelele, Sagnol and Barthez continued to meet for quiet chats away from the training sessions. They were calm. Les Bleus were more motivated than ever, relieved at having avoided an unthinkable disaster.

In knockout games, you need solid morale and nerves, which are acquired in part through experience. Many of the French players were accustomed to tense matches. Most of them played for big European clubs and in the Champions League year in, year out. During qualification, they had also played several matches of this kind, including the narrow victory in Ireland, followed by the draw in Switzerland.

The Spanish were delighted to be facing an ageing opponent whose forces were on the wane. France had not played well in the group stage, with only one win against Togo and two draws. Spain, on the other hand, had been largely convincing, beating Ukraine, Tunisia and Saudi Arabia. Three clear victories in three games, giving them, probably a little too quickly, the unusual status of favourites.

Their manager Luis Aragones kept his starting 11 fresh by regularly leaving out Raúl and the two 'older' players Abelda and Marchena.

'We're going to send Zidane into retirement', *Marca* even dared with its headline.

Would it be the end? Zidane thought about it carefully. He did not want to leave anything to chance and had brought with him a shirt on which were written words of thanks to the people who had helped him throughout his career. He planned to wear it if France lost. He would tell this anecdote on Canal+ once the World Cup was over. 'That shirt helped me a lot. It was in my bag, but it didn't want to come out!'

The Spanish would not get to see it. The stadium in Hanover was located about 50km from France's base. It was a short journey, but one full of expectation. Les Bleus were eager to confront their young and arrogant adversaries.

On 27 June, as always, Zidane looked very serious as *La Marseillaise* rang out, heartily whistled by the Spanish fans. He did, however, greet his former Real teammates, including Raúl, who was back in the starting 11.

The two men, who lived in the same part of Madrid, were both captains of their teams, but it was Zizou who was wearing the same colour shirt as Real that night. Les Bleus were playing in white again.

The Spanish took the lead in the 28th minute, courtesy of a penalty from David Villa. But as the minutes ticked by, the France team and Zinedine Zidane became bolder. Their Madrid playmaker was having a very good day. He distributed the play well, was successful in his dribbling sequences and feints, and fumbled hardly any pieces of control.

Ribéry equalised before half-time. It was 1–1 at the break. In the second half, Zizou played masterfully, like the 'Maestro' he was known as in Spain. He repositioned his teammates energetically, playing with great freedom some way up the pitch, but often falling back to support the defence or organise a counter-attack.

In the 83rd minute, he took a free kick that was deflected to Vieira, who headed it into the back of the net with the unwitting help of Puyol.

While the Spanish were giving their all to equalise, Zizou, applauded by the French fans, treated himself to a wonderful goal in injury time: after a long run, he got past Puyol before wrong-footing Casillas, the keeper: 3–1! The only downside was that Zizou had received a yellow card just a few seconds before scoring.

Spanish excitement gave way to Zidane's jubilation. After scoring his goal, he turned towards the touchline and ran along, waving his folded arms up and down with his tongue out. The celebration was reminiscent of that of his friend Christophe Dugarry when he scored against South Africa at the 1998 World Cup. There was, no doubt, also another similarity: a certain feeling of revenge.

Off the pitch, 'El Maestro' talked about the fact that his opponents had been hoping to send him into retirement: 'I want to tell the Spanish, because they took the mickey out of us enough about it, that I'm not ready yet! The adventure continues and we're delighted. We had prepared for this game in the best way possible.

We wanted to do something, to show that maybe the first stage wasn't easy, but we showed tonight that we've got a good squad and we want to go a lot further.'

The happiness within the team finally found an echo in France. The Champs-Élysées and plenty of other city centres were invaded by supporters. The atmosphere of 1998 had returned, as had faith in the France team and old slogans such as 'Zizou for president!' The audience share recorded by TF1 that night, with 19,564,940 viewers, was the best of 2006, with all programmes and channels combined.

'After the third goal from Zidane, something powerful happened, something we've had deep within us for weeks and months,' said Raymond Domenech. 'We've finally been able to express it. To get this thing out. It can't be explained, it can only be lived. A real moment of collective happiness has spread across France. I'll never forget what happened.'

'Our objective is 9 July.' Why not? The sceptics were becoming fewer and further between.

France, no longer just its footballing public, was suddenly jubilant. Jean Varraud would likely have found this over the top. The day after beating Spain, on an afternoon that was as warm and damp as the eyes of his friends, his remains joined those of his wife Roseline, who had passed away just before the 1998 World Cup. The Zidane family were there, of course. As was Malek, who liked to visit the recruiter. A page had been discreetly turned. A glorious page of anonymous football, of a life without concession to the lure of profit that would return time and again to the nobility of amateur and volunteer sport.

It was to be France–Brazil again. The nobility of the game. Monsieur Varraud would have loved it. For Les Bleus, the tournament would be considered a success if they did not disgrace themselves.

Brazil were the reigning world champions; they had won the Copa América, the South American tournament, to qualify for the World Cup – which now required the holders to qualify, for the first time in the event's history; they had also won the 2005 Confederations Cup. All this inevitably made the Brazilian favourites to walk away with the trophy. But there was no mention of the fact that their so-called 'magic square', Ronaldo – Ronaldinho – Adriano – Kaká, was not on a par with the 2002 trio of Rivaldo – Ronaldo – Ronaldinho. Ronaldo had been sharper then, while Ronaldinho had not been as tired or as much of a star.

Assisted by the legendary Mario Lobo Zagallo – who lost in 1974 and 1998 and was a replacement for Saldanha in 1970, but owed his legendary status to his wins in 1958, 1962 and 1970 – Carlos Alberto Parreira, the World Cup-winning manager in 1994, said only one foreign player would have made it into 'his' *seleção*: Zinedine Zidane.

Brazil wanted revenge for 1998. The Brazilian press picked up on the idea seized upon by *Marca*. One Brazilian newspaper published a photoshopped front page of Zidane queueing outside a pension fund office.

Zagallo, never short of arrogance, explained on television that, as 'the only power capable of saying so', he believed 'Brazil would be the only ones who would turn up'. These comments were in marked contrast with the fraternal atmosphere that permeated this high-stakes match.

The South Americans feared the French, essentially out of superstition. They, and the entire footballing world, remembered their elimination in Mexico in 1986 and the more recent defeat in the final at the Stade de France, thanks to Zidane's famous two goals.

This psychological advantage was given credence in Hameln. 'It's a happy memory for us. We're all fit, we're happy to be here together and it shows,' said Zidane, who would once again face some of his former Real teammates: Ronaldo, who had become the highest scorer in the history of the World Cup with 15 goals, Roberto Carlos, Cicinho and Robinho, whom he believed would become one of the greatest players of his time.

The Brazilians lavished praise on their opponent, who before being feared was respected: 'Zidane is the best player in the world and I think he always will be. As far as I'm concerned, he's a professor,' said Roberto Carlos, his teammate for five years. For Ronaldinho, who played against him for Barcelona, Zidane was 'a player that everyone loves to watch; one of the best in the world. It's a shame that he's retiring. He's a great player both on and off the pitch.'

Zidane was confident. Since the victory against Spain, he had been on fire. Often staying under the radar during previous weeks, he shone in training. Although he had always been one of the guys, this was a side he rarely showed: he had almost become a joker, seen in the kind of images that had been forgotten since his time at Cannes and Bordeaux.

France–Brazil. Zidane looked happy during the warm-up on the pitch at the stadium in Frankfurt. He tapped the ball calmly. He smiled and talked to his teammates, while journalists from TV channels all over the world discussed the 1998 final and only had eyes for him.

Physically, he had lost what tends to disappear with age: energy ... and hair. In terms of football, he had grown. Just as he had when it came to dealing with the media. He had everything needed to join the ranks of the demi-gods.

The France team was to be the now-expected starting 11: Barthez – Sagnol, Thuram, Gallas, Abidal – Makelele, Vieira – Ribéry, Zidane, Malouda – Henry.

Brazil had made several changes with the surprise presence of Juninho. As the 'magic square' had failed to deliver complete satisfaction, the Brazilian manager wanted to strengthen his midfield against the French in the area of the pitch in which they excelled.

After the anthems, Zidane and Ronaldo, the two friends from Madrid, embraced. Kick-off. Brazil started quickly but Zidane started even stronger. Despite missing his first two long passes, he appeared motivated, determined and ready to make the difference with his incomparable vision of the game. With 15 minutes gone, the Brazilians seemed deflated in the face of a conquering France led by an exceptional Zidane. Marseille turns, rainbow flicks, blind passes, outside-foot passes, perfect controls, dribbling and hook turns, short and long passes in abundance: it was the perfect match, or almost. Undoubtedly one of the best of his career, in a France shirt at least. He held his own, preferring to stress the game's important context: 'I don't think it was necessarily my best match ever. But it was in the World Cup, against Brazil!'

At half-time, Robinho jumped into the arms of a laughing Zidane. A World Cup semi-final was at stake, but that the game was played in good spirits on both sides was an added bonus. Zizou was resplendent. Finally, a real celebration of football in the middle of a tournament marked by an overabundance of sanctions.

Victory would suddenly spring up from Zidane's foot in the 57th minute. With a free kick just off-centre to the left, he sent the ball towards the far post, where Thierry Henry met it with a fabulous volley. Goal! It was the first time a pass from Zidane had been converted by Henry in all the time they had been playing together; they had had to wait until the 55th match! For France, it meant qualification, as Brazil, outplayed in all departments, could not pull things back.

France became the only country to have knocked Brazil out of the World Cup three times.

The country exploded with joy. More than a million people gathered in Paris with shouts of '*Allez la France!*' as well as 'Zizou! Zizou!' Just as the French team wanted to take revenge, the fans were also keen to put things right. After the game, William Gallas lamented the fact that popular support, as well as that of the press, had not come until after the win against Spain: 'We didn't feel it in the first round.'

After lingering on the Frankfurt pitch to prolong the happiness, the French players celebrated their win in a jubilant dressing room to which even Jacques Chirac himself paid a visit.

However, just as after the match against Spain, there was no apparent demonstration of warmth between Domenech and Zizou, who, on seeing his manager, gave both him and the other members of the coaching team a simple hand shake. But the two men were united for the better. What about 9 July? Zizou would think about it later. He spent a moment in the Brazilian dressing room, where he spoke to his friends and swapped shirts with Ronaldo. Despite the defeat, the Brazilian knew France deserved the win. Zizou was welcomed appropriately: honoured as the king of the game, without any misplaced bitterness. They were among champions.

In the mixed zone, where journalists wait for the players, one Brazilian was crying over his team's defeat: 'I would have liked to see Brazil win but I can console myself by saying that I saw Zidane play in a way that few people have. It was moving.'

Zidane, who was still very wary of the press and held a grudge against certain media outlets due to misplaced criticism, contented himself with talking to Eurosport's microphones: 'It's huge. We had to play a huge match and we did. We had to hold firm defensively and play well as a team. We deserve our victory. We're going to try to get to the final. We don't want to stop here. It's so fantastic that we want to keep going. We want to go all the way.'

Around him, only praise could be heard. Although still reluctant to talk about individuals rather than the team, Raymond Domenech even added his own: 'That's Zidane. You look surprised? We're not! We know the "extra" he brings. He knows that he's going to stop, so he wants to play to the max. There are no more calculations to be made. Every moment is his last. But that's what you say to every player: play like it's your last ever game. Now he's doing it naturally.'

Carlos Alberto Parreira claimed 'Zidane played his best match for eight years. He kept running throughout and played with great authority. We all knew what Zidane was capable of, and France killed off the game with his free kick.' King Pelé said, 'Zidane was the magician of the match.' All over the world, Zidane's performance astonished pundits, claiming that 'Zidane brought the gods down from the skies.' They talked about his 'magic' and 'genius', and paid tribute to an 'artist'.

'Zidane makes Brazil cry for a second time,' said the Brazilian press, who pointed out, without animosity, that Zidane 'unlike the stars of the *seleção*, had been able to step up to the big occasion'. 'Come here to retire,' offered one newspaper from São Paulo, while another consoled itself: 'We lost, but at least we are going to see

Zidane play one more game.' He had put his farewell shirt away again.

To make it to 9 July, without stopping on 8 July at the third-place play-off, they needed to knock out Portugal in the semi-final, just as they had done in Euro 2000.

The Portuguese were serious adversaries. They had successively knocked out the Netherlands and England, two of the contenders for the title, and were managed by Luis Felipe Scolari, the coach of the defending Brazilian champions. With the likes of Deco, Cristiano Ronaldo, Maniche, Pauleta and Figo, Portugal had reached the semi-finals of the World Cup for the first time since 1966. They were playing well.

Raymond Domenech, former manager of the France Under-21 team, had not forgotten that Portugal had eliminated his team from Olympic qualification in 2003 in Clermont-Ferrand, in conditions that could be described as turbulent to say the least: Cissé's sending-off, a miserable penalty shootout, a brawl, dressing rooms destroyed by the Portuguese and accusations of doping. But only Cristiano Ronaldo and Helder Postiga had been present that day.

It was also a special match for Portugal. Euro 2000, dotted with incidents after Zinedine Zidane's 'golden goal' from the penalty spot, was still a painful memory. Abel Xavier, Paulo Bento and Nuno Gomes – playing in Germany – had received lengthy suspensions.

Nor had the last-16 or quarter-final matches played by the men in red and green been any calmer: a 'historic' game against the Netherlands, with 16 cards, including four reds, and a stormy encounter with England that included Wayne Rooney's relatively harsh sending-off.

However, the goalkeeper Ricardo, his country's hero in the penalty shootout against England, lashed out at a journalist who used the word 'battle'. Scolari resorted to self-deprecation in an attempt to calm the atmosphere: 'It's great to see Zidane and Figo play. The ball doesn't cry at their feet.'

Zidane inspired and exuded confidence: the game against Brazil had brought down every barrier. The World Cup had been a success and he believed nothing could now tarnish the end of his career. Relaxed, he even treated himself to a cigarette at the window of the Schlosshotel with his teammates who smoked, Sagnol and Barthez. Newspapers in the UK and Italy published the photo taken by a paparazzo. But by then nothing could trouble France's serenity.

One of Zinedine's brothers, who attended all the France team's matches, travelling by car from Marseille, was too superstitious to fly to Munich despite being invited by Zizou. He would drive.

In Munich on 5 July, in the magnificent Allianz Arena, Zidane was cheered as he made his entrance onto the pitch. He chatted with his former Real teammate Luis Figo before kick-off. The two men had long got on. Figo did not know it yet, but after Raúl and Ronaldo he was about to receive the 'assassin's kiss', according to the expression coined by the Spanish press.

Zizou did not quite play the same high-flying game against Portugal that he had against Brazil, but he was active and solid. In the 33rd minute, it was he who was charged with taking the penalty won by the Malouda – Henry duo. A mission that was not easy against Ricardo, who had stopped three penalties out of four in the previous round.

Zizou took a very short run-up and kicked powerfully to the left – 'as always', he pointed out. Ricardo went the right way but Zidane's shot was perfect and the strike was so hard that Ricardo could only get a fingertip to it. Portugal played very well, but France held firm. France won and Zizou, after receiving a yellow card against Spain, made it back to the dressing room without getting another. He would play in the final.

Just as he had hoped, this match would be the last of his professional career. In Berlin. On 9 July.

A well-known refrain resurfaced. 'We're in the final! We're in the final!' chanted the French supporters in Munich, in unison with those across France.

The semi-final had been watched by 22.2 million television viewers, a third of the population. It was the highest audience figures in the history of French television since Médiamétrie's measuring scale had been created. It was higher than France–Italy in Euro 2000 (21.4 million). But potentially lower than France–Italy 2006 in the World Cup final.

After the game, Zidane told Canal+: 'You need some pressure to take a penalty. But good pressure. I told myself that if we scored, we would win. We went 1–0 up and if we didn't let in a goal we were in the final. That was all I thought about: that I needed to score my penalty. I was a bit tired. Now the most important thing is to rest. We really gave a lot tonight. It was very hot, so we need to recover.'

The only blemish on the celebrations came in France, where seven people died and more were injured in a number of skirmishes. Sport is not worth that. And Zizou knew it, moderating the excesses wherever possible, just as he did individual roles in team performances. He was not the only one in the team.

But in a world where men can be seen as gods, a group is often symbolised by one name. One individual. One face. Patrick Vieira, the hero of the France–Spain game, had been pushed into the background in summaries of the game, highlighted primarily by an albeit fine goal from its star playmaker, but one scored when the match was already almost won. A goal that was certainly not irrelevant, as it had no doubt given Zizou confidence, but one that was hardly decisive.

The star system leaves no room for nuance. It wants a hero. Someone who can bring the crowd to life with a single gesture. Everything was expected of him. A goal in the final, for example. Before one last lap of honour.

15

THE TRAP

Sunday 9 July. *Finally*. 'We've made it this far because we've all worked really hard and we're going to try to win the cup. It won't be easy. It's going to be very tough, but we have the weapons and we're all really committed to doing it. Our motto is: "We die together,"' recalled Zidane. 'We have to bring the cup home. It would be fantastic! Not for us, not for the squad of 23, but for all the staff and the people who've supported us. I'm talking about those who've supported us from start to finish, not those who came on board halfway through.'

Whatever the result of the match, the final pages in the legend of Zizou would be written in gold letters. His last match was to be a World Cup final. Not even Pelé, Maradona, Cruyff or Beckenbauer had been entitled to such an exit. Other greats, such as Di Stefano, Zico, Van Basten and Platini had never even played in a final. For Zizou, the match was special in another way – he would face Italy: the country where he learned to toughen up, where he became a superstar, where his play took on a global dimension. Once again, he would face his former teammates: Alessandro Del Piero, Gianluca Zambrotta, Pippo Inzaghi, and, above all, he would cross swords with his former manager Marcello Lippi.

Zizou had never lost to Italy. The Italians claimed to have immense respect for him, although behind the scenes they were said to have less respectable and destabilising intentions, both for him and for Thierry Henry. Gennaro Gattuso, whose mission was to mark the French captain, declared that: 'You can't stop Zidane! That's not what I'm planning to do. He's one of the best players in the world. He's had some amazing games at the World Cup. He's 34 and he's played his last three matches at the highest level. I just hope he doesn't have much energy left for the final. I'll need to be lucky because playing against him is a bit like a game of chance. Now you see the ball, now you don't! He's one of those players who make it worth buying a ticket.'

The match was also special for Italy. Not only because it was an opportunity to take revenge on a France team that included Zidane, Thuram, Vieira, Trezeguet and Henry, but also, and most importantly, because of the oppressive situation back home. Since the end of the season, Italy had been shaken by a match-fixing scandal: four big clubs were affected and, through them, many of the internationals playing in the tournament, as well as the manager Marcello Lippi.

Despite everything, the Azzurri had made it to the final. After a lukewarm but effective start to the tournament and a last-16 game won against Australia – thanks to a contentious penalty awarded just a few seconds from the end of full time – they had succeeded in dismissing Ukraine in the quarter-final. In the semi-final, they had knocked out their German hosts in extra time.

With only one goal conceded, Italy had the best defence in the tournament. They had probably the best back at the World Cup, Fabio Cannavaro – a candidate, like Zidane, for the title of best player in the competition – and the excellent goalkeeper Gianluigi

Buffon, seeking the record of World Cup invincibility held, since 1990, by his compatriot Walter Zenga.

The eyes of the world were fixed on Berlin. And, in fact, not just those of the world. During a press conference given in space, the British-born American astronaut Piers Sellers wished 'Good luck to Zidane, Thierry and Patrick', Henry and Vieira, the undisputed star and former captain of London's Arsenal.

On 9 July 2006 at 7.15 pm, a French team with no surprises took to the turf in Berlin's Olympic Stadium. Spared by injuries and suspensions, it was the same team that had lined up since the last 16: Barthez – Sagnol, Thuram, Gallas, Abidal – Vieira, Makelele – Ribéry, Zidane, Malouda – Henry.

During the warm-up, Zizou ran the length of the French half twice and waited for his muscles to spark into life before kicking the ball for the first time.

The cup, meanwhile, had been placed on a table on the touchline.

The Argentine Horacio Elizondo, the first referee to officiate a final after having refereed the opening game, blew his whistle for kick-off at precisely 8pm, after a *Marseillaise* during which the French had their arms tightly around one another.

The Italians were aggressive from the start. Henry fell victim to a heavy challenge in the first minute, but France started strongly. They continued to push. In the seventh minute, they were awarded a penalty for an inconspicuous foul on Malouda, committed by Marco Materazzi. Zidane faced one of the best goalkeepers in the world. He had scored countless penalties in his career, but never in such circumstances. You could have heard a pin drop in the stadium.

Zidane tended to shoot to the left and Buffon knew it. But Zidane knew that Buffon knew it! 'I couldn't take it the same way. Particularly against him [Buffon],' he later told Canal+. He added that he was also anxious about striking it too hard because of the risk of missing, as he had against China. What should he do? He thought about the phone conversations he had had with his loved ones before the final. They had told him: 'Enjoy your last match.'

He made his decision and began his run-up. As his foot connected with the ball, unusually he tensed up a little and flicked it up to the right, floating it against the underside of the crossbar. 'I wanted it to be remembered as a beautiful penalty,' he would later explain. Was his pride his undoing? No. The ball fell back inside the goal before bouncing out, but fortunately the officials confirmed it had crossed the line. Goal!

There was nothing Buffon, who had dived the other way, could do. Zinedine Zidane had had the audacity to try a 'Panenka' in the World Cup final. It was a style of penalty named after Antonin Panenka, whose spot kick had won the European title for Czechoslovakia against Germany in 1976.

Zidane became the fourth player to have scored in two World Cup finals, after the German Paul Breitner (also from the penalty spot in 1974 and 1982), and the Brazilians Vava (1958 and 1962) and Pelé (1958 and 1970). With this 31st goal in 108 caps, he surpassed Just Fontaine and Jean-Pierre Papin to become France's fourth-top scorer behind Platini, Henry and Trezeguet.

The French fans in the stands were close to hysteria.

But the Italians reacted. As they knew all too well how to do, but only did rarely, they temporarily abandoned their so-called 'cynical, almost infamous' style in favour of the sporting ideal, as Jacques Ferran, an editor at *France Football*, had described it after their last World Cup title in 1982. When they wanted to, the Azzurri knew how to attack, and attacked well. France were under the cosh. The run of play saw Materazzi level the score after 12 minutes.

Against Gattuso, who marked him tightly, Zidane was not as decisive as he had been against Brazil. But he was very useful, offensively and even defensively. He put together combinations for his teammates, trying tactical options to recover possession. At the half-hour mark, he opted for a reorganisation and quickly informed Vieira, Thuram and Makelele.

After the break, France finally took control against the Italians, who bent but did not break, neither in the face of Malouda or Henry. Zizou was struggling physically. At the end of the second half, he was in pain, on the point of asking to be replaced after a clash with Cannavaro during which he thought he had dislocated his shoulder. But the Italians did not spare him. He continued almost breathless, but with plenty of courage, panache even.

Once again the French dominated extra time. In the 99th minute, Franck Ribéry came close, stringing together a move and a shot, which flew off to the right of the goal. Les Bleus' best chance came in the 105th minute. It was the work of Zinedine Zidane. On the end of a cross sent in by Sagnol from the right, he aimed a header towards the goal. For that moment, it was as if history was going to repeat itself, that Zidane would once again score two goals in a World Cup final and that France would win. But Buffon pulled off a stunning save.

They were locked at 1–1 at half-time in extra time. The golden-goal formula, ending a match in the sublimest of fashions, was no longer in use. The more time ticked by the more it seemed as if the game was heading towards the lottery of a penalty shootout. A clattered crossbar, a lucky deflection off the post, a fumbled shot, a slip or an unexpected error would decide the winner of this major sporting competition. It was a pessimistic and oppressive feeling: what if Zizou missed this time? There is no crueller fate in football. At least that was how it seemed at that stage in the match.

There were still ten minutes to go before the end of extra time. If the scoreline remained unchanged, the career of Zinedine Yazid Zidane would finish after a penalty shootout at around 10.30pm. During the final, he had scored, harangued his teammates after the equaliser, defended, attacked and suffered. He had taken on his fair share of responsibilities. He would have lived up to his mission, as well as his reputation. Only a missed shot on goal or a penalty could tarnish his exit now. Nothing else ...

The 108th minute of play soon came. Alou Diarra, who had replaced the injured Vieira, neared the opposition goal on the diagonal. He passed the ball to Florent Malouda, whose cross made it into the box. Materazzi held Zidane back by the bottom of his shirt with both hands. The foul may well have deserved a penalty but it seemingly went unnoticed by any of the officials.

Malouda's shot was saved and the ball span off towards the French camp. In Italian, a language he speaks fluently, Zinedine told his opponent that if he wanted his shirt that much, he would gladly give it to him at the end of the game. It was an ironic way of making him understand that his behaviour was unacceptable.

Offended or, as he would put it, annoyed by this response that he found to be arrogant – the great Zidane offering to give his last and so sought-after shirt to poor little Materazzi! – the Italian defender showered him with insults.

This in itself was worthy of punishment but all the officials were ball-watching. Zidane walked slowly back to his position. Suddenly, he turned around and struck a blow with his head in response to the insults slung by his opponent. A head-butt to the chest.

Materazzi is over six feet three. As Raymond Domenech would note ironically, Materazzi may have an imposing physical stature but it didn't stop him falling over. Lying flat out on the pitch, he made a meal of getting up – something the fans in the stadium interpreted as somewhat exaggerated. The game was stopped. A crowd formed around the player on the ground.

The practice of simulation or exaggeration, too widespread in modern football, is particularly prevalent among Latin players. The public knew it. They began whistling.

The Argentine referee, Horacio Elizondo, asked one of his assistants, Dario Garcia, if he had seen the incident. He said no. The fourth official, who as usual was not on the pitch, then intervened. Presumably, and despite his denials, it was a video replay that allowed this fourth official, the Spaniard Luis Medina Cantalejo, to see the blow struck. However, resorting to a video replay was forbidden by FIFA regulations at that time. Otherwise, Vieira's goal against South Korea would have been given!

It was he who told Elizondo what to do. The Argentine referee, who had seen nothing himself, took the red card out of his pocket, held it tightly in his hand and, standing tall with a hard look in his eyes, brandished it at Zinedine Zidane. The verdict had been given. His career would end with a sending-off!

'Zidane grabbed my arm. He admitted having given a head-butt, but asked me: "Didn't you see what happened before?" He didn't tell me if something underhand had taken place or if Materazzi had provoked him. It wasn't a recrimination either. He just explained to me, correctly and in perfect Spanish, why he had reacted in that way,' the referee would later tell the Argentine newspaper *Clarin*.

The boos from the stands got louder. They were not aimed at the perpetrator of the head-butt, which most of the spectators had not seen, but those who had decided on the sending-off that the crowd did not understand, with the exception of those who had access to a television replay.

The cameras had captured everything . . . apart from that sound. Noise can sometimes be more aggressive than a gesture.

Had the Italians, who were familiar with the temperament of Juve's ex-playmaker, adopted a deliberate strategy? Had they laid a trap for him?

The history of football is littered with warlike declarations, admissions by players aware of how to provoke certain opponents and make them crack. Nevertheless, the Italians were careful not to say such things openly. There may have been doubt as to their intentions. But none as to the injustice committed, in the eyes of the French fans.

The imagined farewell with a fanfare, the shirt awarded with thanks, the lap of honour, the possible triumph – that all vanished. Even if Les Bleus won, the party would no longer be the same.

Zizou left the pitch, mechanically rubbing his lips and chin. With his head lowered, he passed in front of the table on which sat the trophy he would not touch for a second time. He went down the stairs towards the dressing room. It was there that he watched the end of the match, on television.

Once the incomprehension had passed, the commentators, without anything to rely on but the images they had seen themselves and no idea what had been said on the pitch, began to condemn someone they had been praising just as exaggeratedly a few minutes earlier. His actions were described as 'unforgivable' and 'inexcusable'. A trial without appeal, even without a hearing, had just begun. Zidane, everyone's favourite, had, as far as the world's television stations were concerned, become Zidane the guilty. To blame, first and foremost, for shattering the French dream. The party was over. The king had suddenly become cursed.

The referee blew his whistle for the end of normal time. There was no winner, but one big loser: football. An exceptional player's final farewell had been ruined. An inopportune, unexpected and brutal head-butt had damaged the image of the world's most popular sport. If only the opportunity had been seized then to get rid of the vices that still threaten the game. Insults are only harshly punished if they are audibly directed at a referee. And, in general, a player who responds comes in for more criticism than one who attacks. 'Dear perfectionists, after video replays, may we soon have sound with microphones that will flay alive these players who too often forget to wash their mouths out with soap before walking out onto the pitch,' was the pertinent insight from the referee Gilles Veissière in his column in *Nice-Matin* the following day.

So it was penalties. All the Italians scored theirs. Almost symbolically, the player who had taken Italy apart at Euro 2000, one of those most feared by the team from the *bel paese*, missed his attempt. Trezeguet, who had not had enough time on the pitch during the competition, would leave Germany with bad memories and the feeling of an opportunity wasted.

For the Azzurri, it was a wonderful success. They won their fourth World Cup, their first since 1982, when an unfairly disallowed goal for Cameroon could have knocked them out of the competition in the first round. Some shameful but incredibly effective marking by Gentile carried them to a surprising coronation.

Back then, the Italians had been nicknamed the 'beloved bandits' by a French football newspaper, and nothing had changed. A week after the final in Berlin, one journalist wrote that Italy, despite being thoroughly dominated, 'deserved their victory', described as a 'triumph' on the cover of another football magazine, whose reporter even went on to point out that 'morality is intact'!

It was glory for the winners. *Adieu Zizou, vive Materazzi!* In Italy this player, sometimes described as a specialist in aggression, low blows and harsh words, was celebrated as a hero. On Saturday 15 July, after qualifying for the German Grand Prix, the motorcyclist Valentino Rossi would even wear a shirt bearing his name.

All the French were left with was regrets. 'I don't know if we could have won if I'd stayed on the pitch for another ten minutes. But I don't think it would have changed much as far as the penalties were concerned,' said Zizou, who would not come back to the pitch to collect his finalist medal.

When his teammates returned to the dressing room, he apologised for leaving them as ten men. 'No one was angry with Zizou. Besides, we don't know if it would have changed anything. He got himself sent off, we know why, but great players are often provoked,' said Florent Malouda. 'He's not leaving through the back door!' said Éric Abidal, with annoyance. 'He's already gone through the front door. We've all seen what he's given to football, even during this World Cup.' Lilian Thuram explained: 'The feeling we had was that he was very disappointed about leaving us as ten men. He realised afterwards that he'd fallen into the Italian players' trap.'

Everyone wanted to focus on his career and forget about the head-butt. In any case, none of the players had heard what had really been said on the pitch.

Alone in the dressing room, Zinedine Zidane had the opportunity to think about what he had done, to reflect on his fate and on men's morals in the days of a modern circus. A circus that was not taking place in a big top but on the World Cup stage.

He was no longer a demi-god. In Marseille, at the deserted Vieux Port, where skips had begun collecting the tons of litter strewn on the ground, a TF1 reporter began sketching out an off-air explanation that would be widely shared: 'We made him France's favourite, the perfect man. Subconsciously, maybe it weighed him down. He cracked under the pressure. In a way, he wanted to be human again.' In the cold light of day, journalists, pundits and reporters alike would attempt to flesh out this quasi-psychoanalytical theory, despite not necessarily having the means, the scientific tools or even all the information ...

Many people agreed that his, albeit informal, status as a worldwide star imposed on him the need for exemplary behaviour. In 1998, Zizou had been a brilliant soloist, finally released during the final. In 2006, he was the captain, the boss, the taker of set pieces, the last star to qualify for the final. One of the most-watched men on the planet. But did he have more responsibilities than others because of his skills or his popularity, the latter of which he had never sought out? Only one role should have compelled him to have more restraint: that of captain.

At midnight, while Marseille's sleep was troubled by nightmares, one man was thinking about the tournament at Roanne, about the first time Yazid was provoked. Almost 20 years of provocation, now. A pensive Fernand Boix returned to his home in Septèmes-les-Vallons, passing the cemetery where Robert Centenero rests. He took some perspective: such a head-butt was hardly serious on the scale of such a long and distinguished career.

Contrary to the media storm that was being whipped up, the wise man of SO Septèmes' prime concern was the limited budget at his club, struggling just like, at another level, AS Cannes, who were vegetating in the National Division. Or like Juventus, relegated in the wake of the match-fixing scandal. Or like Real, who had become an anonymous club in La Liga. Would it be time for regrets all round? For the emotional memory of the passing of Zidane?

The day after the final, the world's press set the standard. There was no restraint on the part of the pundits, who pointed fingers and gave a thumbs-down. Some were ferocious, claiming that Zizou had 'ruined his career'. There was no let-up for two days. The image of the head-butt was on the front page of almost every newspaper. The bloodshed even eclipsed the result of the match, Italy's victory and the assessment of the biggest sporting event after the Olympic Games. 'A criminal head-butt' (*O Dia*, Brazil), '[Head-butt] of shame' (*Publico*, Portugal), 'Stupid' (*New York Times*, US) and 'Barbarian' (*Al-Watan*, Kuwait) were just some examples of the press.

There was a reminder that Zizou had been sent off 13 times during his career; that he had often committed reprehensible actions. There was talk of the 'actions of a madman'.

A madman, or perhaps one that was all too human? The actions of a man who could not bear the injustice of a foul going unpunished, the dishonesty of a shirt-pull or the cowardice of an insult. That was the counter-argument of Zidane's fans.

The question remained. What did Materazzi say? The rumours began to circulate. According to Brazilian lip-reading specialists called in by the Globo TV channel, Materazzi insulted Zizou's sister three times. Other specialists, interviewed in England, thought they had detected the words 'son of a terrorist whore', which he denies.

'I only grabbed his shirt for a few seconds. He rounded on me and said something mocking. He looked at me incredibly arrogantly, up and down: "If you want my shirt that much, I'll give it to you afterwards." Yes, I did reply with an insult, that's true. The kind of insult you hear dozens of times and that often comes out on the pitch,' said Materazzi, back in Italy. His own poor record was finally mentioned.

Zizou would eventually deliver his own version of the 'affair'. He took advice from his team before contacting TF1 and Canal+, the partner channels of Zizou and the French team, and decided he would hold back his explanations for an exclusive with the British press.

In the afternoon of Wednesday 12 July, he recorded an initial discussion with the journalist Claire Chazal, TF1's star presenter, which would be broadcast during the eight o'clock news. He then went to Canal+ for a long interview with Michel Denisot, head of the channel and someone familiar with the ins and outs of French football.

For the first time in its history, Canal+ posted an audience share greater than that of the other terrestrial channels: 33.5 per cent at 8pm, in other words six million viewers, and an average of 24.4 per cent during the programme.

Zizou opened up and told the story of his World Cup before turning to the Materazzi affair and the insults: 'Very personal things. About my mother and my sister. You hear them once and you try to walk away. That's what I did. You can see me walking away. Then you hear it twice, then a third time ...' he explained without explicitly mentioning the words used, but implicitly confirming they were the ones identified by the experts.

'I'm a father. I'm sorry for all the kids who saw it. What I did was inexcusable. Of course, it's not something you should do. I want to say that loud and clear, because it's been seen by two or three billion TV viewers and millions and millions of children.'

Zizou apologised several times on TF1 as well as on Canal+. But despite this, he did not regret his actions: 'I can't, because that would mean he was right to say what he did. And he was not right. Definitely not. I can't regret it, I can't, I can't. Materazzi provoked me. If there's no provocation there's no reaction.'

The inevitable survey claimed that 60 per cent of the French population understood Zidane's actions – a percentage that would climb as high as 82 per cent after his televised explanations.

Zizou's stock was rising once more. 'What he did was reprehensible but most importantly, it's forgivable,' summarised the former manager of the France team Michel Hidalgo. Even Jacques Chirac was questioned on the subject during the French president's customary Bastille Day interview on 14 July: 'I have plenty of admiration, esteem and respect for Zidane and that is nothing new. It probably influences me a little. His actions were unacceptable, that much is clear. Zidane himself has said so courageously. I don't want to pass judgement, but I think FIFA have opened an investigation. We will see if there was any provocation, or if it was insulting. I don't know. We cannot accept it but we can understand it.' Was that really his personal opinion? Or was it demagogy? Gradually, this opinion was becoming widely shared. Especially by those who took the time to review all the elements of what had happened.

On Monday 10 July, the day after the final, the day Les Bleus returned to France, Zidane received the loudest applause at the airport, on the way into the Élysée Palace and then again at the Hôtel de Crillon, on a balcony from which the players were able to thank their fans.

He may have lost some credit among a section of the public not passionate about football, or those who will only remember the altercation for his brutal reaction, but Zidane may have ended up forging an even stronger appeal to those who have always loved him.

The night of the final, one chant resounded around the Arc de Triomphe: 'Zizou, we love you!' Over time, which would mitigate the final image of his exit, this slogan would gain plenty of new devotees.

16

THE CONVERSION

It was over. A lengthy holiday was in order, the first in a long time. Since Zinedine had first stepped off the train at Cannes station in 1987, the summer had been scented as much with physio's massage oil as with sun cream, and had resonated with instructions from his coaches as much as with the song of the cicadas.

He had, of course, taken some holidays in 19 pre-seasons, and in the second half of his career had plenty of money to enjoy them, sometimes on the other side of the world with friends and family. How could he regret that his holidays were cut short when the return to work was always followed by an important goal: a league title to be won and, every other year, a World Cup or a European Championship to play?

As a radical change of life arrived, it was finally time to really enjoy spending time with his family, to try to forget the end of the World Cup and to look to the future. In the summer of 2006, his holidays would not be restricted by preparing for the next match.

There would be no more matches. And on 19 July, the name of the new owner of the Real number 5 shirt was announced: Cannavaro, transferred from Juventus.

Eleven months after the sending-off in Berlin, on 7 June 2007, Adidas organised a promotional tournament in Murcia, Spain, involving young players from around the world. One of the teams in the final was captained by Zinedine. It was managed by his former coach at Juve, Carlo Ancelotti, who had won the Champions League two weeks earlier with AC Milan. The referee was Horacio Elizondo, who had also recently hung up his whistle.

Zizou was not against the involvement of the Argentine former referee, who had been appointed Under-Secretary of State for Sport the previous month. In Murcia, the two men greeted each other with a handshake, followed by some banter.

The big winner in this reunion was Adidas, who focused on the theme of making peace, while Nike, with Materazzi, ambiguously played on the theme of confrontation.

The partnerships continued, with others as well as Adidas.

Zidane's diary was filled not only with holidays but also with advertising campaigns and charity work, as he dedicated the rest of his time to those closest to him. His family stayed in Madrid. Soon there would be four licensed players with the name Zidane at Real, who were crowned champions of Spain once again in 2007 and 2008. Those others were his sons.

May 2009. After the resignation in January of Ramon Calderón and the interim Vicente Boluda, Real Madrid needed to elect a new president. Florentino Perez threw his hat into the ring. He promised to make Zizou his adviser. Perez was well aware of the Frenchman's reputation, and what he meant to the club. Moreover, the roots he had put down in the Spanish capital, where all his sons would share their earliest memories, meant a lot to those who placed importance on 'club spirit', as Real's associates did. One by one, Perez's competitors pulled out and he became the only candidate left in the running. With the result a foregone conclusion, he was once again elected to the presidency he had already held for more than five years. Keeping his electoral promise, Zinedine Zidane became his adviser.

But Real's pomp and financial resources did not prevent recurring instability, which was not in keeping with the tradition of big clubs, where work was often accomplished over the long term. Since the departure of the legendary Miguel Muñoz in 1974, who had been at the helm of the first team for 14 years, the record for a manager was only four seasons, while it was eight at AC Milan, and six at both Barcelona and Bayern Munich. Real's last Champions League title dated back seven years.

Some wondered whether Zizou, who had won the Madrid club its ninth major European trophy and whose career there was often summed up by his stunning goal in the final against Leverkusen, would have a role that would go beyond that of a simple adviser. Would he be able to contribute to stabilising the club's management? To help make it durable?

Zinedine's work at Real gave him freedom and did not leave him exposed to the pressure of results. This was fortunate, as the first season under the returning president was not crowned with a title. Eliminated very early on by Lyon in the last 16, it was not the Madrid team that lifted the cup at the Santiago-Bernabeu, where the Champions League final was played that year, but Inter Milan. Their manager José Mourinho would soon return to the Bernabeu as one of the much-hyped arrivals of the 2010 close season.

Mourinho and Zidane, with different if not opposing characters, did not appear a natural pairing at first glance. But the Portuguese manager spoke eloquently to TF1 when the league season was only six days old: 'I would like to see Zidane out here with me more often, and less with the president.'

The following week, the club released a statement outlining the role of Zidane's advisory role: 'Optimising the working conditions of the first team.' Here he was plunged right back into the rhythm of training and match preparation.

In the spring of 2011, the potential and performances of one young player who was starting to get noticed were pointed out to him by two of his former Bordeaux teammates: Stéphane Plancque, the manager at FC Annoeullin, a town between Lille and Lens in northern France, and Didier Sénac, a scout at Racing Club de Lens, where the 17-year-old defender, Raphaël Varane was playing at the time. Manchester United were so keen on him that a transfer to Old Trafford was considered likely. In May, Zizou convinced Florentino Perez that Real should make a play for him. Varane made his decision in June and became the youngest player ever recruited by Perez, usually more attracted by stars than promising talent.

Ten years after his arrival in Madrid, Zizou had perfected his knowledge of the services and facilities at the Valdebebas training centre, the Bernabeu and, of course, the staff at Real, from the club's directors to its employees, those who remained as star players, managers and even presidents came and went. He was named director of football for the first team.

For the public and observers of Spanish football, however, this role seemed poorly defined, and many saw him more as an ambassador than a real decision-maker.

Zinedine took the time to observe, reflect and define the contours of his professional conversion. His future was becoming clearer. He was now working on acquiring a diploma in sports management, which he studied for in France at the Centre for the Law and Economics of Sport in Limoges. There he was reunited with two former players who had won one of the rare titles missing from his own career, the Confederations Cup: Éric Carrière, who had filled in for him in 2001, and Olivier Dacourt, who won in 2003.

As indicated by the centre's name, the course focused on law, economics and sport. The curriculum never lost sight of the pitch, but it was not the only component of successful management. Nevertheless, it was almost too far away for Zinedine, who did not feel that he wanted to become an administrator. He saw his future closer to the pitch, closer to the players. He saw himself more as a coach than an administrator.

He had, of course, been asked about coaching at the end of his playing career; as if managing a team was the logical next step for an exceptional player like him; some even predicted he would be the future coach of the France team. At first, he didn't think about it, but his mind had become clearer and he now felt ready to take on the role. At the same time, Florentino Perez said he wanted to see Zidane take the footballing helm at Real over the next four years, though there was still a question mark over exactly what that role might be.

He would only be director of football for the 2011–12 season. In 2012 and 2013, he spent most of his time away studying.

He began coaching during the 2013–14 season, initially as assistant manager. Perez offered him the finest setting in which to learn his apprenticeship: the Real Madrid first team. He was appointed to assist the successor to Mourinho, Carlo Ancelotti, who had been his manager during his two last seasons at Juve.

He was back by the turf; sitting by the touchline, where he was joined by Ancelotti, when he was not standing up, giving instructions or watching the game. David Bettoni, his friend from Cannes, was not far away. Part of the club's coaching set-up, thanks to Zizou, who trusted him implicitly, he was responsible for supervising opposing teams.

Those first weeks on the bench were precious, useful and enjoyable as he listened to Ancelotti's tactical subtleties. At the training ground, the team's stars, who had just been joined by the Welsh player Gareth Bale for what was unofficially the largest transfer in history – unofficially only so as not to risk ruffling Cristiano Ronaldo's ego – listened to and respected the former French international.

On 6 December 2013 in Bahia, Zizou once again donned his guise of world champion to take part in the group draw for the next World Cup, to be played in Brazil. A winner of two Champions Leagues as a player and two as a manager, in the time when the trophy had been known as the European Cup, Ancelotti was a model manager, just as European competition was an extraordinary training ground for Zidane when it lasted, as it did that year, until the final.

On 15 May 2002, Zizou's volley had given Real the advantage and the victory over Bayern Leverkusen in Glasgow. Since then images of that goal had been broadcast regularly, particularly on the screens at the Bernabeu, where they were still waiting to celebrate a tenth major European title.

On 24 May 2014 in Lisbon, for the first time in the history of the Champions League, two clubs from the same city competed in the final: Real and Atlético. Down 1–0 during the match, Real equalised in the fourth minute of injury time thanks to a goal from the only player in the team who had played with Zidane: Sergio Ramos, who headed in a corner delivered by the Croat Luka Modrić.

Atlético cracked during extra time. Bale scored first, the Brazilian defender Marcelo widened the gap, before Cristiano Ronaldo sealed the result from the penalty spot in the Lisbon stadium he knew so well and in which, ten years earlier, he had endured a memorable disappointment with the Portuguese national team, beaten in the final of the Euros by Greece. It finished 4–1 to Real.

Twelve years on, Zinedine could hug the trophy once more. The Madrileños celebrated the victory by telling themselves that his presence, whatever his influence, was at the very least a happy coincidence.

In the 2014–15 season, he would lead a team on his own. Zinedine Zidane became the head coach of the Real reserve team Castilla. The team played in the Segunda División B, the Spanish third division that pits 80 clubs against one another in four groups of 20. Promotion to the next level, the Segunda División, was their first objective. In the hope of achieving this, they had to finish among the top four teams in the group in the initial phase. Zinedine had to assume responsibility on his own. His daily life would once again be punctuated by the ups and downs he knew so well. But this time, he would be on his own in the technical area, the space between the pitch and the bench, bounded by dotted lines.

He would now also be on his own when it came to justifying his choices to the media. But he would not be on his own in the dressing room or on the training pitches. Over the years, by observing and studying, he had become convinced that it was impossible to take charge of a squad without being surrounded by a trusted team. He was ready to become a manager, but only if he could count on a man whose loyalty and vision of the game and of life he appreciated: none other than David Bettoni. Twenty-six years after their first meeting in Cannes, their shared passion for football brought them even closer together.

Zizou would also stand alongside someone else he knew well: Enzo, his eldest son, a midfielder for Castilla, who preferred to be called Fernández, his mother's maiden name, or more simply by his first name.

The profession took hold of Zinedine as he learned his trade in stadiums with small stands, in which the players' comments were audible above the noise from the few fans in attendance. At grounds of a size the like of which he hadn't seen since his last season with the Cannes reserve team.

He also continued training, which took him to Marseille where he met the Argentine manager of Olympique de Marseille, the ebullient Marcelo Bielsa, a strong personality and a source of inspiration for Zidane's own concept of the attacking game.

But enemies were lying in wait for Zidane. On 27 October 2014, the Spanish Football Federation suspended him on the pretext that he did not have the necessary certificates to coach a team. The sanction was eventually annulled on 12 November by the Court of Arbitration for Sport. Supported by the French Football Federation, Real argued for the European equivalence of the level-two certificate of which Zinedine was in possession, and which would have allowed him to coach in France at that level. He was also continuing his training and would soon obtain the UEFA-recognised coaching certificate.

Zidane, a leader of men, learned on the training ground and in the dressing room, dealing with confident personalities such as the precocious Norwegian international Martin Ødegaard, who arrived at the club in January 2015, a few days after his 16th birthday. The authority of a player like Zidane, as well as the legitimacy afforded to him by his career and the relationships he forged intelligently with the youngest players, all helped

Ødegaard quickly reach the level he needed to play at in a league as demanding as that in Spain.

In Munich, in March, it was Zinedine who was in the role of apprentice. His training led him to meet the inventive Catalan coach Pep Guardiola. However, learning about Bayern's coaching structures was not the most interesting part of the course. In Bavaria, Zizou met up with Ribéry, who had become a star player at Bayern, where Willy Sagnol, part of the small group of observers, also played.

Also including Bernard Diomède, part of the 1998 World Cup squad, and Claude Makelele, who like Sagnol had been one of Zinedine's closest teammates at the 2006 World Cup, this group of aspiring coaches was placed under the supervision of an even older acquaintance – Guy Lacombe, who had been a federation supervisor for a year and a half. Twenty-five years after sessions at La Bocca, Yazid was reunited with one of his very first coaches.

On 17 May 2015, Castilla had one last victory in Toledo, but only finished sixth in their group, two points shy of the fourth place needed to qualify for the next phase. Zidane's first league season therefore came to an end at an early hurdle. It was a first disappointment, followed two days later by a personal joy: Luca Zidane and his Under-17 teammates were doing well in the final phase of the European Championship in Bulgaria. France played Belgium in the semi-final.

It was 1–1 after full-time, and so went to penalties. Despite being the goalkeeper, Luca was fourth up for Les Bleus, who had a one-shot advantage. If he scored they would go through to the final.

He took his shot … A Panenka! His penalty was just as daring as his father's had been in 2006 … but this time the ball struck the crossbar and failed to cross the line.

If the final Belgian player scored, France would have to try again. He faced Luca, who had returned to the goal.

He took his shot ... Saved! It was the third shot Luca had saved in that shootout. The last French player scored. France were in the final. But more was yet to come: they won the competition for the second time, 11 years after the victory of a team that included Karim Benzema, the striker who had been playing for Real since 2009.

The day after the Under-17 Euros, another young player was being talked about in Madrid: Martin Ødegaard, who came on as a substitute for Cristiano Ronaldo. He made his La Liga debut at 16 years and 5 months. But the road to fame is long. It was with Castilla that the Norwegian prodigy began the 2015–16 season, as Enzo became captain of a team that could take advantage of a prize new recruit. This arrival was not a player but a man of whom Zinedine was very fond: a sports-massage therapist and physio originally from the Comoros but working in France, Hamidou Msaidié, who specialised in fasciatherapy. Little known and not always recognised, this discipline takes a global approach to the body through its fascias, a collection of tissues manipulated by the massage therapist to detect and prevent any underlying physical trauma.

Meanwhile, Carlo Ancelotti had been replaced by Rafael Benítez as head of the first team. Zidane's name had of course been mentioned as a successor to Ancelotti, and it was exactly the same during the tenure of Benítez, whose position was challenged by various disappointments at the club including in La Liga, which was dominated by a superb Barcelona team that seemed to be about to win a second consecutive Champions League – La Liga double.

The weeks passed. The winter arrived. Some players were unhappy with their relationship with Benítez. Some players and supporters were unhappy with the team's play. The directors, players *and* supporters were all unhappy with the team's position in the table. An unsatisfactory third place, behind Barcelona and Atlético Madrid, had been Real's since a humiliating defeat in the 12th game of the season: 4–0 down to Barça at the Bernabeu.

Zinedine knew he was being discussed as a replacement, but his immediate objective had not changed: he wanted to see Castilla finish among the top four in their group. On 3 January, after the first 19 games of the season, this objective was within his sights. Managed by Zinedine and captained by Enzo, given the role in the close season, the Real team were second, one place and six points better off than at the same stage a year earlier. They also had a nine-point cushion over the team in fifth place.

The second half of the season began the following week, with an away game at CD Ebro in Zaragoza. But Zidane would not have the chance to prepare for it: Florentino Perez asked him to replace Rafael Benítez, who was relieved of his duties on Monday 4 January. The president had paid heed to criticism of Benítez, as well as to the chants of 'Perez out' resonating around the stands. Of course, his choice of replacement was considered risky. But he had confidence in Zidane, in his abilities and first and foremost in his aura with the fans. It would silence the whistles for a while at least, and help his own standing.

Zizou was in charge of Real. The manager of a team of stars, and an inexperienced manager who would have to do better than his experienced and acclaimed predecessor, whose merits had been praised by Perez just a few months earlier: it was enough to make you dizzy.

Nevertheless, Zidane's followers believed in his influence, in his authority as a former champion to inspire respect in the dressing room and manage egos. Meanwhile, the sceptics and detractors pointed out a troubling lack of experience, indeed a managerial past without any results whatsoever. Having been a great player was not enough when it came to being a great manager – and Real wasn't just any old team.

Zidane agreed that he was not quite ready – but also noted that if you spent too much time thinking about these things, you would never take any significant steps. It was his first rhetorical subtlety, a dodge and a dribble at the same time, a well-considered entrance into what would become an important game: his communication with the media. Beginning a career at the highest level with Real was a considerable challenge. But Zinedine had the advantage of having played and worked in various positions. He was in his own environment. He had been living in the Spanish capital for almost 15 years.

Zizou left Castilla, but not alone. The team around him there was important, as it would be in his new role. And he would have the people he wanted. So he took David Bettoni with him, the first time he too would be involved with a senior team. Hamidou Msaidié and Bernardo Requena, a physical trainer for Castilla, followed him in the adventure. He also called upon Luis Llopis, previously in charge of the club's goalkeepers but now in charge only of those of the first team. Llopis had contributed greatly to the development of the current first-choice keeper, the Costa Rican Keylor Navas, when he worked with him at Levante.

A season without a title was a failure for Real, but a little less so if they beat their great rival, Barcelona. For the fans, it was almost perfect if they won one or more trophies and the play produced had been attractive. The standards were high.

When Zidane took the helm, Barcelona were one point ahead of Atlético Madrid and five ahead of Real in the middle of the season, and Real were due to play Roma in the last 16 of the Champions League in February and March.

Any newly appointed manager, let alone one who takes over partway through the season, benefits from a certain grace period, even more so when his name is Zizou. But he didn't need to use it: his credit was not used up by his first weeks in La Liga, which were marked by a flood of goals.

The only quibble was an administrative one; another story about certificates, this time for David Bettoni, the assistant manager, who lacked the requisite qualifications. Still keen to surround himself with people he knew well, Zizou invited Stéphane Plancque, then a recruiter at Lille OSC, to join Real to oversee their opponents. Plancque accepted enthusiastically. He immediately made himself available and was not required by Lille to see out his notice.

The team was in place. The players demonstrated a renewed cohesion. But their rivals Barcelona continued winning relentlessly. And their local enemies in Madrid beat them at home on 27 February.

After this frustrating defeat at the Bernabeu against Atlético – 1–0 thanks to a goal from Antoine Griezmann – Cristiano Ronaldo turned on his teammates, whom he described as not sufficiently motivated by the stakes. But he was not irreproachable either: the previous week in Malaga, he had missed a penalty that would have made it 2–0 and Real eventually dropped two points when the game finished in a 1–1 draw. The setback against Atlético made it very unlikely that they would be able to climb up the table.

Twelve: that was both the number of games remaining and the gap in points between Barcelona and Real, who were four behind Atlético.

'La Liga's over,' said Zizou calmly, stating the opinion of every observer. Statistically, Real's chances of becoming champions were almost nil.

Two days after the good news came from the Court of Arbitration for Sport, allowing David Bettoni to take his seat on the bench, the mood improved a little. A very important victory had seen the debutant manager's credit restored: on Saturday 2 April, Barcelona were beaten 2–1 at home at the Camp Nou after 39 games without defeat. For Zizou, it was a psychological victory, even if there was still no reason to believe that La Liga race wasn't over, as Barça still had a nine-point cushion with seven games left to play. There was still the Champions League. Real beat Roma 2–0 in both legs of the last 16. In the quarter-final, the Madrid team would once again play their first leg away and the draw was lenient, on paper at least. They had avoided the feared Barça, Bayern and Atlético in favour of the 'modest' German team Wolfsburg, whom all the clubs still in the running were keen to be drawn against.

But Real failed to win the first leg. Wolfsburg triumphed, without conceding a goal at home, a detail that would be important in the event of a tie after both games. It was difficult to come back from 2–0 down. Statistics were called up. Real had a 20 per cent chance of qualifying. And rumours about replacing Zidane at the end of the season were already beginning to circulate, even with the mention of other names: the return of Mourinho or the arrival of Ernesto Valverde from Bilbao.

The league title seemed lost and the European quarter-final looked unlikely. But a fortnight later, on the evening of Sunday 17 April, Real's situation began to look up.

In La Liga, they had recovered almost miraculously and were within a single point of Barça, who nevertheless still had a much superior goal difference. The Barcelona team, who had successively posted a draw and three defeats, were tied on points with Atlético Madrid, who had knocked them out of the Champions League.

In Europe, Real qualified by beating Wolfsburg 3–0 thanks to a hat-trick from Cristiano Ronaldo and no need for extra time.

Barça reacted with some impressive league wins, including a spectacular 8–0 at La Coruña on 20 April, which allowed them not only to cling on at the top of the table but also to improve their already formidable goal difference. But Real had begun once again to believe in a double. La Liga was not over. The Champions League continued. Zizou, the man born under a lucky star, was determined to seize his chance and, as has often been the case, fate continued to look favourably on him.

Destiny helped once more at the draw. It was a decent draw, offering up the least formidable opponent in the European semi-final. Surely Manchester City would be a better bet than Bayern or Atlético, and Real would once again have the advantage of playing the return leg at home.

This time, fate took the form of injuries. The fortune of some is the misfortune of others. In the quarter-final, Wolfsburg had lost Julian Draxler in the 30th minute. In the semi-final, Manchester City lost their great attacking asset David Silva in the 40th minute of the first leg, which ended 0–0. In the second leg, in Madrid, it was the Manchester City captain and pillar of their defence, Vincent Kompany, who limped off in the seventh minute,

Real won 1–0. They had qualified. Only his seventh Champions League game in charge and Zidane would be in the final.

In the other half of the draw, Atlético Madrid knocked out Bayern Munich, narrowly scraping through thanks to an away goal after the tie ended 2–2 across both games. As in 2014, the two clubs from the Spanish capital would face each other in the Champions League final on 28 May.

Atlético specialised in snatched victories. This clash with their city rivals was even more hotly anticipated by the fans who had seen hopes of winning the league vanish. To everyone's surprise, Atlético had lost away to the team at the bottom of the table, Levante, in the penultimate game of the season, while Barcelona and Real had won.

Barça were out of the Champions League. Atlético could no longer win La Liga. Real were the only club that could still win both. But in La Liga, Real were dependent on Barcelona, who were still one point ahead, making a mistake. The uncertainty would continue until the very last match, where Barcelona grabbed the title with a third goal in the 86th minute. Real, who finished the season with a 12th consecutive win, were virtual champions for 15 minutes when they were 2–0 up and Barça had yet to score.

Despite this, the overall assessment of the new manager was positive. Since Zidane had taken over, Real had banked more points than Barcelona: 53 compared with 49. He had also done better than Benítez: 53 points in 20 games, compared with 40 in 19 matches by his predecessor.

Statistics were summoned up once more: at Real, this record over 20 matches was the best ever achieved by a team managed by a debutant coach. Doubts expressed by some about his ability to manage a major team seemed unfounded. However, Zidane would not become a great manager after six months, 20 games and a statistical record. It would take time to become long-term builders, such as Arsène Wenger at Arsenal, Alex Ferguson at Manchester United, or adaptable and lauded strategists such as Guardiola or Mourinho who had earned respectability over the long haul. Above all, those managers had won many titles. But here, at least, was the opportunity to win one.

On 28 May in Milan, during the Champions League final, Real were expecting to – in the words of Zidane himself – 'suffer'. Many pundits had Atlético as favourites.

After a quarter of an hour of play, Kroos took a free kick on the left that was deflected by Bale. Savić grabbed Ramos by the shirt in the box but the referee neither gave a penalty nor spotted that Ramos was in an offside position when Bale deflected the ball: 1–0 to Real! It was Atlético who suffered, before reacting at the end of the first half.

At the break, Atlético manager Diego Simeone brought on the Belgian Yannick Ferreira Carrasco, who showed himself to be enterprising and threatening. Real began to look weak on the right wing, as Carvajal was forced to leave the field in the 52nd minute with an injury. It looked as if he might miss the Euros and he broke down in tears. He was comforted by Zinedine and replaced by Danilo, whose season had been marked by virulent criticism after the match in Wolfsburg.

The team in white closed ranks and gritted their teeth. Zidane attempted to raise the morale of his ragged troops. He moved around and waved, coming out of his technical area. He was just a few centimetres from the pitch, as if it was all he could do to stop himself from coming on. They had to hold firm but Ferreira Carrasco equalised 11 minutes from the end of full-time, after an impressive move.

As in Zizou's last final as a player ten years earlier, with the French team in Berlin, the score was 1–1 when extra time began. It was painful for Real. Bale was struggling to run. A massage at half-time failed to revive him, and he had fallen victim to cramp. Modrić no longer had the energy to direct the ball in his usual sparkling fashion. Only Isco, who had come on in the 72nd minute, and Casemiro, who superbly justified the trust placed in him by Zizou at the end of the season, seemed able to give the game a decisive boost. In these conditions, penalties were almost a relief. Zidane began the ordeal by displaying a cheerful casualness intended to give his players confidence.

Penalties began, the first by their opposition hitting the left post. Juanfran, whose cross had allowed Ferreira Carrasco to equalise, was the only player to miss. Real had won the Champions League. *Zidane* had won the Champions League.

The Madrid players ran towards the final penalty-taker, a Cristiano Ronaldo recovering from injury and operating far from his usual level. But victory was theirs. And nothing else mattered.

The players piled on top of Cristiano. Zinedine hugged David and Hamidou. The cup reached out its arms to all of them, and Véronique opened hers to those of her husband. Only they and their loved ones remembered that they had been married on another 28 May, and so this was also their 21st wedding anniversary. She was waitng on the touchline, accompanied by their sons Elyaz and Théo. He embraced them all before returning to his squad, whom he led to the rostrum to receive their medals and the trophy. The happy procession passed in front of the officials, whom Zizou greeted with a handshake or a friendly pat, or even a long hug when he got to Florentino Perez.

The cup was placed at the end of the row. He had filed in front of the World Cup 2006 trophy with his head lowered. This was different: he could embrace, and not just with his eyes, this Champions League cup, engraved with the words 'Coupe des Clubs Champions Européens'. David and Hamidou stationed themselves next to him, to the right of the players who had gathered to see the captain Ramos lift the trophy, also testifying to an expertise acquired and developed in France. The statisticians later confirmed that Zidane, Real's first French manager, was also the first Frenchman to win the cup both as a player and a manager.

The ceremony came to an end but the party would continue. The two-hour-long match was followed by two days of jubilation. The players, technicians and their friends and family returned to the pitch to celebrate the victory. The manager reminded everyone that it was first and foremost a victory by his players. Carvajal, Ramos, Modrić, Bale, Benzema, Cristiano, Marcelo and Isco had already won the title two years earlier in Lisbon. Zinedine pointed out that with players like those it was easier to win titles. He recognised their merits but, implicitly, did not forget his own: 'We worked hard.' The late evening was clement at the San Siro.

Back in Madrid it was cold. Day broke over Barajas airport, where fans came to greet the squad excitedly. In the city, a little later, thousands crowded around the bus in which the winners paraded. The Cibeles Fountain was reunited with its familiar flag, hung by Sergio Ramos.

At the end of the evening, a grand ceremony rocked the Santiago-Bernabeu, where the final had been broadcast the day before on giant screens set up in the middle of the pitch. They were topped that night by a podium on which the winners of the *undécima*, the 11th Champions League title, took pride of place. Eleven giant balloons floated above the stadium. On each of them appeared the name of the city and the year in which Real had won its finals, including the last three with Zizou: a player in 2002 in Glasgow, assistant manager in 2014 in Lisbon and head coach in 2016 in Milan. A light show and fireworks punctuated the celebration.

Zinedine Zidane was the first to be announced to the crowd. Introduced as a lifelong 'Madridista', he was given an ovation. His legend continued as he acquired new fans who had not even been born when he had scored his first goals.

After the final, Zidane kept an eye on the club over the summer. He insisted on recruiting the physical trainer from Olympique Lyonnais, Antonio Pintus, whom he had known at Juve, and training could begin in earnest for the new season.

On 9 August 2016, Real won the European Super Cup against Sevilla in extra time after a last-minute equaliser from Sergio Ramos just a few seconds before the end of normal time. The final result was 3–2. Zidane had only been a manager for seven months and he had already lifted his second cup, and there would be another before the year was out. On 18 December, the Madrid team won the Club World Cup against the Japanese team Kashima Antlers. The result was 4–2 after extra time thanks to a hat-trick from Cristiano Ronaldo, who had won the Ballon d'Or for a fourth time a few days earlier.

The third trophy of the year, first place in La Liga ahead of Barcelona and a winning streak for the club. Since 27 February and a bitter home defeat to their rivals Atlético, Real had not lost a single match, going on an unbeaten run of 36 games (though there was a loss to Wolfsburg in the Champions League; Real went on to win 3–2 on aggregate). It seemed as though his transformation to manager was succeeding – but, of course, there were still more titles to win and more trophies to be lifted before this once-legendary player could approach a place in the managerial hall of fame. And football is a curious game.

17

NEW YEAR, NEW HORIZONS

The dawn of 2017 saw Zinedine Zidane's Real Madrid breaking another record. They returned from the Christmas break by beating Sevilla 3–0 in their first leg of their Copa del Rey tie against Sevilla, then defeated Granada 5–0 to equal Barcelona's Spanish record of going 39 games unbeaten. It had been Zizou's Madrid who had ended Barça's own sequence back in April 2016, coming from behind to win 2–1 at Camp Nou. Now Real had the chance to go one better, in their second-leg match against Sevilla.

Real's three-goal cushion saw Zizou rest several key players, a fact that Sevilla took full advantage of. Going ahead through an own goal from Danilo, Sevilla responded to Real equalising by scoring twice more. But with seven minutes left on the clock, Casemiro was brought down in the penalty area, allowing Sergio Ramos to halve the deficit. Then, in the 93rd minute, and with seconds remaining, substitute Karim Benzema was put through by Marcelo to equalise. Real's unbeaten run was preserved and the Spanish record was broken.

For Zizou, it left the Real manager with the remarkable record of having won more trophies (three) than he had lost matches (two). During the 40-match run, he had seen his team win 30 times and draw 10, scoring 115 times in the process. By any measurement it was a remarkable achievement, but particularly so by someone so early in their coaching career.

The run, however, wasn't to continue. Real's next match found them returning to Sevilla for a Liga clash, and this time it was Sevilla who were celebrating an injury-time goal. Stevan Jovetić scored in the last minute of stoppage time to give the home side a 2–1 win. And rather than shake the defeat off, Real found themselves losing twice in a week, this time going down by the same scoreline to Celta Vigo in the first leg of their Copa del Rey quarter-final. With the second leg ending in a draw, Real were out of the cup competition.

That might not sound a big deal, but the curious fact about this defeat was that it meant the Copa del Rey was to be the only trophy Zizou's side weren't to win in 2017.

It had been five years since Real Madrid had last won La Liga. Indeed, over the previous eight seasons, Barcelona had won the title six times: even Real's local rivals Atlético had won it more recently. 'For Real Madrid,' Zizou told Marca, 'because it is the best club in the world, we have to return with this league title.'

Real's defeat against Sevilla left their victors just one point behind them in the table, with Barcelona a further solitary point back. For all the success of the 40-match unbeaten run, Real remained far from the favourites for the title. Described by one newspaper as 'The Tightrope Kings', Real had gone top by winning a remarkable number of points in the last ten minutes of games; seven times in the last ten minutes they scored a winner; twice they came back from losing to draw. These late shows accounted for 17 points, 21 per cent of their final total. But impressive as these turnarounds were, for Zizou he knew the team were playing with fire: 'We're not always going to win late in games,' he admitted.

By the end of April, Sevilla's challenge had faded, leaving Real and Barça to fight it out. In a tightly fought Clásico on 23 April, Barcelona beat Real 3–2 at the Bernabeu, with Lionel Messi scoring the winner in the 92nd minute. It left the two teams level on 75 points, but Barcelona on top via a superior goal difference. Real, though, had a game in hand which seemingly made the maths simple: win their last six games and they would be champions. But they also had a Champions League semi-final to contend with against Atlético Madrid in the middle of all this – a fixture schedule that saw them playing eight games in 25 days. Barcelona, who had been knocked out of the Champions League, had only five games to play over the same schedule. These they won to keep the pressure on Real.

That Zizou succeeded where his predecessors, Carlo Ancelotti and Rafael Benítez, had failed can be put down to two things. The first of these was in his man-management of his star player, Cristiano Ronaldo. In previous years, Ronaldo had faded towards the business end of the season. This time round, Zizou sat down with Ronaldo and explained to him how they needed to better manage his game time. Now in his early thirties, Ronaldo couldn't play every game in the autumn and expect to be at his best the following May. Zizou argued that by resting him for less important games, Ronaldo would not only be sharper at the season's end, but would also help to prolong his career.

That can't have been an easy conversation to have, but who better to give Ronaldo that advice than a fellow Ballon d'Or winner? Over the course of the 2016–17 season, Zizou used his talisman more sparingly. Ronaldo played fewer matches than he had done in previous seasons, but was at his best when it came to the crunch: out of his 40 goals for the season, 14 came in the final 40 days.

At the same time as not playing Ronaldo every game, Zizou also made full use of his entire first-team squad. This was the second reason for Real's success – a fulsome use of rotation that not only kept legs fresh, but also garnered support for his tactics from his players. Zizou trusted them and they, in turn, put their trust in him. Over the course of the season, Real had over 19 different goalscorers on the score sheet; over 20 players played over 1,000 minutes. To keep up with a relentless fixture schedule, Zizou made regular wholesale changes to his side – at times rotating up to nine players between each match.

So when La Liga entered its final throes, with victories required over Deportivo de la Coruña, Valencia, Granada, Sevilla, Celta Vigo and Malaga, Zizou's team were ready. The late goals were replaced by early ones – in five out of the last six league matches, Real were ahead after ten minutes (and within half an hour in the other). The biggest threat to their winning run came from Valencia, who equalised with eight minutes to go, only for an even later strike from Marcelo to give Real victory. As the Bernabeu erupted, with players and substitutes celebrating together, Zizou watched impassively on.

On the final day of the season, the two title contenders both faced mid-table teams: Real were away at Malaga, while Barça were at home to Eibar. A refreshed Ronaldo removed any nerves by scoring the opener in under a minute: by contrast, a nervy Barcelona went two goals down, before eventually emerging 4–2 winners. Their result, however, was academic: Benzema doubled Real's lead and the title was theirs.

'After nine, ten months, to win the league five years later ... there are no words,' Zizou said afterwards. 'When you are at Real

Madrid you know the expectations are high and I like that. I lived that as a player but this is my happiest day because as a coach it changes completely.' While his players celebrated, Zizou told the assembled press, 'I'd like to get up here and dance. I'm not going to, but on the inside, I'm very, very happy.'

Indeed, the only disappointment on a triumphant day was the absence of La Liga trophy. To the bemusement of the Real players, they were told the trophy wasn't there for them to lift. It transpired that the trophy belonged to the Royal Spanish Football Federation (RFEF) and – with the president of the Federation, Ángel Maria Villar, unavailable to hand it over – the trophy remained under lock and key. It was a surreal end to a remarkable season.

La Liga title, however, was just the first of Zizou's trophy haul for 2017. Next up was an even bigger prize: the Champions League. If Real could beat Juventus in the final at Cardiff on 3 June, then they would become the first club to retain the trophy in the Champions League era. On top of this, Zizou's side would become the first Real team to be both champions of Spain and Europe for almost six decades.

Zizou had Ronaldo to thank for getting them to the final – or maybe Ronaldo had Zizou to thank for keeping him in shape for the big matches. In the quarter-final, Zizou found himself up against Bayern Munich and his former boss, Carlo Ancelotti. Ronaldo scored twice in Germany to give Real a 2–1 win, then three times back in Spain as Real won 4–2 after extra time. That set up a semi-final that was a repeat of the previous year's final against Atlético Madrid. This time, Ronaldo settled the tie with a hat-trick in the first leg. And while Atlético briefly threatened a recovery in the return leg, an Isco goal gave Real a two-goal cushion that they never let go of.

Juventus, however, were the toughest challenge of the lot. In their twelve games en route to the final, Juve had conceded just three goals; in knocking out Barcelona over two legs, they stopped Messi and co scoring a single goal. If anyone was going to stop Real, it was going to be Juve's classic Italian back line of Barzagli, Bonucci and Chiellini, backed up by Gianluigi Buffon in goal. Further up the pitch, there was former Barça player Dani Alves to deal with, and one-time Real striker Higuín with a point to prove against his former club.

Zizou, though, had faith in his players. The only real decision to make on the starting line-up was whether to include Gareth Bale, who hadn't played since coming off injured in April's Clásico match. Bale was desperate to play in his home city, but Zizou eschewed sentimentality, selecting Isco instead and leaving the Welshman on the bench.

For the first half, the match was relatively balanced. Ronaldo put Real ahead in the 20th minute, only for Mario Mandžukić to equalise with a remarkable overhead finish seven minutes later. As both teams traded shots and cynical fouls, neither team were able to gain much advantage.

At half-time, however, Zizou made the decisive change. Tweaking the Real tactics, he told his team to be more aggressive and push higher up the pitch. Modrić, meanwhile, who'd had a relatively quiet first half on the left of midfield, was switched by Zizou to the right-hand side of the pitch, with Kroos told to play more centrally and Isco shifted across to the left. Zizou's tactical switch bore fruit: Real were rampant in the second half, Casemiro restoring their lead with a deflected shot, then Modrić picking out

Ronaldo for his second, decisive goal. By the time Asensio scored a fourth goal in the 90th minute, Real were out of sight.

Real's success was a personal triumph for Zizou. In less than 18 months as manager, he had as many Champions League titles to his name as Alex Ferguson, Pep Guardiola or José Mourinho. Yet his modesty at his achievements continued to prevail. 'I'm happy,' he told the press. 'You may not see it, but inside I feel a great satisfaction.' Asked if achievements made him the best coach in the world, he demurred: 'No, no, not that.' Instead, he heaped praise on his players: 'the key is that they get on bloody brilliantly'.

The trophies continued to arrive. In early August, Real travelled to Skopje to take on Manchester United, winners of the Europa League, in the Super Cup. Goals by Casemiro and Isco helped Real to a 2–1 victory. Next up was the Spanish Super Cup, an early-season match-up with Barcelona. Over two legs, Real defeated their great rivals by five goals to one. To cap off a trophy-laden year, Real followed up retaining their Champions League title by winning the FIFA Club World Cup title for a second year running – Gremio were despatched in Abu Dhabi, thanks to a Ronaldo free kick.

Yet if the history books suggest that the second half of 2017 was a continuation of the first, on the pitch it was a different story. Real had started the 2017–18 season as overwhelming favourites to regain their Liga title. Their victories in the Super Cups suggested they were picking up where they left off, while all the crisis talk surrounded Barcelona: Neymar had stunned the club by demanding and getting a transfer to Paris Saint-Germain. Defender Gerard Pique, meanwhile, said that, 'in the nine years that I have been here, it is the first time that I feel inferior to Madrid'.

Yet even in that Super Cup victory over Barcelona, the first problems for the season were emerging. Sent off for pushing the referee, Ronaldo found himself suspended for five games. A combination of that and injuries to Karim Benzema and Gareth Bale meant that the famed 'BBC' frontline didn't play together until well into the season. Real dropped seven points in their first five games, including a surprise loss at home to Real Betis. This defeat wasn't an isolated one: in October, Real were beaten by Girona; in November, Tottenham defeated them at Wembley in the Champions League. Then in December, the freshly crowned World Club champions were brought back down to earth by Barcelona, who beat them 3–0 at the Bernabeu. It left Real finishing the year in fourth place, 14 points behind Barcelona.

When quizzed about Real's form, Zidane was circumspect: 'Maybe last year we won some games we didn't deserve,' he said. 'Now it's the other way round.' Certainly, the team weren't short of shots: by early January 2018, Real had registered 348, more than anyone else. The problem was that they'd only converted 29. Ronaldo, normally so rampant, was their joint-top scorer with just four league goals.

Barcelona might have lost Neymar over the summer, but Real had suffered some important departures, too: Alvaro Morata had been sold to Chelsea: James Rodriguez had gone to Bayern Munich; Pepe, meanwhile, turned down a one-year contract extension to move to Besiktas. Zizou had been hopeful of bringing in Kylian Mbappe, but the rising French star opted to join PSG instead. All of which left Zizou a little light in terms of options from the bench, and reliant on the rest of his squad to return to form.

The year ended with Zizou facing the first real test of his managerial career – and at a club not known for indulging managers when things go wrong. While 2017 had begun in record-breaking fashion, it was finishing with rumours as to when Zizou might go, and who could be lined up to replace him.

For Zizou, it was a time to stay true to his principles. He announced that he didn't want any new players in the January transfer window, preferring to stick to the squad of players he already knew. 'I won't ever change,' he once said, a phrase that frustrated those who wanted different tactics and fresh blood in the team. But that was Zidane's way: quiet, but determined. And however the season ultimately turns out, one thing remains certain: he will do things his own way, whatever the outcome.

ZINEDINE ZIDANE'S CAREER AS A PLAYER

Clubs

Under-9s 1980–1981: AS Foresta (Marseille); 1981–1982: US
Saint-Henri (Marseille)

Under-11s 1982–1983: US Saint-Henri (Marseille); 1983–1984:
SO Septèmes-les-Vallons

Under-15s 1984–1986: SO Septèmes-les-Vallons

Under-17s 1986–1987: SO Septèmes-les-Vallons; 1987–1988: AS
Cannes

Under-19s 1988–1991: AS Cannes

Senior

1991–1992: AS Cannes

1992–1996: Girondins de Bordeaux

1996–2001: Juventus

2001–2006: Real Madrid

Titles

1996–1997: Intercontinental Cup, European Super Cup, Italian Championship

1997–1998: World Cup, Italian Championship, Italian Super Cup

1999–2000: European Cup of Nations

2001–2002: Intercontinental Cup, European Super Cup, Champions League, Spanish Super Cup

2002–2003: Spanish Championship

Player of the year by FIFA in 1998, 2000 and 2003 (voted for by managers)

Goals

League: 95 goals (6 with Cannes, 28 with Bordeaux, 24 with Juventus, 37 with Real Madrid) in 506 matches (61 with Cannes, 139 with Bordeaux, 151 with Juventus, 155 with Real Madrid)

In European cups: 18 goals (4 with Bordeaux, 5 with Juventus, 9 with Real Madrid) in 108 matches (4 with Cannes, 18 with Bordeaux, 39 with Juventus, 47 with Real Madrid)

With the France A team: 31 goals (5 during his time at Bordeaux, 13 during his time at Juventus, 13 during his time at Real) in 98 matches (17 during his time at Bordeaux, 49 during his time at Juventus, 32 during his time at Real)

Matches for France

Friendlies

7 August 1994 in Bordeaux: France–Czech Republic, 2–2, he played the last 37 minutes. While France were behind 0–2, he scored the first goal in the 85th minute with his left foot, and the second in the 87th minute with his head from a corner (1st cap)

22 July 1995 in Oslo: Norway–France, 0–0, he played the first half (4th cap)

24 January 1996 in Paris: France–Portugal, 3–2 (9th cap)

21 February 1996 in Nîmes: France–Greece, 3–1, he played the second half and scored the goal to make it 3–1 in the 49th minute (10th cap)

1 June 1996 in Stuttgart: Germany–France, 0–1, he played the first half (11th cap)

5 June 1996 in Villeneuve-d'Ascq: France–Armenia, 2–0 (12th cap)

31 August 1996 in Paris: France–Mexico, 2–0, he played the second half (18th cap)

9 October 1996 in Paris: France–Turkey, 4–0, he played the first 80 minutes (19th cap)

9 November 1996 in Copenhagen: Denmark–France, 1–0 (20th cap)

22 January 1997 in Braga: Portugal–France, 0–2 (21st cap)

26 February 1997 in Paris: France–Netherlands, 2–1 (22nd cap)

2 April 1997 in Paris: France–Sweden, 1–0, he played the first 55 minutes (23rd cap)

3 June 1997 in Lyon (Tournoi de France): France–Brazil, 1–1 (24th cap)

7 June 1997 in Montpellier (Tournoi de France): France–England, 0–1, he played the last 15 minutes (25th cap)

11 June 1997 in Paris (Tournoi de France): France–Italy, 2–2, he scored the first goal (26th cap)

11 October 1997 in Lens: France–South Africa, 2–1, he played the second half (27th cap)

12 November 1997 in Saint-Étienne: France–Scotland, 2–1 (28th cap)

28 January 1998 in Saint-Denis: France–Spain, 1–0, he scored the first goal in the history of the Stade de France with his right foot in the 20th minute (29th cap)

25 February 1998 in Marseille: France–Norway, 3–3, he scored the goal to make it 2–1 in the 28th minute (30th cap)

22 April 1998 in Solna: Sweden–France, 0–0 (31st cap)

27 May 1998 (Hassan II Tournament in Casablanca): Belgium–France, 0–1, he scored with his right foot in the 63rd minute (32nd cap)

29 May 1998 (Hassan II Tournament in Casablanca): Morocco–France, 2–2 (33rd cap)

5 June 1998 in Helsinki: Finland–France, 0–1 (34th cap)

19 August 1998 in Vienna: Austria–France, 2–2 (40th cap)

20 January 1999 in Marseille: France–Morocco, 1–0 (44th cap)

10 February 1999 in London: England–France, 0–2 (45th cap)

13 November 1999 in Saint-Denis: France–Croatia, 3–0 (49th cap)

23 February 2000 in Saint-Denis: France–Poland, 1–0, he scored in the 88th minute (50th cap)

26 April 2000 in Saint-Denis: France–Slovenia, 3–2 (51st cap)

28 May 2000 in Zagreb: Croatia–France, 0–2 (52nd cap)

4 June 2000 (Hassan II Tournament in Casablanca): Japan–France, 2–2, he was substituted in the last minute before the penalty shootout (won by France), which was not preceded by extra time; he scored the goal to make it 1–1 in the 61st minute (53rd cap)

6 June 2000 (Hassan II Tournament in Casablanca): Morocco–France, 1–5, he played the last 30 minutes (54th cap)

16 August 2000 in Marseille: France–FIFA team, 5–1, although it was not played between two national teams, this charity match was counted by the French Federation as an official cap (60th cap)

2 September 2000 in Saint-Denis: France–England, 1–1, he played the first 65 minutes (61st cap)

15 November 2000 in Istanbul: Turkey–France, 0–4, he played the first 63 minutes (62nd cap)

27 February 2001 in Saint-Denis: France–Germany, 1–0, he played the first 82 minutes and scored in the 27th minute (63rd cap)

24 March 2001 in Saint-Denis: France–Japan, 5–0, he scored the first goal from the penalty spot in the 9th minute (64th cap)

28 March 2001 in Valencia: Spain–France, 2–1, he played the first 62 minutes (65th cap)

25 April 2001 in Saint-Denis: France–Portugal, 4–0, he played the first half (66th cap)

15 August 2001 in Nantes: France–Denmark, 1–0 (67th cap)

1 September 2001 in Santiago: Chile–France, 2–1 (68th cap, 1st as captain)

6 October 2001 in Saint-Denis: France–Algeria, 4–1, he played the first half (69th cap)

11 November 2001 in Melbourne: Australia–France, 1–1, he played the first 80 minutes (70th cap)

13 February 2002 in Saint-Denis: France–Romania, 2–1, he played the first 70 minutes (71st cap)

27 March 2002 in Saint-Denis: France–Scotland, 5–0, he played the first 80 minutes and scored the first goal with his left foot in the 11th minute (72nd cap, 2nd as captain)

17 April 2002 in Saint-Denis: France–Russia, 0–0 (73rd cap)

26 May 2002 in Suwon: South Korea–France 2–3, he was replaced in the 38th minute due to a right-thigh injury (74th cap)

21 August 2002 in Tunis: Tunisia–France, 1–1 (76th cap, 3rd as captain)

12 February 2003 in Saint-Denis: France–Czech Republic, 0–2 (80th cap)

20 August 2003 in Geneva: Switzerland–France, 0–2, he played the first 70 minutes (83rd cap)

15 November 2003 in Gelsenkirchen: Germany–France, 0–3 (86th cap, 7th as captain)

18 February 2004 in Brussels: Belgium–France, 0–2, he played the first 70 minutes (87th cap)

20 May 2004 in Saint-Denis: France–Brazil, 0–0, he played the first 69 minutes (88th cap)

6 June 2004 in Saint-Denis: France–Ukraine, 1–0, he scored in the 87th minute (89th cap, 8th as captain)

17 August 2005 in Montpellier: France–Côte d'Ivoire, 3–0, he scored the second goal with his left foot in the 62nd minute (94th cap, 12th as captain)

1 March 2006 in Saint-Denis: France–Slovakia, 1–2, he played the first half (99th cap, 17th as captain)

27 May 2006 in Saint-Denis: France–Mexico, 1–0, he played the first 52 minutes (100th cap, 18th as captain)

31 May 2006 in Lens: France–Denmark, 2–0, he played the first 66 minutes (101st cap, 19th as captain)

7 June 2006 in Saint-Étienne: France–China, 3–1 (102nd cap, 20th as captain)

Competitions – qualifying matches
EURO 1996
8 October 1994 in Saint-Étienne: France–Romania, 0–0, he played the last 18 minutes (2nd cap)

26 April 1995 in Nantes: France–Slovakia, 4–0, he played the first 74 minutes (3rd cap)

16 August 1995 in Paris: France–Poland, 1–1 (5th cap)

6 September 1995 in Auxerre: France–Azerbaijan, 10–0, he scored the seventh goal in the 72nd minute (6th cap)

11 October 1995 in Bucharest: Romania–France, 1–3, he played the first 85 minutes; in the 73rd minute, he scored the goal to make it 3–1 (7th cap)

15 November 1995 in Caen: France–Israel, 2–0 (8th cap)

EURO 2000

5 September 1998 in Reykjavik: Iceland–France, 1–1 (41st cap)

10 October 1998 in Moscow: Russia–France, 2–3 (42nd cap)

14 October 1998 in Saint-Denis: France–Andorra, 2–0 (43rd cap)

4 September 1999 in Kiev: Ukraine–France, 0–0 (46th cap)

8 September 1999 in Yerevan: Armenia–France, 2–3, he scored the goal to make it 1–2 to France in the 67th minute (47th cap)

9 October 1999 in Saint-Denis: France–Iceland, 3–2 (48th cap)

EURO 2004

7 September 2002 in Nicosia: Cyprus–France, 1–2 (77th cap)

12 October 2002 in Saint-Denis: France–Slovenia, 5–0 (78th cap)

16 October 2002 in Valetta: Malta–France, 0–4 (79th cap)

29 March 2003 in Lens: France–Malta, 6–0, he scored the fourth goal with his right foot from the penalty spot in the 57th minute; he scored the sixth goal with his head in the 80th minute (81st cap, 4th as captain)

2 April 2003 in Palermo (due to security concerns in Israel): Israel–France, 1–2, he scored the last goal from the penalty spot in the 45th minute (82nd cap, 5th as captain)

10 September 2003 in Ljubljana: Slovenia–France, 0–2, he played the first 78 minutes (84th cap)

11 October 2003 in Saint-Denis: France–Israel, 3–0 (85th cap, 6th as captain)

WORLD CUP 2006

3 September 2005 in Lens: France–Faroe Islands, 3–0, he played the first 57 minutes (95th cap, 13th as captain)

7 September 2005 in Dublin: Republic of Ireland–France, 0–1, he played the first 70 minutes and came off with a right-thigh injury (96th cap, 14th as captain)

8 October 2005 in Bern: Switzerland–France, 1–1 (97th cap, 15th as captain)

12 October 2005 in Saint-Denis: France–Cyprus, 4–0, he scored the first goal with his right foot from the penalty spot in the 29th minute (98th cap, 16th as captain)

Competitions – final stages

EURO 1996 (in England)

10 June 1996 in Newcastle: France–Romania, 1–0, he played the first 80 minutes (13th cap)

15 June 1996 in Leeds: France–Spain, 1–1 (14th cap)

18 June 1996 in Newcastle: France–Bulgaria, 3–1, he played the first 62 minutes (15th cap)

22 June 1996 in Liverpool: France–Netherlands, 0–0 (16th cap)

26 June 1996 in Manchester: Czech Republic–France, 0–0 (17th cap)

WORLD CUP 1998 (in France)

12 June 1998 in Marseille: France–South Africa, 3–0 (35th cap)

18 June 1998 in Saint-Denis: France–Saudi Arabia, 4–0, he was sent off in the 70th minute (36th cap)

3 July 1998 in Saint-Denis: France–Russia, 0–0 (37th cap)

8 July 1998 in Saint-Denis: France–Croatia, 2–1 (38th cap)

12 July 1998 in Saint-Denis: France–Brazil, 3–0, he scored the first two goals, both with his head, in the 27th minute and the first minute of injury time at the end of the first half (39th cap)

EURO 2000 (in Belgium and the Netherlands)

11 June 2000 in Bruges (Belgium): Denmark–France, 0–3 (55th cap)

16 June 2000 in Bruges: Czech Republic–France, 1–2 (56th cap)

25 June 2000 in Bruges: Spain–France, 1–2, he scored the first goal, with his right foot from a free kick, in the 32nd minute (57th cap)

28 June 2000 in Brussels (Belgium): Portugal–France, 1–2, he scored the golden goal that brought an end to extra time from the penalty spot in the 117th minute (58th cap)

2 July 2000 in Rotterdam (Netherlands): Italy–France, 1–2 (59th cap)

WORLD CUP 2002 (in South Korea and Japan)

11 June 2002 in Incheon (South Korea): Denmark–France, 2–0 (75th cap)

EURO 2004 (in Portugal)

13 June 2004 in Lisbon: France–England, 2–1, he scored the equalising goal from a free kick in the last minute of normal time, then the winning goal from the penalty spot in the 3rd minute of extra time (90th cap, 9th as captain)

17 June 2004 in Leiria: Croatia–France, 2–2, he scored from a free kick deflected by a Croatian player in the 22nd minute; for this

disputed reason he has not been officially credited with the first goal (91st cap, 10th as captain)

21 June 2004 in Coimbra: Switzerland–France, 1–3, he scored the first goal with his head in the 20th minute (92nd cap, 11th as captain)

25 June 2004 in Lisbon: France–Greece, 0–1 (93rd cap, 12th as captain)

WORLD CUP 2006 (in Germany)

13 June 2006 in Stuttgart: France–Switzerland, 0–0 (103rd cap, 21st as captain)

18 June 2006 in Leipzig: France–South Korea, 1–1 (104th cap, 22nd as captain)

27 June 2006 in Hanover: Spain–France, 1–3, he scored the third goal in the 91st minute (105th cap, 23rd as captain)

1 July 2006 in Frankfurt: Brazil–France, 0–1 (106th cap, 24th as captain)

5 July 2006 in Munich: Portugal–France, 0–1, he scored the first goal from the penalty spot in the 33rd minute (107th cap, 25th as captain)

9 July 2006 in Berlin: Italy–France, 1–1, he scored the first goal from the penalty spot in the 7th minute and was sent off in 110th minute (108th cap, 26th as captain).

PICTURE CREDITS